How to Profit
from... *Auctions*

HOW TO PROFIT FROM...
Auctions

By
Fiona Shoop

REMEMBER WHEN

First published in Great Britain in 2009 by
REMEMBER WHEN PUBLICATIONS
an imprint of
Pen & Sword Books Ltd
47 Church Street
Barnsley
South Yorkshire
S70 2AS

Copyright © Fiona Shoop, 2009

ISBN 978 1 84468 024 5

The right of Fiona Shoop to be identified as author of this work has been asserted by her in accordance with the Copyright, Designs and Patents Act 1988.

A CIP catalogue record for this book is available from the British Library.

All rights reserved. No part of this book may be reproduced or transmitted in any form or by any means, electronic or mechanical including photocopying, recording or by any information storage and retrieval system, without permission from the Publisher in writing.

Printed and bound in Thailand
By Kyodo Nation Printing Services Co., Ltd

Pen & Sword Books Ltd incorporates the Imprints of
Pen & Sword Aviation, Pen & Sword Family History, Pen & Sword Maritime, Pen & Sword Military, Wharncliffe Local History, Pen & Sword Select, Pen & Sword Military Classics, Leo Cooper, Remember When, Seaforth Publishing and Frontline Publishing

For a complete list of Pen & Sword titles please contact
PEN & SWORD BOOKS LIMITED
47 Church Street, Barnsley, South Yorkshire, S70 2AS, England
E-mail: enquiries@pen-and-sword.co.uk
Website: www.pen-and-sword.co.uk

Contents

Introduction		8
Acknowledgements		11

SECTION ONE – AUCTION BASICS   13

Chapter 1	– Why use Auctions?	15
Chapter 2	– How to Find an Auction House	20
Chapter 3	– First Steps – Parking and Other Must-ask Questions	23
Chapter 4	– Beware of the Auction Ring and Other Auction Trickery	30

SECTION TWO – BUYING AT AUCTION   39

Chapter 1	– Why Buy at Auction?	40
Chapter 2	– What to Do Before Buying	47
Chapter 3	– Getting to Know the Porters	51
Chapter 4	– Viewing and Catalogues	54
Chapter 5	– Buyer Beware	60
Chapter 6	– What to Buy at Auction	62
Chapter 7	– What Not to Buy If You Want to Make a Profit	70
Chapter 8	– When You Arrive	73
Chapter 9	– Buyer's Premium and Other Costs	76
Chapter 10	– If You Can't Go to the Auction	78
Chapter 11	– The Modern Auction House – Internet and Live eBay Sales	81
Chapter 12	– Bidding and How to Get Noticed	86

Chapter 13	– Collecting Goods, Including Paying, Packaging and Delivery	90
Chapter 14	– Staying in Touch – Mailing Lists and Newsletters	95
Chapter 15	– Your Rights	97
Chapter 16	– Ideas for Where to Make Your Profit	100

SECTION THREE – SELLING AT AUCTION — 103

Chapter 1	– Why Sell at Auction?	104
Chapter 2	– How to Choose the Right Auction House/s	109
Chapter 3	– Negotiating Better Commission Rates – and Other Vital Questions	114
Chapter 4	– Should You Set Reserves?	120
Chapter 5	– Protecting Your Interests	124
Chapter 6	– What Happens to Unsold Lots?	129
Chapter 7	– When and How You Get Paid	131
Chapter 8	– Your Rights	134
Chapter 9	– Tax Matters	139

SECTION FOUR – ESTATE AUCTIONS — 143

Chapter 1	– What Happens When Someone Dies? Estate Auctions	144
Chapter 2	– Why Sell at Auction?	149
Chapter 3	– Choosing the Right Auction or Auctions for Your Needs	160
Chapter 4	– Probate and Other Legalities	167
Chapter 5	– How to Get Lots to Auction	171
Chapter 6	– Protecting the Interests of the Estate	173
Chapter 7	– Getting Paid and Paying Tax	179
Chapter 8	– Conclusion	181

Section Five – Information & Auction Directory — 182

Glossary	183
Publications and Websites	187
Auction Directory	189
Permissions	233
Index	235

Introduction

AUCTIONS are wonderful places to be – if you know what you're doing. If you don't, they can be uncertain territory, places for the novice buyer to lose money or for the beginner to miss out on vital profits. It doesn't matter who you are or how much you're worth, there's always money to be made – as long as you know how.

But who am I to show you the tricks of the trade and the best ways to earn extra money as a career or hobby or to tell you just when it's the right time to buy or sell at auction? My name is Fiona Shoop and I'm a TV and radio antiques expert. I have also written several books about antiques and over 4,000 articles on the antiques trade, including many on making money at auction and how not to make mistakes. Above all, I've been dealing in antiques since 1982, so I've learnt from my own experiences. I've also had to use auctions for reasons other than business, such as when I move home and don't want to take everything with me.

There was also the time when my father died. This is often the first auction experience for many people because the bereaved family has to clear the estate. It's a difficult time and full of pitfalls for the unwary. Because of my own experience and the questions my sisters asked me at the time and because it is a regular topic on my radio phone-in shows, there's a section dedicated to dealing with estate auctions. It's the hardest possible time to start using auctions and I don't want anyone else to get caught out. I was able to prevent my dad's other heirs from losing thousands of pounds through bad cataloguing and other methods. Hopefully, with my help, you'll also be protected.

But auction houses are also really enjoyable, and I'll show you what to spot – and what to avoid – when buying for profit. I'll teach you the hidden tricks, not just of the auction houses themselves but of your fellow buyers. It can be full of costly pitfalls if you don't know what to spot.

I always get asked when I'm on the radio how to find the right auction house. That's one of the reasons there's a directory at the back of this book. But it's not just about location. I'll reveal what questions you need to ask when choosing an auction house for selling your goods and how to spot those auction houses where you shouldn't buy anything – unless you want to pay over the odds or get ripped off. My advice could save – or make – you a fortune.

So read on and you'll discover how to profit from auctions – and have fun doing so.

Good luck,

To my mum who introduced me to auctions – and has been regretting it ever since. With grateful thanks and love for all your help over the years, especially recently.

And in memory of dad whose collections I finally got to see in detail when clearing his estate. I wrote the section about estate auctions because of my experiences then, and those pages are dedicated to him.

Acknowledgements

Writing a book relies on the help and kindness of others and I would like to thank the following, not just for their help with writing this book but, in many cases, for their assistance over the years when I was an antiques journalist and editor:

Sandra Shoop for teaching me to bid when I was six. More than three decades on, I've definitely got the knack.

Lisa Freeman-Bassett of Cheffins and Bruce Cairnduff of Dreweatts, and its various incarnations, who have been a delight to deal with over the years and who supplied dozens of images for various publications, including this book. They work for two of the best auction houses (or several in Bruce's case) in the country.

Mark Oliver at Bonhams for showing me how to catalogue properly and for helping to turn my china collection into an Eighteenth Century thatch cottage when I was only 21.

Gorringes of Lewes and all of their staff for allowing me to take so many photographs.

George Kidner in his Lymington saleroom for his help over the years with buying and selling, writing articles and books and even filming TV shows. George Kidner Auctioneers is still one of my favourite auction houses.

Charles Ashton and Sarah Flynn at Cheffins for their advice, images, information and, in Charles' case, for helping me sell my dad's estate.

And to everyone else who has sent me press releases and images for this book and various publications since I started writing about antiques in 1992 – a decade after I started dealing. Thank you.

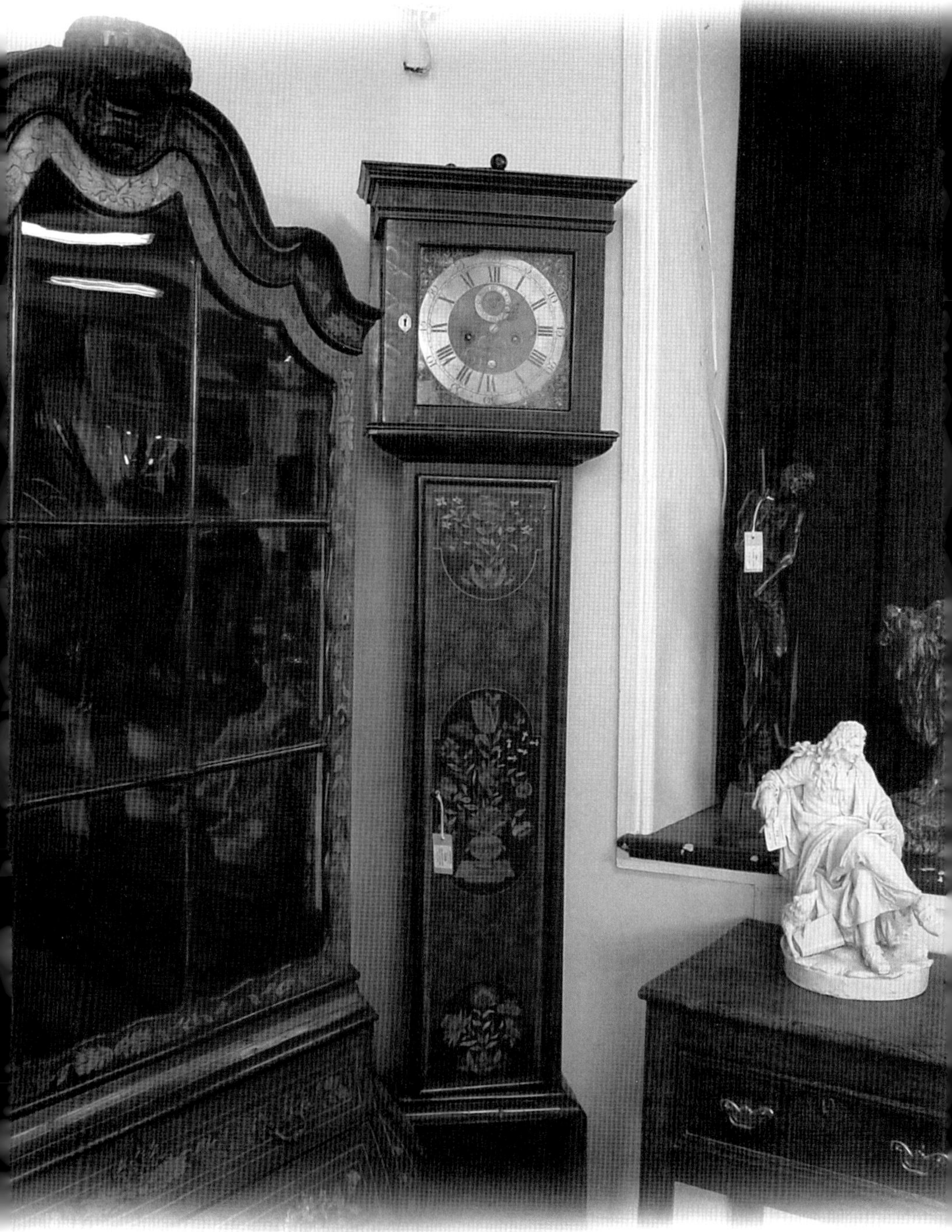

SECTION ONE
AUCTION BASICS

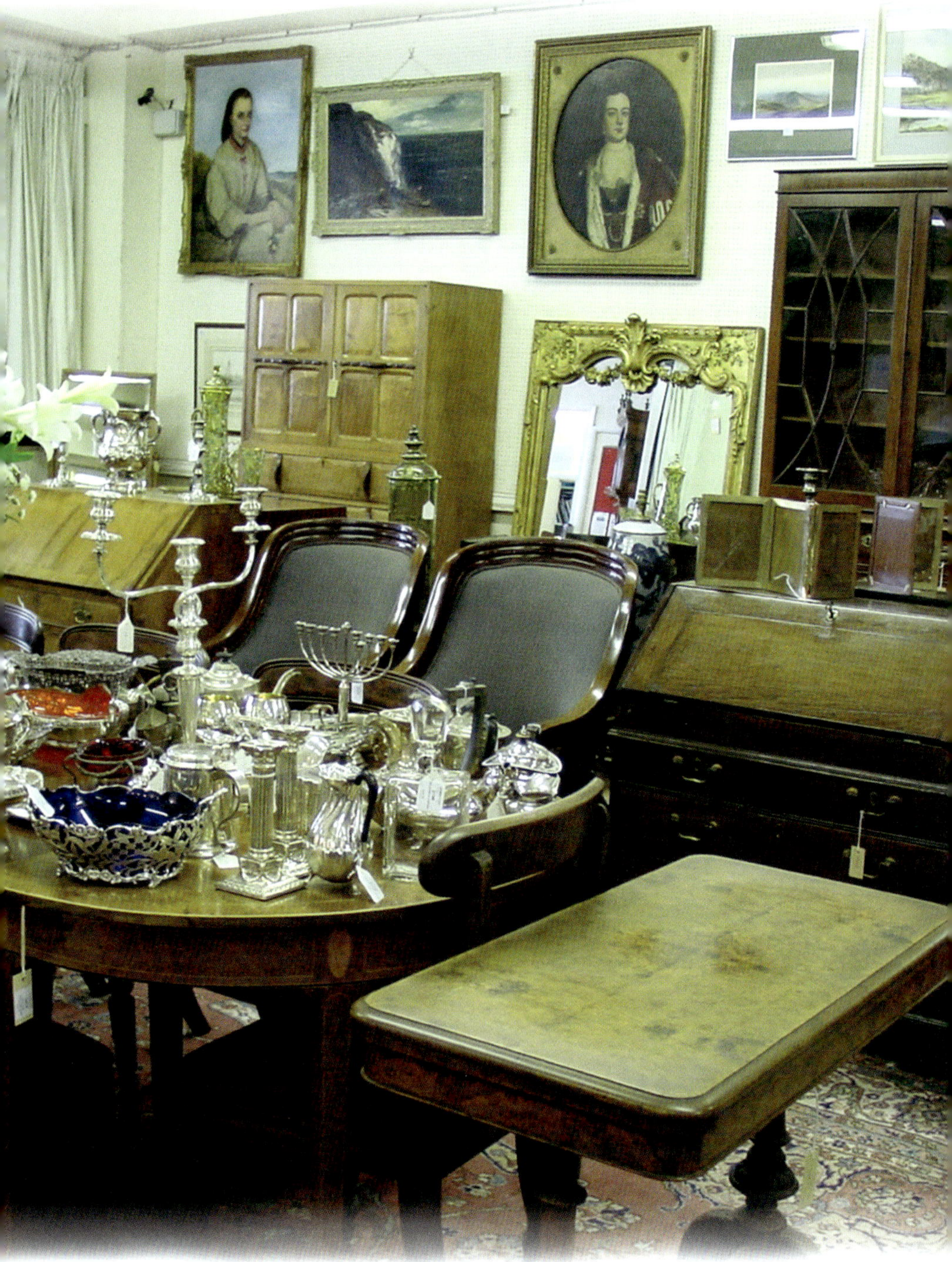

CHAPTER 1

WHY USE AUCTIONS?

FOR MANY people, the auction world is full of potential traps but, once you know what to spot, it's an easy way of making money – which is why I've been going to auctions for most of my life. And it's not just for making money but saving it. There are lots of different types of people who could benefit from auction houses, not just the obvious ones, and that's what makes them such exciting places.

WHO USES AUCTIONS?

- **Antiques dealers** – Auctions are obvious places for buying cheap lots to sell on for a profit
- **Interior designers** – For quality or 'do-up' furniture, fabrics and accessories with a difference so houses become homes, not replicas of each other, as well as for bargain appeal
- **Students** – For cheap essentials such as crockery and furniture (including desks) for a fraction of the primary market (i.e. retail shops) and they love having something different from everyone else. Bargains with character
- **Fashion buyers/designers** – Even Kate Moss buys vintage clothes. Auctions are a great way to find something which sets you apart. You can also find retro fabrics at rock bottom prices
- **Prop buyers** – Whether it's a major film, period drama or school play, auctions are fantastic places for picking up props at a good price
- **Hotels** – It's amazing how many hotel/bed and breakfast owners buy pieces of furniture and even crockery from auctions, especially if they want to improve their star ratings with a few pieces of antique furniture without the cost of buying direct from dealers
- **Families** – They find auctions a great opportunity to buy something for the home which not everyone else has. Ikea has its place but everyone recognises where you've got your furniture from and for how much. Auction buys set you apart and show originality
- **People moving house** – If you're downsizing, changing eras (will your modern furniture look right in a modern, minimalist house?) or just fancy a

change, auctions are fantastic places to find what you want easily. And there's no waiting for goods to become available, no trawling around antiques fairs, shops or centres. You find everything you want in one place – or a few if, like me, you just love auctions

- **Need a change** – When the state of the housing market or your own needs stop you from moving but you're bored with what you've got, set a different mood for your home by buying and selling through auction
- **Inheritance** – If Great Aunt Mabel's Victorian jewellery isn't your style, sell it at auction and buy something you love with the money. You will still remember her but her inheritance won't languish at the back of a drawer
- **Estates** – One of the hardest parts of dealing with a loved one's death is where and how to clear their goods whilst honouring their memory and protecting the estate (see Section Four)
- **Clearing space/goods** – Reasons can include needing extra space when you have more children, having visitors come to stay or simply wanting to de-clutter your home. Sell unwanted goods at auction instead of giving them away
- **Buying history** – There are some auctions where prices reflect the importance of the person whose goods are being sold, such as royalty and entertainers, or who have a place in history (e.g. Jackie Onassis). The same applies to items from places of interest such as London's original Savoy Hotel (where there was a rush to collect the beautiful Art Deco furniture, fittings and a host of other items when it closed for refurbishment) or from stately homes. People get to own a little piece of history or something someone they admire has touched
- **Just to make a profit** – You don't have to be an antiques dealer to make a profit from auction, whether it's a one-off or a regular habit. Everyone can do it

WHAT ARE THE ADVANTAGES?

This will be covered in more detail at the beginning of the 'Buying' and 'Selling' sections, but there are some excellent reasons to buy and sell via auction, including those listed above:

WHEN BUYING

- You get what you want in one place, all at the same time
- There is the opportunity to add a touch of originality to your home
- Unusual presents which show that you've thought carefully about what you're buying. Much more personal than a gift voucher

Save money by buying good quality furniture at auction for a fraction of the price of some flat pack stores. Or make a profit by buying where the dealers go.

- You get what you want for your budget
- Auctions are great places to buy goods which you can sell for a profit elsewhere, especially job lots which often include fantastic bargains

WHEN SELLING

- You know you're not being cheated. The person buying is not the one valuing, unlike selling direct to a dealer (see p152)
- The convenience factor. Someone else does all the work (pricing, advertising, describing, selling)
- A one-off effort. Everything goes to one place so it's out of the way in one go instead of you having to find individual buyers/dealers
- Vital paperwork. There's a paper trail which stops disputes when dealing with estates or other parties such as the tax office or divorce lawyers

WHAT ARE THE DISADVANTAGES?

Ironically, auction houses work for both buyers and sellers. You win some, you lose some. The way this works is that not everything does well at auction. I'll

> ## *What it means*
>
> See also Glossary, p183.
> **A lot** – The name given to individual listings in auction catalogues
> **Job lot** – The term used for several goods sold together in one go or 'lot'

be giving you more information about this later when discussing what to buy and what not buy at auction. For example, ordinary tea and dinner services go for a pittance at auction which is fantastic if you're buying but obviously not if you're selling. But it does mean you get rid of the sets all in go instead of risking a single piece breaking en route to car boot sales, antiques fairs or in the post when sold via an internet auction (where, incidentally, the cost of postage is often higher than the price received). It's not just about money but convenience. But there are disadvantages and I'm going to show you how to make the most out of auctions so you're aware of the risks

- You might fall in love with something and not be the highest bidder which can be frustrating, especially for novice auction-goers
- You don't always get the highest price. Some goods just don't do well at auction, such as lesser quality diamond rings
- Specialist auctions (e.g. musical instruments) are excellent when selling rarer pieces but more ordinary items don't make the money. However, they will at general auctions
- Not all auctioneers are equal and the wrong one could lose you money. But don't worry, I'll show you how not to get caught out
- Commissions and lottage can add up. But at least you'll have sold the goods if clearance is your main reason for selling
- You have to wait for your money. It depends on the auction house but expect to wait three-four weeks before your cheque comes. You might get cash when selling direct to a dealer, but will you get as much as you could through auction? It depends on your needs

OTHER FACTORS

I love going to auctions, whether I'm buying or selling. It's a good place to meet people and find out what's happening in the antiques world or your particular field of interest. It also gives me ideas for articles or books. Auctions provide ideas for designers and those decorating their own homes and the chance to buy interesting goods at affordable prices. I'm not just talking furniture, but also rugs and carpets (antique, vintage and brand new, the latter for bargain prices) and attractive curtains for a fraction of the price of new ones – or in some cases, even the cost of material. But it's not just the place for buying goods to put in the house. You can also buy garden statues – my stone bird bath cost me £5 and a similar one at the local garden centre, cost over £100. If you want to age stone or concrete garden ornaments or furniture quickly just add yogurt and they look antique in weeks. Lawnmowers sell at some general auctions for under £20 and I've even seen second-hand Dyson vacuum cleaners sell for £25 which is a tenth of their price new. A friend bought all her fitted carpets for her four-bedroom house from an auction for under £300. You can also buy double-glazing, stained glass windows, UPVC doors and a host of other goods. One restaurateur bought everything he needed at an auction house which specialised in selling commercial goods such as cookers, tables, chairs, crockery and cutlery, Again, all were obtained for a fraction of the cost, leaving the businessman more to spend on staff, advertising and food. It's all about knowing where to look.

Auctions aren't just great places to buy bargains, sell at a profit or to offload goods for practical reasons. They really can be exciting. I love nosing through job lots such as folders of art (better known as folios) and talking to the porters to find out what the latest trends are, what's coming in later auctions, what specialist auctions are coming up and what they're buying themselves. It's a fascinating world and, with my help, you can make even more money from it.

Specialist knowledge is not uniform so ask around to find the best auction house for your needs.

CHAPTER 2

How to Find an Auction House

THIS MIGHT not be as simple as it sounds. On a very basic level, if location is all that matters, check my directory (see p189), your phone directory or your local newspaper. For some of you, finding a convenient auction house is the most important aspect. For others, locating specialist auctions or auctioneers is more vital. As well as the directory, personal recommendation or word of mouth is ideal. Speak to dealers in the field in which you're buying or selling, but be aware that not all dealers like others to know their business. I buy a lot of pictures from one dealer and wanted to research a particular artist. I looked through my reference books, then clicked on Google (www.google.co.uk) and, quite by accident, found out exactly from which auction house he'd bought the painting, what else was in the lot and how much he'd paid. If I wanted to, I could bypass him completely and buy from his source – which is why not all dealers want you knowing where they go. Some may find it offensive to be asked. Don't be surprised at this as many dealers earn their entire living from the antiques trade so can't afford to lose you as a valued customer. Others, like me, just like sharing information. What I will add, though, is that I don't necessarily recommend all of the auction houses listed in the directory but have tried to make it as full as possible. I know from experience that auction houses can change. Both good and bad auctioneers can leave which makes a difference, so ask around and trust your own judgement. I may like some auction houses but not necessarily all of their auctioneers, so I try and work with them accordingly. And I use a variety of auction houses to sell my range of goods. For instance, if I have a specialist item such as Garibaldi's signature, I won't sell it at my local auction unless it has a specialist department. I want to reach the highest possible price, which means selling through a specialist books and ephemera auction.

I've written lots of articles and news stories about books and ephemera, so I know to sell them through top specialist auctions such as Bloomsbury Auctions, Cheffins and Dominic Winters. But that's knowledge through experience. How do you find out where to go if you don't have contacts?

What it means

See also Glossary, p183.

Ephemera – The name given to items meant to have been ephemeral, i.e. not long-term. Autographs, letters, diaries, postcards and cardboard or paper packaging (e.g. cereal boxes) come under this heading. Ephemera is best sold at specialist fairs or auctions as it tends to get ignored or under-valued in general auctions and needs an expert auctioneer to catalogue it to reach its best potential.

PUBLICATIONS

There are several antiques publications which carry auction directories, information or advertising which show what specialist sales are forthcoming and, even if you miss the latest one, at least you'll know where to go in future. For more details, see p187. It is not an exhaustive list as distribution for antiques publications is not always extensive, so I've based it on what's easier to find and what the trade use. These are worth buying for details of both specialist and general sales.

Whilst these are the main general antiques publications, there are many specialist clubs which contain details of relevant auction houses and specialist sales, many of which have websites. Search on the internet or simply ask around at antique fairs. You can also ring some of the auction houses listed in the directory for advice, asking if they have specialist departments or specialist sales – not necessarily the same thing as some auctioneers, whilst listed as 'general', have excellent specialist knowledge.

I also read newspapers, not just for listings but for the latest information on sales. If I want to sell a first edition Harry Potter for example, who better to go to than someone who has recently made the news for achieving high figures for one they've sold? It means they have the right market and know how to sell what you're selling. It's also a case of 'taking coals to Newcastle'. If I want to sell Rye pottery, I'll sell it in Rye which has an established market. But if I want to buy it, I know there's more competition in that area. There will also be more knowledge about those particular items, meaning prices will be higher. It's still worth looking there but I'd also check other auctions further away where I'm more likely to find a bargain – if the auctioneer has enough knowledge to catalogue it correctly.

THE INTERNET

In the earlier days of the internet, there were several sites which acted as a personal auction search engine. Either for free or for a small fee, they'd search auction catalogues on your behalf, letting you know when your chosen objects were due at auction, where, and their estimated price. That way, I discovered

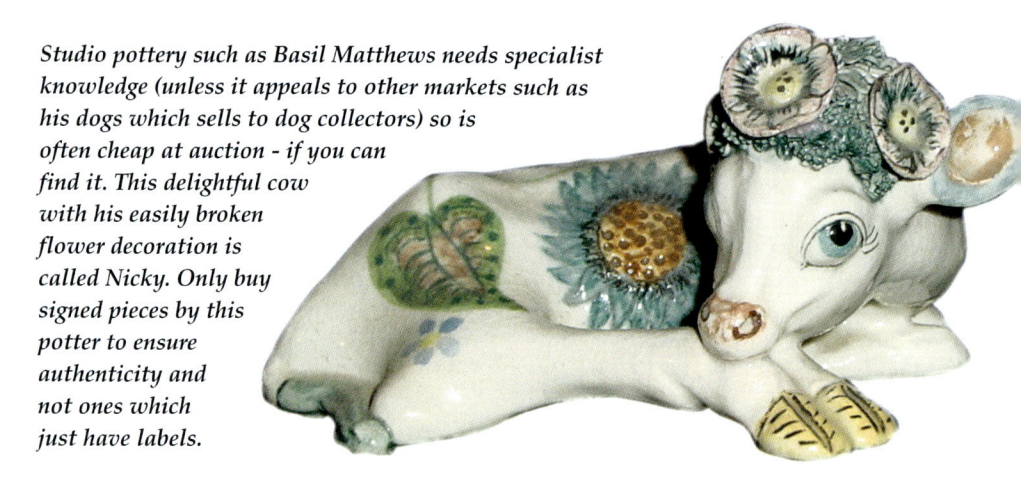

Studio pottery such as Basil Matthews needs specialist knowledge (unless it appeals to other markets such as his dogs which sells to dog collectors) so is often cheap at auction - if you can find it. This delightful cow with his easily broken flower decoration is called Nicky. Only buy signed pieces by this potter to ensure authenticity and not ones which just have labels.

three rare Basil Matthews figures were coming up at auction hundreds of miles away that very morning. Had I searched earlier, I could have attended the auction, but I still had time to speak to the auction house, determine their condition and bid for them.

What surprises me is how few of those sites now survive. There are websites which fulfil this need but there's also a gap in the market for a really good one. Some auction houses now have Live eBay (see p81) but sites like iThesaurus which promised so much just didn't last.

However, the following are worth checking out for auction details:

- www.artfact.com – Subscription needed but the free newsletter is useful
- www.auctionlotwatch – Only searches online auctions like eBay
- www.governmentauctionsuk.com – Subscription needed to search for amazingly cheap liquidated and government-seized goods
- www.invaluable.com – Subscription needed
- www.ukauctioneers.com – Free registration

I have also signed up to auction houses' own websites and receive their catalogues by e-mail. This means I can then do a search within the catalogues if I'm looking for something specific. I also speak to porters who are the mainstay of the auction world. They are often overlooked by novice buyers who assume it's the auctioneer who has all the knowledge. Whilst many do, the porters cover the entire sale, not just specific subject areas. They know what's coming up and can also warn you of damaged lots. They'll also ensure that you know what's coming up at auction which is of particular interest to you. Remember, it's in their interest for the sales to do well so they'll want to make sure you're there not just once but every time it's useful for you. If you collect in specific areas, see if there are relevant websites, not just official collectors' clubs but those belonging to dealers and fans who might choose to list relevant auctions. Some collectors' clubs hold their own auctions. Just ask or look at their websites or newsletters for more details.

CHAPTER 3

FIRST STEPS – PARKING AND OTHER MUST-ASK QUESTIONS

IN AN IDEAL world, all auction houses would have decent parking. The reality is that those who have their own car park get full very quickly. Depending what you're buying, the parking situation is important to know. Jewellery is light and easy to carry but I wouldn't want to walk to a distant parking spot with £10,000+ worth of jewellery in my bag when people have seen me buying it. And when purchasing pictures, who wants to risk carrying them to or from a nearby car park in the rain – even if they are small enough to be manageable? As with antiques fairs, the key is to ask the right questions and then arrive early – just like the pros. If there isn't a car park or it's 'staff only', the auction house can advise you of the best places to park. This might not be obvious from a map as not all car parks are good to use for auctions. They may not be safe or well lit, may have height restrictions, steps or time limitations etc. One auction house has parking outside with an hourly cost the same as the all day car park just yards away. You won't know unless you ask. The auction house will know where the best places are. I'm always allowed to park in 'staff only' car parks. I just ask the porters.

It's not just securing the parking space that matters. Make sure you can get out easily. At the end of the auction, the buyers will cram into the car park, not caring whom they block in. I always park right by the exit, facing out but with access to my boot so I can load the car easily and still get out without problems. Those who park right by the doors might find it easier to load their vehicles, but are virtually guaranteed to be stuck there until the other vehicles have left – which can be hours if dealers have trapped you and aren't prepared to miss their vital lots. The auction house might not be as co-operative as you'd like as their business is to make money and regular high buyers will take precedence over new or irregular ones.

> ## Make the Most of Parking
> Another reason to befriend the porters. You might be able get into the car park before it's officially open, secure your spot and always have extra help loading. That's what I do.

Parking costs

If the auction house doesn't have its own parking or says it is for 'staff only' – which might not always be the case, ask the porters – find out where both the nearest and cheapest parking is. To be honest, it depends what you're buying and how often. You're normally there for two days – viewing and buying – which adds up if you go to every auction be it weekly, fortnightly or monthly. If you're buying for a profit, those £5+ parking fees really do cut into your profits. If you're buying from a London auction, you'll be paying a lot more, possibly including the congestion charge. That said, it's all relative. I drive when I can, not just for convenience and a way of staying dry – not all auction houses being near bus stops or train stations – but because, if I find out about a 'must-visit' event happening locally, I can get there with ease. I've even met people at the auction and then visited their home or business to buy more goods. I only do this if I feel safe doing so and even then I always tell people where I am.

Jewellery precautions

Buying jewellery from an auction without its own car park needs to be planned more carefully because of the higher risks. Of course, most of the time, it's perfectly safe, but buyers have been robbed by people who note what they've bought at auctions, fairs or shops. Jewellery is an easier target than any other type of antique because of its size and relative value of the object. I've left Bonhams with £12,000 worth of jewellery in a small bag and jumped straight in a cab. If you're not happy, ask the auction house to order you a cab and don't leave there until it's arrived. Just be sensible.

Other questions

I'll be covering some questions in the 'Buying' or 'Selling' sections such as how to register, how to pay and when you get paid. The questions in this section relate to both buying and selling at auction.

Be careful when buying jewellery, such as this £9,200 diamond bracelet, at auction. If driving, always park nearby. Otherwise, ask the auction house to call you a cab. DN.

WHAT SORT OF SALES DO THEY HAVE?

Most auction houses have general sales. These can have a variety of names from General Auction to Fine Art and Antiques or a not so obvious one such as Blenheim Auction (Bonhams' version of the general auction). These can be weekly, fortnightly, monthly, or less often, but are generally a regular event. They can also have specialist auctions which vary hugely both in quality and content. Gorringes in Lewes holds weekly sales at its Garden Street auction, and more specialist and fine art sales less regularly over three days at its North Street saleroom. It's a case of asking or looking at the auction's website or sales brochure if they have any.

WHO ARE THE BUYERS/WHAT IS THEIR MARKET?

If it's antique dealers, then, as a buyer, you've got competition – but for a good reason. It means the auction house is known to be worth buying from. The good news is that as a seller, you know that the buyers are there. But if your goods are not particularly unusual, be realistic about the price you'll achieve. The auctioneer will talk you through the estimate based on what they can achieve (see next question). Remember, it's in their interest to get the highest price as the more you make, the higher their cut – both from your commission and the buyer's premium.

What it means

- **Hammer price** – The price achieved for a lot before extras are added/deducted (commission/premium etc). See also p184
- **Commission** – The percentage the seller has to pay based on the hammer price. This varies from 8% upwards. 12.5-15% is normal
- **Buyer's premium** – The percentage added to the hammer price – 10-15% is normal. This premium is often forgotten by novice buyers who end up with a larger bill than expected, especially if they got carried away and exceeded either what they intended to pay or the number of lots they'd decided to buy before the auction started. It really is a case of buyer beware

Note, VAT is added to the commission and buyer's premium.

ESTIMATING ESTIMATES

One question to ask is how realistic the estimates in the catalogue are. This might seem an odd thing to ask, but there are three ways of setting estimates:

- Too low – This tempts the novice or greedy buyer into bidding for the lot, believing either that they can afford it or that they've found a bargain
- Just right – Basically, how much the goods should achieve
- Too high – To tempt the buyer into paying too much, especially if they are a novice and trust the auction house to guide them

There are also what we term 'guestimates'. This is when similar goods haven't been sold at auction before and the auctioneer takes a guess as to their value. This is particularly the case when collections are sold. Then the market establishes itself and determines the 'worth' of the lots in question. If you are the person selling these items, it's best to sell just a few initially to set a precedent and see how the lots do. You could lose a lot of money otherwise if the market is overloaded with unusual goods and you have no clear understanding of their desirability. When it comes to auctions, precedence is vital because it reassures both the auction house and buyers that there is an established market – even if you were the one to set it initially.

As a consultant for Bonhams in the days when it was owned by Phillips, and when working as a cataloguer on various TV shows, I always set accurate estimates because I feel it's the most honest way to work and shows the would-be buyers if they have a chance of getting the goods. If the prices are too aspirational, I don't think you'll get as many bidders. If they are too low and there are not enough bidders, they might not get up to the right level. If

The estimate on this pierced silver basket being sold at Gorringes a couple of years ago shows what the auctioneer thought it would achieve based on his experience and the state of the market at the time. The number 2230 is the lot number. The long number at the bottom is the seller's identification number.

reserves are set, your goods won't be sold or you might not achieve a good price. I worked on one TV show where the auctioneer started far too low and we didn't have a chance of achieving the right price. That's why I don't recommend estimates that are too low. Some auction houses insist on setting estimates either too high or too low but, if this doesn't work for you, try a couple of lots or buy or sell elsewhere. You could be wasting your time and money otherwise.

Are lots catalogued?

This might seem a strange question as you'd expect all auction houses to catalogue their goods. This is true in most auction houses. They're not only catalogued, but divided into handy sections such as china, jewellery, paintings and prints, or books to make life easier for the buyers. However, I was once offered a job to turn around an auction house. One of the reasons it was failing was that it didn't have a catalogue. I'm not talking a glossy, heavily illustrated one, but nothing whatsoever – not even the self-typed and printed A4 sheets of paper which are used at many weekly or fortnightly general auctions. There was nothing. In fact, one of the jobs I was given at the two days I spent there was quickly to put lot numbers on items – as the auction was in progress. This is a hopeless way of doing business as no one knows where they are, there are no descriptions of the goods as a reference and, as a seller, there's no real record of your goods for buyers – or if they were even sold. I couldn't take the job, partly for this reason. If you see an auction where the lots are not numbered and there are no catalogues, my advice is the classic auction one – buyer beware. I'd also advise a would-be seller to steer clear and find a more organised auction house where buyers can find their goods clearly listed so they don't miss them and you know they've definitely been shown to would-be buyers. Proper paperwork is vital when buying or selling at auctions and the catalogue helps to establish this. If the auction house can't even get a catalogue written, will they ensure your buying or selling details are accurate? Personally, I'd advise you to avoid selling through any auction house which doesn't even follow this most basic rule of auctioneering – that of having a catalogue.

What it means

Reserve – The lowest price at which a lot can be sold. Some auction houses don't recommend setting reserves but, if you're selling a lot with a £800-1,200 estimate, this allows them to sell it for £300. Some auction houses will have a discretionary reserve which allows them to sell the lot for 10% (or an unspecified amount, watch the paperwork) lower than your reserve. I always use a 'set reserve' meaning that they have to stick to my figure, or, if they ignore it, make up the difference themselves. I *always* do this when selling for myself or on behalf of someone else. It doesn't matter whether I am acting for a member of the family or working as an antiques consultant on a TV show. It just means that your interest is protected.

If you just want to clear low value lots, don't establish any reserves or you could be stuck with unwanted goods (see also p129).

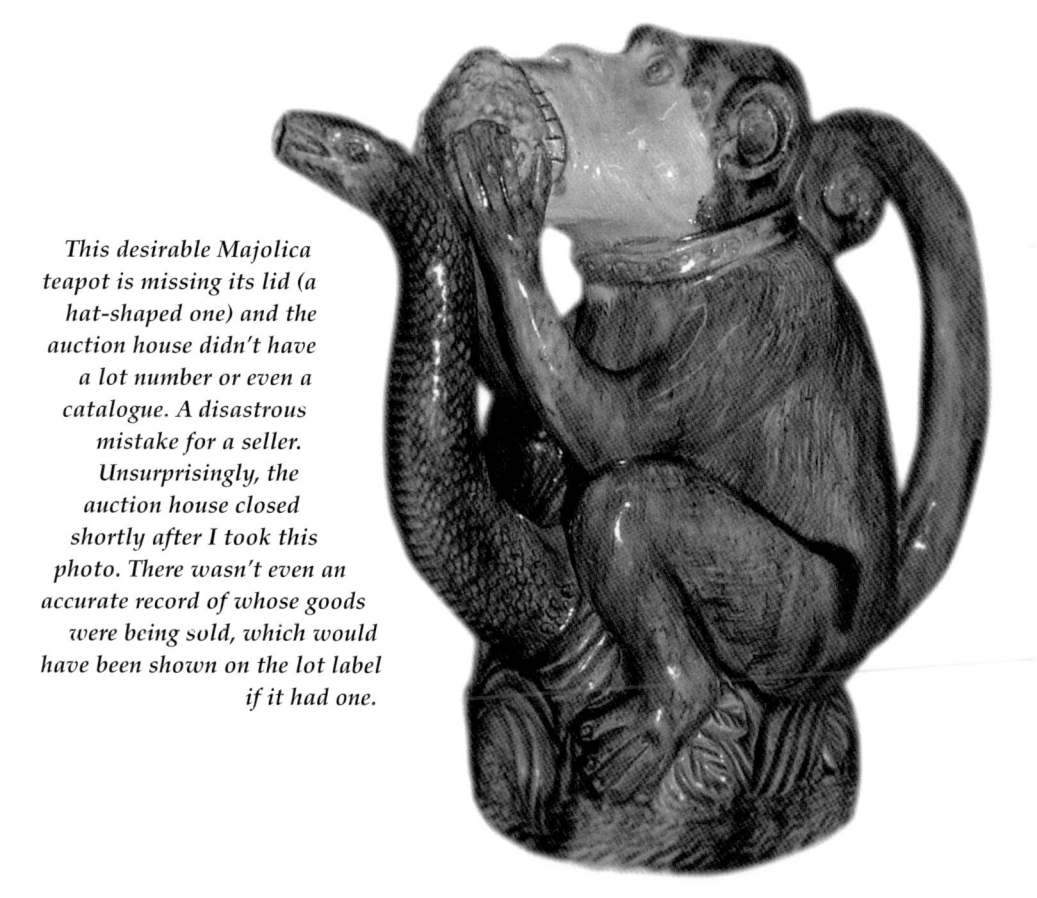

This desirable Majolica teapot is missing its lid (a hat-shaped one) and the auction house didn't have a lot number or even a catalogue. A disastrous mistake for a seller. Unsurprisingly, the auction house closed shortly after I took this photo. There wasn't even an accurate record of whose goods were being sold, which would have been shown on the lot label if it had one.

CHAPTER 4

Beware of Auction Rings and Other Saleroom Trickery

AUCTION rings damage auctions and their reputations. They are also harmful to buyers and sellers alike but you needn't be a victim to one. I love watching rings as most of them are really not that clever – not even the ones where the auctioneer is involved. Don't let rings worry you. Just follow this advice and you won't get caught out. But first, what is a ring?

Types of auction rings

There are actually different types of auction rings and they've been around for years, especially in the silver world. Basically, their aim is to:

- Drive down prices of particular lots
- Raise prices of particular lots
- Drive away competition

Driving down prices

The best-known form of the ring keeps down prices. Instead of competing against each other as they would normally do, the ring members unite so only one buyer bids for the lot in question. This is then sold on, either by one of the ring's dealers with the price being divided between all of them or, rather unpleasantly, they then sell the lot within their own ring. This is sometimes done blatantly in the auction house's own car park. The idea is that all of the ring members bid for the lot and the highest bidder pays for it. The money is then divided amongst the ring – after the original buyer has been repaid. This means everyone profits. If you're the seller, this is not where you want to sell your goods or you could lose money.

Raising prices

Ring members also help each other to reach the maximum possible price at auction by bidding for each other's lots, forcing up the price. By sitting at the back of the auction house, you can actually see this happening. In this case, I just don't bid, but not everyone is aware of what is going on concentrating, instead, on the lot in question. Two or more of the ring members will bid to try to make it less obvious. If they accidentally drive the price too high and are the highest bidders, they have to buy the lot which they'll simply resell either at that or another auction. I was working on a TV show when I realised that our contestants had brought along their friends not just for support, but to act as a ring. I watched the friends bidding for two of our featured lots before I could prove it and then quietly signalled to the auctioneer not to take their bids before speaking to the friends. To be honest, when they were lumbered with buying back one of their own lots at an inflated price, I wasn't too sorry but I stopped them bidding for any more. What they were doing was illegal – and we had it on camera. It was stupid but it shows just how greedy people are. For some dealers, it's a very profitable way to earn a living.

Intimidation and other methods

Not all auctioneers are ethical. Sometimes they are either ring members or are paid off by the ring to do their bidding, turn a blind eye to the ring's activity or keep out other buyers. Again, this is not in the interests of the seller or the auction house. As an antiques journalist, I've had complaints from dealers – not just members of the public – whose bids were 'not seen' at auction. It doesn't mean that if your bid was missed, there's a ring or a complicit auctioneer. I've been caught out when the auctioneer was too vain to wear glasses. I just call out to draw attention to my bid and it's taken. What I'm talking about is far more serious. It's when the auctioneer deliberately avoids taking bids for anyone but a ring member. It's the ultimate way of keeping prices down. They might take one or two bids initially to make it look more legitimate, but they don't welcome new buyers or let them bid.

At least that's a gentle way. In other cases, would-be buyers are warned off more aggressively, sometimes by violence, but that is very rare.

The positive news

The positive thing is that rings are normally easy to spot and, once you've done so, you don't buy or sell at that auction. I believe, possibly naïvely, that the auction houses have got to take responsibility for the rings. They don't have to let members buy or sell through them. The trouble is, many auction houses do because the bidders don't always operate as a ring and tend to be good buyers. It's profitable. I just won't buy or sell if I suspect something is going on. I once went to review an auction house for *The Antiques Trade Gazette*, but I phoned my Editor to say that I couldn't review it as there was a ring. I accept that many good auction houses have them but this one was blatant. If I can spot a ring, so can you.

How to spot rings

It really can be easy to spot all but the most professional rings.
• Sit at the back of the venue so you have good, all-round sight of the bidders
• Look for dealers exchanging glances before one or two of them bid. This is the most telling sign. They always look at each other but are rarely seated or standing next to each other
• Watch how the auctioneer or other dealers respond to them. You might see some people stop bidding as they know they won't get it, know the price is being driven artificially high, or feel too intimidated
• See what happens in the car park after the sale. They sometimes sell the

Don't let your goods be knocked down to an auction ring. Visit the auction house and observe the action in the room before selling. If you're a buyer, spend your money elsewhere or you could either be intimidated or forced to pay over the odds.

goods on in the car park itself. It's not just a normal sale where someone approaches you after the auction to offer you a higher price for what you've just bought (this is normal), but a whole group of people buying the lot or lots. It looks as questionable as it actually is.

Auctioneer tricks

There are many tricks by auctioneers which most of us take for granted – even though we shouldn't. They're so common but make sure you don't get caught out. I bought a lot at an auction and, afterwards, the smarmy auctioneer admitted he'd deliberately driven up the price. I had been aware of this and made a conscious decision to carry on bidding, even though I ended up paying a far higher price than the legitimate bidding. But, in this case, I also knew the auctioneer had catalogued the goods wrongly. His estimates were not only completely off but he'd missed a painting by a very good artist in the box I was buying so it was still extremely profitable. It was just not as good as it could have been with a more honest auctioneer. I profited simply because he wasn't as good at his job as he thought he was. Ultimately, it's your choice if you continue bidding. I did because I wanted the goods and knew what their real value was. In the same sale, the auctioneer ended up paying £600 himself by bouncing a bid which I didn't top.

Bouncing bids

'Bouncing a bid against the wall' is when the auctioneer takes imaginary/fake bids to up the price, often to reach the reserve. The pretend bidder is usually at the back of the hall unless the competing bidder is, in which case, the fake bid is taken from another part of the floor. Many auctioneers see this as a normal part of bidding, I always think it's unethical and it can backfire. I once went to an auction where the auctioneer was trying to force up my bid for a Charlotte Rhead jug this way. I knew what he was doing and stopped bidding. His fake bid topped mine as he didn't realise I wouldn't be trapped this way. In the end, one of the porters came and told me the auctioneer had 'made a mistake' and the jug was mine for my final bid if I wanted it. I didn't. So they were stuck with an unsold lot and had to explain this to the seller. As far as I'm concerned, an auction is a business and not a place for playing games, especially with good, regular buyers. I stopped going to the auction after that until it changed hands.

Other tricks

I'll be covering some of the common tricks used by auctioneers to hide damaged items later (see p61), but there are other ways for people to get caught out at auctions apart from rings and bouncing bids. If you're aware of these traps, you can avoid them – or accept them when it's in your interests to do so. I'm not talking about agreeing to something illegal or unethical, but it can be in your interests to accept an auctioneering trick if it means that you get what you want. It's up to you to protect your own interests and to be aware of exactly what is happening both before and after the auction.

Running down goods

When one of my friends submitted lots for the first time, she wanted to see how an auctioneer conducted business. Had she been happy, she'd have used that auction house again. As it was, she was horrified at having the auctioneer mock her items when he put them up for sale. By doing so – even though they were not damaged and were perfectly good stock – he ensured they would not reach their full potential. My friend had the confidence to stand up and withdraw her lots – all of them – there and then, humiliating the auctioneer in the process but protecting her own interests. I've never heard of this before but a good auctioneer doesn't have to like what they're selling, they just have to sell it. The lot in question was decent glass. It wasn't 'faddish', brand new, or anything else objectionable. Most importantly, the auction house had agreed to sell it and had catalogued it for a good estimate. There was no reason for the auctioneer to behave in such an unprofessional way. It also damaged the auction house as she told other dealers and we all refused to buy or sell there ourselves.

Hiding goods

One of the worst scams I ever heard about was when an auction house laid off a lot of staff. This was known in the trade as 'The Night of the Long Knives'. There have been a few instances of this in the trade in the last 30 years. In one case, a young auctioneer was disgruntled at losing his job and, knowing that he was leaving at the end of the week, decided to make a profit before he went – at the expense of the seller. He deliberately mis-catalogued three boxes of good quality studio pottery by Lucie Rie. Their value is such that they shouldn't be sold in a job lot of more than two or three pieces, let alone three boxes. He didn't put the boxes on display so no one knew what was in them. Then he bought them for himself at a knock down price. No one had seen them, they were wrongly catalogued and the poor seller, who had trusted the auctioneer, lost out. The lesson here is don't buy from an auction house which has laid off staff until after those staff members have left. Once, when I was offered a job to save a failing auction house, I discovered the unpaid staff were collecting their wages by stealing lots from sellers. They knew that the auction house would have to honour those debts with the sellers, even if they wouldn't pay their own staff or would just cover it up. Unsurprisingly, the auction house went out of business shortly after that.

Once an auction house has lost its reputation, no decent dealer will buy or sell there. That means only novice buyers and sellers get caught out – unless you ask the right questions. If you like the auctioneer, ask how long they've been there and what their future plans are. If they're about to leave, wait for a while before selling there.

MISSING GOODS

When I was running the advice column for the now defunct magazine *Antiques & Collectables*, I had a couple of letters from people complaining that

Lucy Rie bowl. Her simple designs are much in demand, so expect competition.

they'd put things into auction which went missing before being sold. In each case, it was when an auctioneer had just left the auction house. I'm certainly not saying that they stole the items when they went, but I've seen how some auctioneers treat their areas as kingdoms with no sense of order and can imagine that the items in question disappeared in the chaos. Neither of the sellers had delivered their goods personally. There are times when this can't be done, especially with a specialist auction some distance away, or when the items are too heavy to carry. It makes sense to have them couriered. Just make a note of exactly what was sent. It's amazing how a follow up phone call, e-mail or letter – or several, in some cases – can get results. If the items have been listed by the auction house with an estimate, then you can either claim off their insurance or take them to the small claims court. At least you'll get your money back if the auction house has a record of receiving them. It is unprofessional and it does happen, just persevere. It took me several calls and e-mails before one auction house found a lot they'd collected from my house. They finally found it after I refused to take no for an answer. Losses are rare, but you need to be aware of how to handle the situation. Don't let them get away with it.

Now, whenever I deliver goods to auction, I make staff list the important pieces. Ten or 15 years ago, I used to send boxes with the receipt just listing 'x boxes of china but have learnt to ask for specifics so I have a 'paper trail'. For example, 'a collection of autographs including George IV and Victorian Prime Ministers, plus an autograph album' - not just 'ephemera' but specifics. Of course, I trust the auction houses I choose but you can never be too sure, not just about things going missing but other unexpected problems. For instance, if there's a fire, the insurance company knows what it's covering and I know exactly what's gone where – particularly if I'm selling at three or four different auctions at a time. Relevant paperwork is important, not just for my own records and the auction house's but the taxman (see p139).

AND FINALLY

I don't want you to think that auctions are places of pirates and thieves with the auctioneers waiting to rip you off. Far from it, most are wonderful, friendly and informative venues with auctioneers and porters there to help you not just make a profit but to enjoy doing so. As with all ventures, as long as you're aware of the pitfalls, you can look out for them. I don't enter into any business without doing my homework and buying and selling at auction, even an internet one such as eBay is no different. Just be sensible – and enjoy

Silver can offer bargain buys at auction but check for dents and 'ringers' (p185) before bidding.

Be practical when buying. Don't waste your money on anything you haven't inspected. How can you tell if these chairs are comfortable when they're hanging up? Ask for help or you could be throwing away your hard-earned cash.

SECTION TWO
BUYING AT AUCTION

CHAPTER 1

Why Buy at Auction?

THERE are many reasons to buy at auction but many revolve around the same issue – you can save a fortune. I'm not just talking cheaper antiques (buying where the dealers do) but household goods, quality furniture at bargain prices – even really basic furniture at student-friendly prices. But it's not just about the money, there are other reasons as well, including:
• You (and the competing bidders) determine the price, and not a single dealer in a shop, fair or centre, so you're not relying on someone else's opinion or profit margin
• Apart from rare pieces such as Fine Art, many antiques are cheaper at auction than buying direct from dealers (they have to make a profit to pay their bills, after all)
• Auctions are a great place to buy household goods – from plant pots and garden ornaments to carpets, double glazing and electrical goods such as fridges, vacuum cleaners and televisions
• A great opportunity to accessorise your home. You can find cheap pictures, many sold F&G (framed and glazed) saving you the cost of framing them; attractive rugs, curtains, linen and cotton sheets
• There is always affordable crockery which is different to everyone else's. Buy it by the boxful at a fraction of the cost
• Jewellery is a great buy, especially engagement rings and strands of pearls
• With few exceptions, which are clearly marked in the catalogue (generally with a sword mark), goods sold at auction are free from VAT apart from the buyer's premium
• Even if you can't afford the top pieces, you can see and handle them in the company of experts. It's a great place to network, as well as learn
• Great finds and amazing buys
• The entertainment value. Whether you're people watching or learning about antiques, the auction world is always entertaining
• It's fun. I love the buzz of auctions, not just the savings I make there

Types of auctions

As I mentioned before (see p20), there are different types of auction from general (no matter what they call it) to specialist. Both offer money-making or saving opport-unities but they also offer other benefits. No matter what your specialist field is or whether you're buying to collect, for your home or business, it's worth knowing what's out there.

People watching is an important part of buying at auctions. You need to see who's buying what and if anything else is going on. Sit at the back of the room for the best position and so only those standing right at the back can watch when you bid.

General auctions

These offer amazing opportunities but the quality varies hugely, not just between auction houses but also between sales. Some auction houses have several different salerooms (branches) which allow them to regulate quality. Cheaper goods which are fine but might be aimed more at home use than the middle to higher end trade will be in more frequent sales (weekly or monthly), whilst other salerooms hold less regular sales, allowing them to build up more choice lots. These can still be general sales but with specialist divisions (e.g. pens, pictures, books etc). Both types of sales allow for bargains but the better quality ones will also bring in the better dealers – and more knowledgeable competition with deeper pockets but that doesn't mean they want the same lots as you.

There are bargains and potential profits at every single auction, no matter who the other buyers are or what goods are for sale. The trick is knowing what you want and why you want it. Sometimes, it's worth buying something like a centrepiece that catches your eye which you can use to attract people to your antiques stall. Or maybe something unique for your office. No matter what, it is often worth paying more for a stylish piece which will capture other people's interest. I paid slightly over the odds for an amazing Art Deco bowl by Charlotte Rhead. I used it to draw people to my stall where they'd buy cheaper goods – ironically, ones with a higher profit margin. I loved that bowl as its bright, attractive colours had so much appeal. It was perfect for attracting attention to my stall and that's what I paid for. Part of me wishes I hadn't sold it, but being a dealer means learning when to let go. But that doesn't mean that I don't buy for myself, as well as for profit.

I love general auctions because of the wealth of goods on offer. I have specialist fields both as a dealer and a collector but still find general auctions very successful. One of the reasons is that there's less competition than at a specialist sale.

SPECIALIST SALES

There are specialist sales in most areas of antiques and collectables. What's interesting is how the market has changed. There are now specialist sales aimed at the interior design market catering for professionals and people who want to buy something with extra style or character – as well good quality curtains, linen and lighting. These are the auctions worth watching if you're in that trade, buying for yourself or are a specialist dealer. There is often very good furniture available and the term 'interior design' could alienate some of the more macho dealers who assume it's too frou-frou for them.

Some of the best bargains can be found at general auctions but, if you only buy particular goods, a relevant specialist auction is often the best place to find what you want.

WHAT IS A SPECIALIST SALE?

There are various specialist sales. Most general auctions have specialist sections of china, glass, jewellery, books and pictures. Some also have other specialist areas in only a few of their general sales a year, for example stamps or entertainment. It gives them time to build up enough good quality lots to attract the serious buyers (trade or collectors) which they wouldn't be able to do if they had fewer lots but on a more regular basis. It's a matter of quality over quantity. Some auction houses can have dedicated stamps and entertainment sales for which they have a good reputation, enabling them to build up the lots and attract more important pieces. If I were buying a famous dress from a famous film (e.g. Audrey Hepburn's black dress from *Breakfast at Tiffany's* or Judy Garland's Dorothy outfit from *Wizard of Oz*), I would rightly expect them to be at these specialist auctions where they would gain more attention and, therefore, higher prices, than in a specialist area of a general auction. It's a question of knowing who's selling what and when. You need to get yourself on the lists of auction houses which deal with your particular field of interest. To be a good buyer on a regular basis, you have to do your homework.

Buyers must be on mailing lists, in contact with the auction house or buy *The Antiques Trade Gazette* (see p187) to keep up to date with auctions which are not planned months ahead. The 'lead time' of magazines (time between going to press and publication) might not allow for updates where the date is set less than two months in advance. Speak to the specialist auctioneer and ask them to keep you informed or put you on their mailing list and watch their websites. That's the best way to ensure you don't miss out.

> *This is an iconic dress from the classic film,* The Wizard of Oz *as worn by Judy Garland who played Dorothy. It exceeded its £35,000 estimate and went on to sell for £140,000. It is one of six gingham dresses worn by the star in the film. One of the others is owned by Debbie Reynolds.* **BN.**

The advantages of specialist auctions

A specialist auction is an auction dedicated to a particular field. Its advantages include:

- Every lot covers the same field e.g. coins, medals, stamps, blue and white china, Art Deco, jewellery, Fine Art etc
- Having catalogues which are a useful guide to what's available and current market prices
- Presenting a good opportunity to network with people with the same interests, including dealers who might have what you want or want to buy what you're selling
- Getting the chance to see some of the best pieces in your market
- The opportunity to discover pieces you didn't know existed
- More information about lots, together with better cataloguing, specialist auctioneers and specialist buyers (some of whom will be happy to share their expertise)
- More common pieces are often cheaper than at a general auction because most of the buyers already have them and want the rarer pieces

Ultimately, specialist auctions offer the dual opportunities of buying and learning. Also, the chance to network can lead to further buying, friendship or just good business links whether with dealers, collectors or, if interior design, potential suppliers and clients. They can also give you ideas of what's available and what you yourself can achieve.

The disadvantages of specialist auctions

There are just a few:

- There is more competition for what you want
- You'll discover more knowledgeable cataloguing so more people know what's worth buying than at general auctions where things get missed more easily (no one can know everything)
- Higher prices are realised for more desirable goods because of more competition, better marketing and better cataloguing
- There is no privacy, unless you leave commission bids. Competing collectors and dealers can see what you've bought – and for how much

Specialist or general sales?

To be honest, there's no point limiting yourself just to specialist auctions, as you'll miss some great bargains. Depending on how specialist your area, general auctions are always worth watching. Apart from anything else, you could find some amazing buys which have nothing to do with what you're officially buying. I've seen brand new, quality electrical goods, still in their boxes, sell for a tenth of what you'd pay in the shops (admittedly, with no guarantee offered but I've always been lucky) and other great bargains, even if it's just a coffee table or comfortable armchair for your house. I once bought a camera tripod for just £8 – a similar one would go for about £40 in a shop – and used it when filming a 'recce' for a TV show a few days later. I've also bought attractive, beautifully framed paintings for £2 (plus buyer's premium of 10%) – not what I was there to buy but that's the joy of general auctions, you never know what you'll find. Even if you're buying solely for business, you can benefit from looking at other lots. There are bargains everywhere if you look for them.

This arcade game was sold in a general sale but would have attracted more buyers at a specialist sale.

General auctions can have fantastic and unexpected bargains. Cheffins' ran a house sale in Cambridgeshire which had stunning furniture such as this four-poster bed (buyers take note, antique beds are generally too small for modern mattresses so you might have to pay to have one specially made). But it was the rocking horse that proved the best buy as there were seven in the sale and it's a fairly specialist market. I phoned a dealer who bought nearly all of them at knock-down prices as there were no other serious buyers there. CH.

Chapter 2

What to Do Before Buying

Before buying anything at auction, you need to ask some basic questions. All auction houses have different Ts&Cs (terms and conditions) so never take anything for granted. Before buying, always ask:

- How do I register?
- How do I pay?
- When can I collect the goods?
- Do they supply packaging?
- If not collecting the goods yourself, do they post them?

How to register

This varies greatly between auction houses. I was once caught out by one of the most unusual terms – paying cash to register. I've only ever encountered two auction houses where this happened and the only reason they agreed to waive the condition was because I was writing an article on them. Otherwise, I wouldn't have been able to bid as I wasn't near a cashpoint and didn't have the necessary £35 on me. Another auction house charged £15. The logic behind this is that anyone not willing to pay a fairly low sum might not be a serious buyer. But 'cash only' demands were made on these occasions even though a credit card or a cheque are acceptable forms of payment when buying goods at those auction houses. It was a rare scenario, but that's why you really do need to ask about registration before turning up.

Most auction houses now require you to fill in a form before bidding, giving details such as home address and phone number. Once you've registered, many of them retain your details on computer meaning you don't have to fill in a form every time you go. This also means they can give you computerised receipts quickly at the end of the auction without having to ask for your details again.

Some will require you to have ID. Again, this differs between auction houses. Some will accept a driving licence; others also want a recent utility bill. Ask before turning up so you know what to take with you. The good news is that, once you've registered, that's it – unless you move.

I carry two forms of ID with me just in case I hear about an auction when travelling around. Although there is a directory at the back of this book, it obviously doesn't cover impromptu auctions – those with handwritten signs on the side of the road. I might not always be asked for ID but it's on me just in case. It means that I never need miss out on the chance of a bargain.

How do you pay?

Surprisingly, not all auction houses accept credit or debit cards. Some won't take cheques; others insist that the cheques must clear before the goods are collected – no matter how many times you've bought from them before. With cheques being gradually phased out, this will one day be irrelevant but if, for the time being, you prefer to pay by cheque, just ask before buying. It's not always convenient to return to an auction house to collect goods if it's not local. Some will also accept a banker's draft – fine if you're near a bank and the auction finishes in time but don't count on it unless returning the day after the auction.

Most salerooms take cash but some won't for amounts over £5,000 because of money laundering laws which, apparently, are open to interpretation judging by the fact that some will accept cash for any amount up to £9,000 – some higher. It differs. Just ask in good time before attending the auction so you have time to go to the bank if necessary.

Not all countries have 'Chip and Pin' for cards which means that there are ways of over-riding the system when paying by credit or debit cards if you're not a UK resident or, like all of us, occasionally forget your Pin number. I was at an auction house with a new debit card and the new Pin number hadn't come through in time. I bought over £4,000 worth of paintings but it wasn't a problem as they over-rode the system and, instead of typing in a number, I simply signed in the old-fashioned way. Not all auction houses will think of this so, if you don't have 'Chip and Pin' or don't know your Pin number, ask to sign instead.

When can you collect the goods?

Generally only after your cheque has cleared if paying by that method. Different salerooms allow goods to be collected at different times, but always after payment when you can present the payment slip as proof of purchase

(not just that you've paid but which lots you've bought):
- During the sale
- Immediately after the sale and/or a day later
- Only a day after the sale

DURING THE SALE

Depending on the saleroom and what you've bought, you can collect your goods during the sale. This tends to be based on levels of disruption so don't expect to buy chairs people are sitting on or the table on which everything has been loaded until after the sale.

AFTER THE SALE

This can either be immediately after the sale finishes or a day later. However, some auctions, such as those held in village halls, have to vacate the venue after the sale has finished so you must collect your lots then. Others allow you to collect everything the day after the sale, especially if buying furniture, for minimal disruption.

ONLY A DAY AFTER THE SALE

This can be the best time for collecting larger goods as there won't be as many cars around and the porters will be less busy so can help more. There are some sales where you are only allowed to collect the goods on the following day. This is especially true of chairs, which although catalogued lots, are also used as seats during the auction and the saleroom obviously can't allow them to be collected early. Tables laden down with various lots often can't be collected early for practical reasons – not just because they'd have to move every single lot on top of them which would be disruptive, risk damage and theft but also because carrying a table across a busy saleroom would be very disruptive and a health and safety issue in a crowded hall.

Failure to collect according to the Ts&Cs can result in fines/storage charges.

DO THEY SUPPLY PACKAGING?

People get caught out when auctions don't have any packaging or boxes for goods being collected. If driving, just put boxes and packaging in the car. I tend to carry extra bubble wrap and if I am buying paintings, special carriers too, so

I can unload the other end. Bubble wrap is often in short supply and, if your goods aren't newspaper-friendly (because it might cause staining or they need extra protection) come prepared. I have been at auctions which have no packaging whatsoever which is why this question is listed. Some salerooms are very well organised so might be amused to be asked but they'll understand that not all auction houses take as good care of their clients.

IF NOT COLLECTING THE GOODS YOURSELF, DO THEY POST THEM?

In an age where auction houses sell live via the internet, I am still stunned that not all of them post goods. I'm not even talking breakable china but flat, unframed pictures. You will either need to collect them yourself or arrange for them to be couriered to you – if the auction house will agree to pack them. Always take out enough insurance if not collecting the goods yourself just for peace of mind. I have seen too many accidents not to recommend this. But some auction houses will be happy to post goods. Ask before bidding.

Don't feel that you have to limit yourself to auctions within easy driving distance. There's always a way to get the goods to you; some just a bit easier than others.

Breakages do happen so take your own boxes and packaging if you can – or you might get a single, scruffy sheet of newspaper for a fragile piece of china like this Minton bone china plate with pierced trellis work border. **WW.**

Chapter 3

Getting to Know the porters

FIRSTLY, you don't have to go to an auction house to leave a bid. If you can't get there, ring the saleroom and ask someone to tell you whether the lots you are interested in are in perfect condition. Most auction houses count on reputation and return business so will be honest. In almost 30 years of dealing, I've only ever been caught out once and have never bought from that auction house again. Incidentally, they were closed down by the police for fraud after too many people were conned by misdescriptions and fraud. Reputation is everything.

Most people think of the auctioneers as the people who run the salerooms and who are responsible for their reputation, but it's also down to the porters. A good porter will advise you what to buy and what not. When I arrive at my regular auctions, I get greeted with a cup of tea (note, this is not mandatory so don't expect it) and tips on what's hot at that auction. They also tell me about reserves so I know if it's worth my while bidding or not. This is not just legal but advisable, as it separates the serious from the amateur. You could argue, as a seller, that this could mean there might not be as many bids but, as a buyer, it saves you time and money. If you go in with limited funds, this knowledge helps you to concentrate your resources so you don't hold out for unattainable lots. Not everyone knows you can ask about reserves – but now you do and this could help you to get what you want.

Porters are also able to tell you what lots not to buy. This is very useful, especially when there is something wrong with the lot or it's an impulse buy and the lot is completely over-priced. They will also warn you if the lot is a second i.e. not perfect according to the pottery – this could be everything from a pin prick to poor painting, depending on the pottery. Sometimes, it's almost impossible to spot why a piece is marked down as being a second. This might seem obvious to those who know that a scratch through a backstamp means the china is a second, but some auction houses deliberately put the lot sticker over the backstamp to hide the scratch. A good porter will alert you to the problem – especially if they know you.

It's the porters who allow me into salerooms early and before they're even officially open. I get into the private staff car parks as well. I can't guarantee that you will enjoy get these perks but it does show that the porters can, in some instances, be much more helpful than the auctioneers. They know a lot about the business and know their customers. I also get warned about competition and who's worth watching. I don't pay for this information; I'm just polite and smile. I've been giving this advice for years but a smile doesn't cost anything and can get you a lot in return. Besides which, I like porters – no ego, just friendly people happy to talk about the business they love and share their knowledge with those who appreciate their expertise. I also get extra help packing and tend not to have to queue, depending on the auction house and how busy it is.

The porters are in charge of the cabinets and will talk about what you want to see and how much interest there's been in it – vital information when sussing out the competition – the more competition, the higher the price. They'll also let you know if there's something wrong with it. Most buyers love to show off when they spot damage – some to 'prove' their expertise and others to deter the competition. The porter will also alert you to something you might have missed, not just in that cabinet but another one. And everyone has favourite items. I always get told about them and make a point of asking to see them. Porters have generally been in the business for years and work in the saleroom alongside the buyers, so often spot something the general auctioneer has missed – and it's interesting to know what other people like, especially when buying to sell. It's also a good way to nurture a relationship. The porters relish the chance to show what they know and they want friendly people to win; it's not about money but relationships. To be honest, I often prefer the porters to the auctioneers. They have nothing to prove and love learning so they want to talk. Auctioneers can often be insecure about people with greater expertise; porters aren't and they're a lot more helpful in those instances.

I'm short and not very strong and I need help reaching items and lifting them. I also normally have a friendly porter in each area of the saleroom and get help readily. It saves time and provides further opportunity to gather information. I have big ears – not literally – but I love eavesdropping; it shows me who's buying what, what to buy and what to avoid. They can be incredibly indiscreet as more dealers are so interested in what they're doing that they don't pay any attention to anything but the lots. I've learnt so much by listening in. Especially what lots are worth considering – and might not be marked up as so in the catalogue.

Porters are in charge of the cabinets and will even point out desirable lots you might not have noticed once they get to know you.

It's also worth watching porters during the auction. Some will bid on behalf of commission bidders and it's useful to know which one the auctioneer pays more attention to. I've seen auctioneers ignore some bids and look at certain porters before accepting others. I know which porter to ask to bid on my behalf to get the best results – they can often be better than the auctioneers who can also be used for commission bidding, with worryingly varying results.

At the end of the auction, porters are the ones who will pack up your lots (instead of leaving you to do it yourself) and carry them to your car. Other buyers have to do that all by themselves. I never have to for which I am very grateful as I buy a lot at auction and they also help me to load my car.

Get to know your porters, they will help to make you money and will also make the whole auction experience a lot more interesting and enjoyable.

Chapter 4

Viewing and Catalogues

MOST AUCTION houses have viewing days before the auction. Some have viewings just a couple of hours before (usually if held in church or village halls, not permanent salerooms). In these days of absentee bidding (e.g. Live eBay or commission bids), you can't always follow basic principles but, when you can, always obey the most important yet simplest rule of them all:
- Never bid without inspecting an item

Now, the reality is that you will, at some time or other, ignore this rule. I know you will because I still occasionally do it – and almost always regret doing so. Why? Because you won't know if what you're buying is damaged or not. That's the whole point of going to viewings.

Viewing basics

Viewings are an essential part of auctions and are not worth skipping to save time. You could lose money. Here are some viewing basics:

- Always allow plenty of time for viewings
- If possible, attend on the first day of viewing and double check your intended lots on the day of the auction. Why? Because goods can get damaged or go missing between the first and last viewing times
- Always buy the catalogue. Never rely on the ones they have around the auction room as you'll need to make notes and read the full catalogue to ensure you haven't missed an interesting lot
- Handle every single lot you intend to buy to check for damage and 'feel'. This will be covered in more detail in the next chapter, but it is important to ask yourself if the weight is right, if the item feels smooth when it should, if there is an unexpected dip and if you like how it feels. The latter is more for people buying for themselves as it is obviously important that you like the texture of the item before buying it – velvet versus velveteen, for example

- Don't let people see what you're doing. I'll be discussing this under the 'catalogue' section of this chapter but one of the most important things to remember during viewings is that you don't want to alert anyone else to an exciting find
- Ask the porters questions. What the reserve is, how much interest has been shown, if they know of any damage and what lots you should be looking at. The latter is a useful question to ask when first buying at an auction house before the porters get to know you; it also shows that you respect their advice which will reap rewards as they'll be eager to look after your interests, tell you what to buy and what to avoid
- If buying furniture, look under the auction's lot labels. Are they hiding scratches or other damage? If you are new to that particular auction house, ask the porter before removing the sticker or it could look as though you are doing something underhand such as swapping labels with a lesser or more important lot (see Chapter 5 – Buyer Beware)
- Watch other people (subtly) to see if they're excited about a particular lot
- When buying folios or a job lot of pictures, look at every single picture
- Check every item in a job lot. The most interesting ones tend to be near the bottom as dealers try to hide them. A better dealer won't hide the best item right at the bottom, but just above it
- Open cupboards. It's amazing how many auction houses will use the space – or unscrupulous dealer try to hide lots inside them
- Open all drawers in desks or chests of drawers. Has the seller forgotten to take something out? Do the drawers fall apart when removed? Better to find out now than after you've bought them when it's too late to do anything about it
- Use viewings to check out the auction house if you haven't been there before. Find out about parking, registration, payment, auction times etc

Never buy anything you haven't inspected or you could end up wasting your money on something damaged and hard to sell like this Royal Winton basket with a broken handle.

Viewing protocol

As with all businesses, there are dos and don'ts when it comes to viewings, especially if you're not known to the auction house:

Do

- Be polite. People will be more inclined to help you. Always thank the porters for their help with opening cabinets or handling larger lots on your behalf
- Ask questions of porters or the auctioneer (as long as they're not serving someone else)
- Rearrange folios or job lots. It is perfectly legitimate behaviour; just do it subtly and never put the most interesting lot on the bottom – it's the first place the experienced buyers look
- Wash your hands before handling fabrics or folios. I'm not casting aspersions, but auctions can be dirty places. Just check before touching anything where grime can rub off
- Admit if you've broken something – or you might not be welcome back
- Find out what you need to know before bidding e.g. when the auction starts, how to register, payment etc (see p47)

Don't

- Join in a conversation unless invited to do so or you know the parties involved. Dealers and auctioneers don't welcome interlopers and this could count against you when bidding (an unprofessional auctioneer will miss your bid or deliberately 'up' the bids)
- Interrupt auctioneers or porters when they're with someone else, even if it looks as though they're just having a friendly chat. Keeping regulars happy is big business for them so don't cause offence by demanding service
- Open cabinets full of smalls (e.g. china). Ask for help, even if they're not locked
- Remove labels to look for damage underneath without asking
- Look over another buyer's shoulders. Wait until they've gone before going through folios or job lots
- Show off your expertise – keep your valuable knowledge to yourself
- Ask anyone else what they're buying. People don't like to tell potential competition or warn others what's worth buying
- Ask for impromptu valuations during viewings. There's too much going on and the auctioneers generally don't have time to deal with anything other than the viewing – unless you've made an appointment ahead of time. It depends on the size of the auction house and how many auctioneers they have

How to use the catalogue

I'm always surprised how many people want to 'save' money by not buying their own catalogue and use the auction house's one instead. Most, if not all, auctions will have a copy or two of the catalogue tied up around the room for reference. Depending on the saleroom and the quality of the catalogue, this can range from £1 for a cheaply printed A4 text copy with no images to £8-20 (or more) for a heavily illustrated, glossy catalogue. I can virtually guarantee that this minor investment will pay for itself. Apart from the information it contains, it also enables you to keep a record of what sort of prices that auction house achieves – useful for both buying and selling there.

I never read the catalogue before I go round the auction for the first time. This is a personal choice and means that I don't unintentionally limit myself to the items of obvious interest. It enables me to take in everything that's up for sale in my own time. I mark my intended lots in the catalogue as I go. Only when I've finished my first round, will I find a quiet corner and read through the catalogue properly, noting any missed lots and reading the description of the lots in which I was already interested. These can be hugely different from their reality and that's why I prefer to form my own impression first before relying on the 'expertise' of the auctioneer. You'll be surprised how often a fascinating lot has been missed by a general auctioneer or a dud lot marked up as being something far better than it actually is.

Misdescriptions

There will be more about this in the next chapter but it's amazing how often goods are described as being 'Victorian' and 'Edwardian' when they were made in the last decade – if that long ago. Let's just say that it's impossible that the Edwardian period (1901-10) could have been that productive. Reading the Ts&Cs (terms and conditions) in many catalogues makes it clear that the auction house 'cannot take responsibility for the descriptions' of its lots. I disagree, but do understand that not everyone can know everything and that there are cases when the auctioneer really didn't know what they were selling – and that's why I never rely on a catalogue.

Marking your catalogue

I love watching people who don't normally go to auctions as they make the classic mistake of being worried they'll miss their lot so circle what they want several times.

What's wrong with that? Well, not only have they alerted themselves to a choice lot but also the people standing either side and behind them. People will look over your shoulder and see what you're buying – or ask to borrow your catalogue if they don't have one of their own. Don't tell them what's worth buying by making it obvious what you want.

I don't even make notes in front of the lots I want but make a point of picking up something near them and making marks in my catalogue which people assume to be about that lot, not the one I was handling previously. This might sound like an unnecessary game but I've had people admit to looking at lots simply because I did or bidding because I was.

I also don't use obvious symbols for the same reason. I use marks which only I understand – and that's all that counts. But I also know that there are lots I would normally buy almost without thinking because I know what I collect, sell or want for myself. However, by handling every lot I want, I also know if these are damaged. If they are, I make a note in my catalogue to remind myself not to buy them. This is a mathematical symbol of an equal sign with a slash going through it ($\neq$) – this means 'not equal to', or in my language, 'no'. It's a useful reminder as I might automatically bid for it knowing that I had handled it. I don't usually make a note of my maximum bid in advance in case someone asks to borrow my catalogue – annoyingly, it is not the done thing to refuse, even if you want to.

Kitty Evershed signed studio pottery figure, est £200-400

Don't Always Trust Catalogues

Catalogues don't always tell the truth and not all auction houses admit if goods are damaged or fake, like these 'Guinness' toucans. Check everything before you buy and don't forget to look at the backstamps. Fakers don't always put much effort into them and, in the case of these so-called Carlton Ware pieces, they made obvious mistakes – genuine ones would have a script signature, not this 'older' mark. Check if goods feel imbalanced or if their colours (like these) are just too bright which are good pointers for fakes. If in doubt, save your money and don't buy them. Estimates are not always good indicators as some dishonest auctioneers will try to get the same for fraudulent goods as real ones or they might not realise they're fake.

What else the catalogue tells you

Catalogues will have the auction's Ts&Cs, times of viewings, contact details and, often, details of forthcoming sales, as well as the actual lots. The language used in catalogues can be confusing until you get used to it, for example, 'F&G picture' (framed and glazed). See glossary for further details (p183) or just ask the friendly porters – they love people who are learning the business, if they're polite, and love sharing their expertise so will translate any unknown phrases.

Some will also list details of their auctioneers' expertise which is worth knowing for when you want to sell lots.

CHAPTER 5

BUYER BEWARE

IN AN IDEAL world, all auction houses behave scrupulously but the reality is that not all do. Some use trickery; others make mistakes. I'm an experienced auction goer and I'm constantly amazed how easy it is to catch out novice or less experienced buyers. These tips will save you money and ensure that you don't get caught out by some of the oldest and most annoying tricks of the trade – not just by the salerooms' but also by dealers and other buyers.

JOB LOTS

When buying job lots, keep an eye on what's in them. Some dealers will try to move things around to suit their needs. I bought one lot of five items but a dealer had moved one of the stickers and swapped it with a lesser item. Not just moved it across the table but actually swapped the labels (with smaller lots, all of the pieces should have a lot number on them with the number of pieces in the lot e.g. 166/5). The porter didn't believe me and insisted that I was wrong, but I had bid for that lot because of the particular piece which had now been re-labelled. I was able to prove my case by pointing to the photo in the catalogue which clearly showed what items should have been in that lot. I have sometimes taken photos (with the auction house's permission) of job lots to avoid such problems. As I'm an antiques journalist, I never have a problem and many of the photos you see in this book are of job lots for that reason. Not everyone wants to take a camera into every viewing, especially as it draws attention to the lots you want to buy if you go at busy times. So do what I also do and record details of what's in each lot. Don't do it in front of anyone but move to one side and make notes. Contemporaneous notes can prove your case if you need to. Swapping lots is common practice, more so than most auction houses will admit, so be aware of it.

SWAPPING LABELS

All lots are labelled and smaller job lots, as I've just said, have every item stickered with the number of items in the lot (e.g. 166/5) or just the seller's code. These are easily removed so double check that what you're paying for is the same for which you were bidding. This can also happen with individual

When buying job lots, check that what you thought you were buying is still there when you collect it and complain to the auctioneer before you leave the auction house if it's missing or it will be hard to prove your case. WW.

lots and unscrupulous dealers. As you would when paying at a shop or restaurant, check the invoice before collecting. You have to pay before collecting lots, but don't leave the auction house until it's sorted out. If the piece you thought you were buying is no longer there, demand your money back.

Hiding damage with labels

This is a common saleroom trick where the damage on furniture, china or glass is hidden under the label. It is especially common with tabletops as scratches can be easily obscured with labels. They are easily fixed but at a price and you should know all the facts before bidding so you can take this into account with your highest bid. I've also seen expensive Wedgwood Fairyland pieces have their scratches hidden by lot numbers and the scratches on these are harder to restore. China restoration is expensive and, unlike French polishing furniture to remove damage, drastically affects the value.

Damage

Not all auction houses catalogue damaged lots. They're not being underhand; it's just how they do things. Always inspect lots before bidding or, if a commission bidder, ask about damage before leaving a bid. If you're caught out, remember that age-old warning *Caveat Emptor* – buyer beware. Check before buying to save your profit margin.

Bad lighting

If something is displayed in a dark corner, ask to see it in better light as the dim conditions could be used to hide damage.

CHAPTER 6

WHAT TO BUY AT AUCTION

THIS IS a general look at some of the best bargains in the auction world. You might think that it doesn't concern you as you only want to buy Nineteenth Century medals, blue and white china or First Edition children's books. However, the auction world offers more than just your obvious area of interest and there are some great deals to be had. Furniture dealers view auctions as some of the best places from which to buy. But if you want to sell a top quality table for top money, display it properly – with an epergne or other table setting and a beautiful dinner service. And where is the best place to buy cheap but good quality dinner services? Auctions.

How to profit from auctions

The best way is simply by keeping your eyes open. If you only look for one particular thing, you could miss out. It's not just about selling on for a profit but buying to save money. The whole joy of buying at auctions is the wealth of goods on offer which sell for less than in shops (primary and antiques), at antiques fairs or interior design shops – because the experts buy their goods from auctions. I have also bought much of my crockery, accessories and furniture, many of my paintings and even some of my garden ornaments and electrical appliances from auction. And I've saved a fortune by doing so.

What to buy at auction

Obviously, buy what you specialise in but also look at the following for added savings and profit. All prices quoted for auctions are exclusive of buyer's premium and VAT:

Job lots. Often a highly profitable buy, but be prepared to buy a lot of rubbish with the choice items. Bear in mind that auctioneers can make costly errors. Items in job lots which should have been sold for far more money individually

One of my favourite auction buys was this bird bath which cost me £5 over 10 years ago. Similar ones cost around £90 in garden centres at the time.

include a single chess piece (worth £170,000), a Moorcroft vase (worth £400) and a collection of 13 Kitty Evershed studio pottery figures, sold for £90 the lot and worth £200-400 each. Always look at collections of jewellery in job lots as most general auctioneers don't know costume jewellery and can often miss expensive, signed pieces. It's all about expertise and, if you know more than the auctioneer (and other people don't), you could make a fortune.

Art Deco. Apart from specialist Clarice Cliff sales, Deco is surprisingly cheap at auctions. A Wade Carmen figure which sold for £65 at one auction would sell for £200-300 at antiques fairs. Deco furniture and lighting is also cheap. The auction of goods from the Savoy Hotel in London saw astonishingly good buys with Deco lights selling for around £120, despite their history and quality. Expect to pay £300+ for similar, without the history, at fairs or more from upmarket interior designers.

Musical instruments. If you have children, you know how expensive 'cheap' violins are, but you could buy a Victorian one with much better resonance, feel and weight, for a fraction of a price either at a general sale or a specialist musical instruments one. Upright pianos can sell for as little as £50 – so much cheaper than a brand new one from a music shop or even a second-hand one from specialist dealers. Just remember that they'll need to be tuned when you get them back (as would any piano but this should be included in the price from many music shops) and play before bidding to ensure none of the keys are stuck or don't sound.

Electrical goods. Most salerooms state in their Ts&Cs that they don't guarantee electrical goods so check they work before bidding if possible (you obviously can't do this with items such as washing machines but you can check they don't spark when plugged in). Some auctions specialise in 'ex-shop' stock – either over-ordered stock or that left over when shops close down – and are great places for cheap TVs and vacuum cleaners. A Dyson vacuum cleaner costing around £200-250 in the shops goes for between £50-75 at auction.

Garden ornaments and equipment. These crop up at general auctions with surprising regularity. Expect to pay under £20 for a stone bird bath (£90-150 from garden centres or shows); £5 for garden loungers; under £15 for lawnmowers and £5-10 for strimmers. At the time of writing, garden ornaments were selling very well at antiques fairs. Just add yogurt to age them if you think they look too new. Antique garden ornaments and furniture are also available at specialist sales and general auctions.

Books. Whole boxes of books can sell for as little as £5 and I've even seen a batch of three boxes go for that small sum. Do what the experts do, snap them up, take what you want and sell the rest at the next auction. You don't even have to take the remaining ones home, so storage isn't a concern.

Carpets. Antique rugs tend to do well at auction but modern fitted carpets are also a great buy as stores and suppliers put 'end of line' rolls into auction.

Curtains. You can often find good quality ones and those that fit larger than average windows. Curtains at auction may not always be obvious bargains, but consider the amount of material used in them, their quality and the fine work involved in making them. If buying for yourself, make sure they fit, or factor alterations into the cost.

Double-glazed windows and UPVC doors. Just ensure you have accurate measurements.

Pictures. A cheap and attractive way to liven up your home and also make great deals for profitable sales. Look for signed lots which are already framed. Landscapes and animals sell better than portraits if you're thinking of selling on. Folios can be excellent buys. To maximise your profits, frame the pictures before selling them; it's a small investment for a major return. I count on making at least 10 times my original investment when buying job lots or folios at auction. Individual paintings are often great buys as well. I'm not talking Francis Bacon or Monet of course, but Victorian and later artists. I also buy to suit my personal taste so can enjoy the pictures on my own walls before selling them on. That way, I get to rotate my art so I don't get bored. And I make lots of money as well.

Curtains can be surprisingly good auction buys, especially if looking for larger ones or vintage material like these 1960s Winnie the Pooh children's curtains.

Stylish, signed china figures. Named pieces always sell better than unmarked ones but stick to style, no matter what the name, for best bargains.
Animals. Whether in pictures or china, animals sell but, as with everything, stick to quality, style and signed or backstamped goods. Beswick Beatrix Potter figures which sell for around £35-75 each at antiques fairs (for the more common ones) can be had for a similar price for a collection of 10 at auction.
Engagement rings. Why spend a fortune on a new diamond ring when you can buy a bigger one for less? Auctions are fantastic for stylish, quality engagement rings without the High Street price to match. Expect to pay under £150 for a £500-£750 insurance-value emerald or diamond ring. Leaving you more to spend on the wedding or honeymoon.
Dolls. General auctions offer superb value for doll collectors as the competition is relatively small and general auctioneers don't tend to know as much about dolls as they do about other toy markets such as teddy bears and model trains. For the same reason, job lots of toy cars can contain fantastic bargains if the auctioneer hasn't sifted through them carefully enough – but there will be more competition for toy cars than dolls.

Expect to pay about £10-15, or even less, for one of the more common Beatrix Potter ornaments by Beswick, like this Benjamin Bunny one. Sell it for £35-45 at antiques fairs – almost three times what you paid after the buyer's premium is taken into account.

Chinese and other Oriental porcelain. This is a very specialist area and one very few auction houses have a great deal of knowledge about, meaning it is a lucrative field for those who do have the right expertise. I went to one auction where pieces estimated to sell for £50-70 went for thousands with two knowledgeable bidders (neither in the room) bidding against each other, much to everyone else's bemusement, including the auctioneer's. I never value Oriental pottery for this reason; it is too specialist.

Ephemera. Paper goods, including diaries, letters and autographs are often sold by the box – sometimes because the auctioneer hasn't had the time (or interest and knowledge) to sort it out. Take your time, as there could be treasures. These go for surprisingly little, even in specialist auctions, and could reap rewards for the person patient enough to sort through them.

Display cabinets. Why pay £50-250 for an attractive display cabinet when you can buy them at auction for £20 or less?

Studio pottery. This is another area often overlooked by non-specialist auctioneers and dealers but which offers good profit margins. Stick to better known makes or stylish designs (the two don't always go together) but avoid unsigned lots, unless they are particularly attractive, as they are much harder to sell. Even stylish unsigned lots can struggle – but buy them if you really like them and don't need a fast turnover.

Crockery. Why spend £8-12 on a new dinner plate when you can buy a whole dinner service, plus extra pieces for £25? Most of my own crockery was bought at auction (and thoroughly cleaned before use) but I've bought and sold Denby, Poole, Royal Doulton and blue and white crockery, bought by the job lot at auction and made at least 10 times what I paid for it – even including buyer's premium. I've sold it to people who want to build up their existing

Unsigned goods are far harder to sell than signed ones, so stick to studio pottery and other china with backstamps, even if they're not signed with their full names like this Aline Ellis monogram.

This studio pottery terrier by Aline Ellis is signed so it's worth £100-200. Unsigned, I'd be lucky to get around £30-50 for it.

sets or replace broken pieces. Stick to the most common patterns for best returns; you'll have more customers that way, or add to your own, out of production dinner service. There are companies who buy job lots of discontinued crockery for people who need more of it. They can also make a fortune if buying job lots of 1950s+ crockery at auction and so can you.

Smoking-related goods. Unless they're particularly stylish, smoking goods are out of fashion, especially with smoking now banned in so many places. In short, the potential market is dying out. Interestingly, stylish glass opium pipes are still good sellers, probably because they are beautiful talking points and bought for decoration, not use.

Goods with local interest to your selling area. They'll be more expensive to buy locally but cheaper away from source. Then sell them where the highest demand is.

Christmas decorations and other seasonal goods. As long as you have the storage, you can pick up great buys after the holiday period. Not just modern

These Ugly mugs might not look like much and will sell for around £3-5 in most places but, near Llandudno where they were made, they're worth £5-15 each. Not a bad profit when buying a cheap job lot. These only cost £35 for five big boxes, although not all were signed.

decorations, cards etc but also antiques and collectables, for far less than you'd expect to pay at the height of the season. Sell when demand is at its highest for maximum profit.

Children's games. Buy 10 jigsaws or five board games in job lots for as little as £2. Perfect presents for kids. Don't forget to look for TV or book-related games.

Ex-restaurant or shop display goods. If you're setting up or redecorating your business, visit commercial auctions for superb savings. I kitted out most of my first shop that way (£5-10 for card and postcard stands, against £75-100 for new ones). Sadly, so many restaurants failing in their first 18 months, means new restaurateurs can save a fortune by buying their equipment second-hand – everything from furniture, ovens and other appliances, to knives, linens, crockery, cutlery and even chef's whites. Save around 75%+ – crucial extra cash for a new or expanding business.

Cars. There are specialist car and classic car auctions, but vehicles are also sold at some general auctions as well – presenting the chance of a great buy for those who know their way under a bonnet (or know someone who does).

Houses. Follow the same rules as normal auctions and NEVER buy without viewing. Know how to pay, don't bid more than you can afford and, hopefully, you'll get a bargain. You also have the advantage that, once the hammer goes down, you have around 28 days to pay. And unlike the traditional housing

Games such as this vintage Victory wooden Magic Roundabout *jigsaw sell for a song at auction. Buy them for around £2-5 and sell them to a specialist market for £30-50 at antiques fairs or internet auctions such as eBay.*

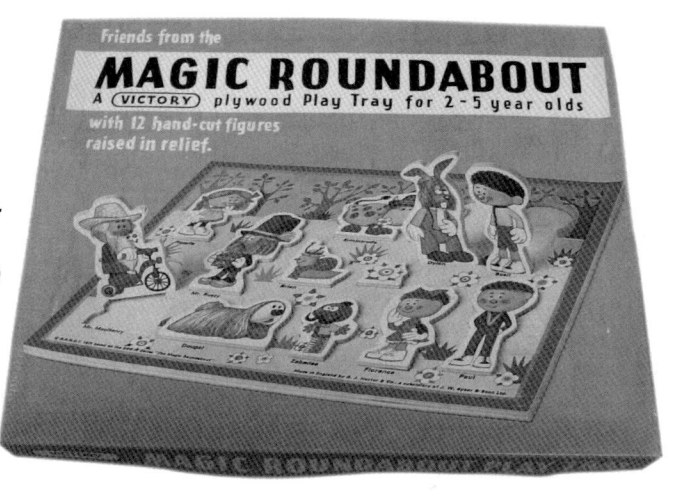

market (apart from Scotland), you can't get gazumped, so there are no wasted legal and surveyor fees. Just do your homework first and know exactly what you're getting yourself into. I sold my first house, an Eighteenth Century thatched cottage, at auction as I wanted to know that it would sell for a particular amount (actually higher than the reserve) and on a set day. It was surprisingly non-stressful and I'd do it again if I had another 'classic' house.

Buying cars at auctions can save you a fortune, but get them checked thoroughly before you buy or a dream car could end up being an old banger with essential parts costing more than the car itself. This beautiful vintage Austin Morris sold at a specialist car auction house. **BCA.**

CHAPTER 7

WHAT NOT TO BUY IF YOU WANT TO MAKE A PROFIT

IT DOESN'T matter how much experience you have, there will be times when, no matter how much you know, you won't be able to resist a profit. I call these bargains white elephants because there's a reason why certain lots are so cheap – they just don't sell. But it's fine to buy them if you're buying for yourself and not thinking about potential profits. Some of these lots are great bargains if you're considering buying similar goods new; they just don't have resale value.

WHAT NOT TO BUY

We all love a bargain but there could be reasons why a lot is just too cheap. The following advice is mainly based on those wanting to sell for a profit. If you're buying for yourself, then it is different, but it's still worth being aware of market needs:

Anything you haven't handled or seen. Whether it's china or a house, don't buy anything you haven't either inspected or read a sales report about.
Tea sets, unless Deco spectaculars. The reason they are so cheap is not many people use traditional tea sets. They either drink from mugs or want all of their crockery to match. I have bought too many tea services over the years which just don't sell even though they're pretty and by good makes such as Royal Doulton or Tuscan Ware. The demand isn't there and I have to resell them at auction. The problem with sets which don't sell is that it just takes one chip to devalue the lot. Unless buying for yourself, don't buy tea services at auction.
Dinner services. Unless they are for you own use. Services simply do not sell (apart from stunning ones). And be practical. They take up a lot of room on a table at an antiques fair or in an antiques centre, often need more than one box

Burleigh, like Paragon, is one of the few tea or dinner services worth buying because of its stylish designs and good quality.

in which to be transported (taking up space needed by better items), are too hefty to sell on internet auctions because of postage charges and, if one piece breaks, that's your profit gone.
Top makes but wrong styles. A name isn't enough in itself. Shelley is superb but only does well if it's Deco. Avoid their Victorian-style goods unless you want to be stuck with unsaleable goods.
Jug and bowl set. In a world of en suites and modern plumbing, these large objects have little appeal and take up too much room on a stall or in the car to be good buys for little (if any) return. Avoid.
Large furniture. If you need furniture for yourself, measure your doorways. Will that exceptionally cheap Victorian wardrobe fit through them or up the stairs? If buying to sell, it's the same thing. Unless buying at the top end of the market for people who have huge homes or hotels, stick to practical pieces which will fit into most houses.
Dark furniture. Think of your home and modern tastes. Dark, Victorian mahogany furniture doesn't work in light, modern or minimalist homes. Pine and other light woods, such as ash, suit the modern market. They can offer great bargains if buying for your own use or (purists, look away), you want to paint them.
Royal Dux. Famous for its embossed pink triangle, this make of china has

What might seem like a great bargain could be a mistake as dinner services take up a lot of room when selling on and they're not practical to sell via the internet because, if one piece breaks in transit, you're in trouble. That said, this Susie Cooper set is a good buy as she's always a popular name and you can split it up into several trios (cups, saucers and plates) and sell the coffeepot by itself, the plates as a set and the tureens individually (you'll make more than selling them as a pair).

flooded the auction world since the Czech Republic (where it's made) was formed in 1993. Some auction houses sell it as Art Deco, despite its newly formed nationality being on the backstamp. The quality is not nearly as good as it used to be which is why it's hard to sell on. Avoid, as it's very hard to sell and the quality of the modern pieces isn't good enough to collect for investment (or in the hope of getting your money back in some cases).

Damaged goods. These can be very hard to sell on, even if good quality, stylish pieces. You can buy them if you're a good restorer or know of one, but take the extra cost into account and be aware that some people won't touch restored china. Furniture is another matter, just ensure that it's fit for purpose – for example a chair can be restored so you can actually sit on it.

Something which doesn't look or feel right. This comes with experience but trust your instincts. If it doesn't 'feel right' (wrong texture, weight etc), leave it alone; you won't be able to sell it.

CHAPTER 8

When you Arrive

ON THE day of the auction, make sure you double-check everything you want to buy. Goods can get damaged during viewings, go missing or be swapped around by other buyers. This is especially true of folios where all the best pictures miraculously end up in one, previously dull folio (it's one of the reasons I try to buy all similar folios at auctions). If this is the first time you have been to the viewing (you couldn't get there before or the auction house only does viewings on the day of the sale), look at everything thoroughly – as described in chapter three of this section (see p51).

Try to arrive as early as possible to get the best seat and to avoid queuing for registration. I always arrive before the auction house is open – and generally get let in early by helpful porters. This also means that I secure a good parking spot (see p23) and seat which saves time, energy and, depending on the auction house, money.

On arrival

Before you view, there are two things you must do:

- Save your seat
- Register

No matter what the weather, always take a coat or other layer which you can put on the seat you want as soon as you arrive. This ensures that you have a seat where you want to be.

Where to sit

Some dealers stand all the way through an auction. I choose not to – not just because I couldn't stand for two-three hours (or more) but because, as soon as you move, you lose your place and there's no privacy. I sit in such a way that no one can see what I'm writing in my catalogue, such as reminders of what to buy (tiny marks but marks, nevertheless), what not to buy etc. I also write down every price achieved during the sale to keep track of market prices or that auction's specialist areas/weaknesses – useful for both buying and selling.

This is so much easier and more comfortable to do when sitting. Auctions are long affairs so I also take a bottle of water with me. It's up to you, but I always sit. It's just more practical.

I always sit at the back. However, every auction house is different so although I try to sit in the aisle where I'm more likely to be seen, there are salerooms where this is not practical e.g. right by the reception which could mean you can't hear the bidding if people are talking, registering or paying. The latter can get very noisy if there are disputes. I also don't sit by toilets (noisy, disruptive and not pleasant) or by doors – another distraction which could lose you a bid. I sit at the back, in an aisle or as close to those positions as practical. Novice buyers sit at the front, but it's not a concert. By sitting at the back you get to see the sale, not just the auctioneer and can take note of who else is bidding, what else is going on in the room (rings, porters moving up to make several commission bids, dealers working the room). It's amazing what you can spot if you're in the right place – and that could save you money. I also watch the auctioneer's interaction with the porters, any sign of bids being bounced or items not meeting their reserves. I also note if the auctioneer is flagging as bids gets missed at that point or lots sold too quickly because the auctioneer just wants to finish their allocated lots (though most auctions

Take your time at viewings and check every single piece you intend to buy. Don't rely on catalogue descriptions but make your own judgement, as even the best auctioneers can miss 'must-buy' pieces – known as 'sleepers' – if they raise a lot of unexpected bids.

change auctioneers during the sale to prevent this problem and to work their areas of expertise). You need to be aware of all of this so you don't miss anything, and the easiest place to spot that is at the back of the room, ideally in the middle if there are aisles on both sides. Avoid getting tucked into a corner where it's hard to get out and your bid can be missed.

How to register

Once you've saved your seat, register. You should have discovered in advance how to do this (see p47) so have everything ready. Registration may take place at a desk in the saleroom or lobby while other auction houses have offices. If they're not clearly marked (especially if you arrive early), just ask.
- In rare cases, pay a cash registration deposit (I've seen it from £15-35). This will get repaid at the end of the sale or deducted from your total if you buy goods
- If you're new to the auction you may need to show some ID. This is generally a driving licence and/or utility bill showing your home address
- Some auction houses will ask for method of payment at this stage. You might be asked to show a credit card or cash in advance simply so they can see you have the means to pay. This is rare but it does happen so be prepared
- Give your details (name, address, phone number and, sometimes, e-mail address). If you've been before, your name and first line of your address will usually suffice as you'll be on their computer records
- In return, you'll be given a bidding number, either printed on a piece of card or on a paddle. If you're a regular, you might have a set number but not all auction houses work that way. If it's a multi-day sale and you're going for more than one day, ask if you can hang on to the number for the whole sale. That way, you don't need to register every morning

And finally

After you've viewed everything but with time to spare before the sale, go to the toilet. Then you won't risk missing a lot if you suddenly need to go mid-auction, you won't disrupt the room or lose your seat (if you don't leave a coat on it) and you can just concentrate on what's important – making money.

Chapter 9

Buyer's Premium and Other Costs

WHAT you have to remember when bidding is that the hammer (highest bid) price is not what you actually pay. The extra costs are covered in the Terms & Conditions (Ts&Cs), generally to be found on the IFC (inside front cover) of the catalogue. Some auction houses have signs near the payment area to remind buyers that a lot which is knocked down at £100 will cost them more than that – at least £111.75 if the buyer's premium is £10 and depending on the level of VAT.

Extra costs

As well as charging the seller commission (see p26) and other charges such as lottage (p115) or insurance (p116), auction houses also charge buyers a fee. Known as the buyer's premium, this can vary considerably but expect it to be between 10-15%, although some houses charge more. However, not all auction houses charge these extra costs on top of the commission for sellers.

You will also have to pay VAT on top of the premium, though some small auction houses might not be making enough to make this charge. See their Ts&Cs for details. Note, this is not on the whole hammer price, just the premium.

- Hammer price – £100
- Buyer's premium (e.g. 10%) – £10
- VAT on premium – £1.75
- Total to pay – £111.75

Or is that the total? Some auction houses charge for credit cards sales but never for debit cards and cash. Ask before the auction so you can take any credit card charges into account when bidding.

VAT lots

Some lots are subject to VAT on the whole item. These will be clearly marked in the catalogue, usually with a dagger (†) and the auctioneer will also mention this before starting the bidding so everyone is aware of the extra charge.

Please note, some auction houses only charge 12.5% VAT on the daggered lots or even the premium, but most charge the standard UK VAT of 17.5%. This will be made clear in the Ts&Cs.

DO YOUR SUMS BEFORE BIDDING

Before the auction, work out your maximum spend per lot or sale. I do both so I don't make a mistake or over-extend myself. Then factor in the premium and VAT on the premium. That way, you know exactly what you can afford. Most novice and even experienced auction-goers forget to add the premium when setting themselves limits.

Keep on top of the paperwork when buying at auction. This rosewood Edwardian desk is a good auction buy because it combines style with practicality so working on your laptop becomes a pleasure. **LW.**

Chapter 10

If You Can't Go to the Auction

THERE will be times when you can't attend an auction because you live too far away or have commitments on that day. In that case, leave a commission bid or, if you really want that lot, arrange a phone bid. Or use Live eBay (see p81) if the auction house has that medium.

When you read the Terms & Conditions, you'll discover that many auction houses won't allow phone bids under a set amount. This can vary hugely but is often around £200. Ignore this and speak to the auction house if you're serious about the lot or lots in question to see if they'll let you be a phone bidder. I once went to an auction where the phone bidder wouldn't go over £20 and the auctioneer was not happy. For lower value lots (under £50), either go to the auction or leave a commission bid.

What it means

- **Commission bid** – Someone from the auction house bids on your behalf up to the amount you listed on the commission bid form
- **Phone bid** – You 'bid' on the phone with someone from the auction house passing it on in the room
- **Live eBay** – Just like real eBay, this is a live internet auction which also takes into account the bids in the room (see p81)

Commission bids

You will be given a set form to fill in. These vary slightly depending on the auction house, but they all mean that there is a written record of your bid which you cannot retract later. Just sign that piece of paper, hand it in and the auction begins. That's it. You cannot change your mind, so ensure that you can afford to pay if all of your commission bids are successful. And don't forget the buyer's premium and VAT on those fees.

Pros ✓	Cons ✗
You can bid for lots when you can't attend the auction	You don't get a chance to up your bid if it goes slightly higher than expected
It can be more reliable than Live eBay where the internet connection can go down (either at the auction house or your end) or the auction house can't reach you by phone for the phone bid	You have to rely on the auction house not to use your highest bid as a starting point. You generally don't stand a chance if that happens
If you can unexpectedly attend in person, it's easy to cancel your commission bid before the start of the auction by letting them know that you're there and will be bidding for yourself	You have to rely on the auction house not to lose or forget your bid. This happens occasionally, even to regular buyers
An experienced member of the auction house will be bidding on your behalf. The auctioneer won't miss their bid and, if you're not confident enough to bid for yourself, this is a useful alternative	You might be on the wrong 'leg' (see below) and miss the lot, despite it selling for your highest commissioned bid

What it means

The Wrong leg – If you have left a bid for £100 and the auctioneer bidding on your behalf bids £90, they cannot then bid again on your behalf against themselves to secure the lot if it sells at £100 – they're on the wrong leg.

To stand a better chance of getting your lot, give the auctioneer the flexibility to beat the wrong leg by adding 'plus one' or even 'plus two' to your bid. This means that they can bid once or twice more than your signed highest bid. In the case of £100, that would be £110 or £120 (if the auction house bids in increments of £10 after £100 is reached). You might wonder why you can't just write £120 as your maximum bid but you could still be on the wrong leg. It is frustrating to lose by a single bid and the dealers will be watching the person bidding on your behalf to see if they're slowing down so they beat you by one bid. The 'plus' option could stop this from happening. It increases your chances. I always go for 'plus two' when leaving commission bids.

Phone bids

Phone bids have more flexibility than commission bids, but that isn't to say that they can't go wrong. Armed with the right information, you can decide for yourself what works best. Phone bids are a very good option, but if you really want the lot, the best way to get it is actually to be there. I've even been to auctions when I'm really unwell just in case anything goes wrong. Sometimes, it really is the only valid option for those 'must-buy' lots.

Pros ☑	Cons ☒
More flexibility than commission bids	The auction house must be able to contact you. If they can't, you won't get the lot and will alienate the auction house
No one can see who's bidding so you retain your privacy	The auction house might have a set lowest limit they'll accept for phone bidding
You get to bid 'live' when you can't get to the auction house	You must be able to think fast and know your limits. But don't feel pressurised

I've been at an auction when the bidder couldn't be contacted by phone. Either they were engaged speaking to someone else, or they just didn't answer. The auctioneer refused to allow this to disrupt the flow of the sale for long so, after three failed attempts, the phone bid was abandoned and the bidder lost out. Don't let this happen to you as you won't be allowed to do it again. If you're going to be a regular phone bidder, you might consider buying a spare mobile just for this purpose. You can buy a 'Pay as You Go' phone very cheaply.

Live auctions on eBay

This is covered in the next chapter. It is the way that the auction world is going to capitalise on the success of eBay and reach an international market. It's definitely worth looking at to see what's going on and if it appeals to you. Its pros and cons will be discussed on p82. Even if you don't choose to bid, you can see the auction live so know exactly what's sold and for how much. See www.ebayliveauctions.com for more details.

CHAPTER 11

THE MODERN AUCTION HOUSE – INTERNET AND LIVE EBAY SALES

AUCTION houses have responded to the threat of internet auctions in different ways. Most accept that eBay has changed the antiques world, but some also know that their regular clientele will always prefer to handle the goods before buying – for instance the regional auctions selling large pieces of furniture or auction houses selling top quality jewellery where diamonds need to be assessed before thousands are spent on them. But there is a compromise in which the client base is increased and eBay embraced into the heart of the traditional auction house. This is Live eBay which combines the live sale at the auction house with eBay itself.

How do you find Live eBay sales

It might have changed by the time you read this, but my initial thoughts were that eBay needs to work on this with better marketing and mapping. When I tried to find it, I couldn't actually find an easy link on their homepage and only knew about the concept from visiting Gorringes in Lewes. They set up a screen to show Live eBay running alongside the auction in the room. I only found the address (www.ebayliveauctions.com) through another website as there was not an obvious way to discover it via the eBay site itself. However, it not only brings in a wealth of buyers, but forces buyers in the room to bid earlier than they might have done traditionally so they won't be beaten by a last minute eBay bidder – competition they can't see.

Your auction house will advertise the fact that their sale is also available on Live eBay, either at the venue or in their catalogues. Most do both and that's fine if you already know about that auction house, but look on eBay to see which auctions are coming up.

LIVE EBAY PROS

There are many advantages to Live eBay:

- It is 'real-time' bidding so you don't have to guestimate your bid as you do when leaving a commission bid
- You are more likely to get the lot than with a commission bid because you can react to the room
- No one can tell who is bidding. Your auction name is listed and you have some anonyminity. In phone bidding, the winning bidder's name can be called out
- If you're a renowned expert, by bidding in the room, making a commission bid or bidding by phone, you could be letting the auction house know that the item is more important than they realised. This can result in lots being pulled, the price increasing through bouncing bids against the wall (see p33) or even friendly dealers being warned. Whilst rare, this does happen. Live eBay allows you to be anonymous and you might want to set up an eBay identity separate from a normal eBay name to retain this anonymity. Most of us try to keep our identities a secret so people can't see what we're buying and try to outbid us or see what we've paid
- You can leave a website bid in advance in case you can't get to the computer in time, and then you can just pick up when the auction starts and your highest bid is exceeded. This is my personal recommendation based on my own experience (see below)

LIVE EBAY CONS

Once, I couldn't make day two of a three-day auction and didn't want to leave a commission bid. The reason for this was because the prices of the rugs I was bidding for were too variable to guess without seeing who the other bidders were. I didn't want to leave a phone bid either, having seen the auction house experience problems reaching people the day before. So I went to bid on Live eBay. I learnt the system is not perfect – and discovered flaws in the concept apart from the difficulty in finding its eBay address:

- Live eBay doesn't always function as it should and you can't bid when the system freezes for several lots
- The sales can accidentally skip lots if the auctioneer presses the wrong buttons or their system goes slow. Your system might be slow too, meaning you miss your lot
- Your eBay identity can be exposed for the competition to see in the room if

you don't have a special eBay identity kept purely for such sales or the auction house arranges for bidders to be listed as 'bidder 1' etc
- You have to rely on the auction house's description pre-sale. Going to the auction means you can spot damage incurred between the viewing and the sales. The same goes for commission and phone bidding
- Some auction houses don't post lots so you still have to travel to collect them
- Not all posted parcels are packed properly or arrive safely. I know one American buyer whose one-off studio pottery designs arrived in pieces and she struggled to get recompense from the auction house. She also lost all of her potential profit margin
- Prices can be far higher than for normal auctions because the saleroom is opened up to an international market. This is great for sellers, not so good for buyers
- This is a small point, but it's actually very dull when you're in the room as the auctioneer spends a lot of time looking at the screen and you're bidding against a silent competition
- If you don't register or log on early you'll miss lots which can whiz by, depending on interest in the room. Some can be knocked down very fast before you've had a chance to press that vital 'confirm bid' button

LIVE EBAY – THE CONCLUSION

I love the idea of Live eBay as it gives the bidder more freedom. But I have missed lots when the auction house's system froze for over 50 lots and, on

Use the internet to hunt down those must-buy items for sale at auctions like this papier maché hunting tray. SW.

another occasion, their system missed out a couple of lots. So I wouldn't trust it. What I would do is leave a 'highest bid' just like a normal eBay auction, and then log on early, picking up where the highest bid finished if I think it's worth paying more at that stage. Some markets, such as rugs and carpets, are very hard to guess at as they depend more on competition than other areas and it really depends who else is there. Most auction houses know the right level of estimates to set for goods, but the market is very different and can vastly exceed expectations which is why Live eBay, when it works, is so useful.

Auction internet sites

Not all auction houses have internet sites and there is a lot of work to be done in this area, especially with the competition from eBay. The most useful forms of information are maps and directions showing where the auction house can be found, whether parking is available, dates and times of sales and of course, the catalogues. You can search all of this online and see in advance if the auction is worth attending. The catalogues are generally available on the auctions' websites before they're printed so you get an advance preview. If you can't get to the auction, you get the chance to see what's for sale and leave a commission bid in plenty of time. This isn't always possible for sales where printed catalogues are only available on the day.

The quality of sites differs hugely. Some are difficult to search whilst others have a more useful keyword search and are sensibly divided into sections such as furniture and jewellery. Auction houses need to review their websites and their search factors. I use one where I have to go through all of the pages because there is no keyword search and I have to guess where the section divisions are to find what I want. I'm probably more persistent than many would-be buyers so, if you're looking for a job in the antiques or auction world, look at designing user-friendly websites. That's what the market needs.

Unlike auction houses, auction internet sites can be accessed anytime. Some allow for live bidding, but not many. They are also great for spotting market conditions and I regularly search archives to see what's sold for what, and to assess if the auction house sells the type of goods I want and for prices I'm willing to pay. I also use them to search for prices when wanting to buy goods elsewhere, especially paintings, as prices are variable and information often scarce. A site can tell you if goods come up too often to be really interesting or if they really are as rare as a seller is telling you. You will also get an idea of the age of the items which is useful if you're not sure of the subject matter. Not all auction houses have the same amount of knowledge but a quick read of the catalogue will expose what their 'expert' really knows. These free catalogues also give you an idea of what sells well in which parts of the country.

THE INTERNET AND AUCTION HOUSES

As I wrote in my first book almost a decade ago, the auction world has to catch up with the rest of the world where the internet is concerned. Some internet facilities are superb and, over time, Live eBay or its ilk will be a vital part of that world. But it all needs a lot of work and some basic common sense. I spent ages finding the link to show you and even longer using different auction house websites trying to figure out just who they thought was accessing them. Accessibility is the key and, once the salerooms realise that and actively create user-friendly websites, then the auction world will see far better returns and a larger market share.

FINDING WHAT YOU WANT

If you already know which auction house or houses appeal, or only want to buy locally, look for their websites which are listed in the back of this book in the county by county auction directory (from p189). Otherwise, either go to www.google.co.uk and input your area of interest (e.g. Lalique), followed by auction and press 'UK search' to see what crops up. Or take a look at the following websites and consider joining their newsletters (see p95) which are e-mailed on a regular basis and record which auction houses are selling what. In theory, it tends to be only auctions which are signed up to their service and too many of these, I find, are American. This immediately makes me think of postage and Customs charges, as well as not necessarily being the right market for what I want to find or sell. But the following sites are useful for discovering what is happening in the auction world. I primarily use *The Antiques Trade Gazette* and Artfact websites.

www.antiques-info.co.uk – Subscription service
www.antiquestradegazette.com
www.artfact.com
www.governmentauctions.com – Subscription service
www.ukauction.info
www.ukauctioneers.com

Chapter 12
Bidding and How to Get Noticed

EVERYONE is nervous about bidding at their first auction. When the daytime TV auction-based series, *Cash in the Attic* first started, I took one of their researchers to his first ever auction and ended up bidding on his behalf because he was scared of making a mistake. There are a lot of urban myths connected to bidding but they're scare stories. Just be sensible and bid clearly. There's no point going for secret signs at an auction house where you're not known as the auctioneer will assume you are rubbing your nose because you have an itch, not that you're bidding very discreetly.

How to bid

Until the auctioneer knows you, bid as clearly as possible:
• Make eye contact with the auctioneer – No matter which of the three following bidding methods you choose
• After catching the auctioneer's eye, nod clearly. Just ensure that they can see you. If not, raise your hand for the first bid and nod subsequently
• Raise your hand. It worked at school and it works in the auction house
• Raise your catalogue in the air

How not to bid

Until the auctioneer knows that this is a bid, not an involuntary twitch, do not bid by:
• Scratching your nose
• Nodding without making eye contact. It can look like a nervous tick
• Lifting a finger in front of your body. This is too easy to miss if unexpected
• Scratching your head whilst looking at or deliberately ignoring the auctioneer. Too many people do this by accident for an auctioneer to take it as a bid unless they know the buyer

What to do if the auctioneer misses your bid

I always sit on the end of a row to act quickly if I think the auctioneer simply isn't seeing me. I can also lean out into the aisle if there's a tall person in front of me obscuring the auctioneer's view. If the auctioneer misses your bid, just shout out something simple like 'Here!' or 'Yes!'

Did you still miss out? It's easy to assume that the auctioneer is taking your bid – but they might be looking at another bidder just behind you. A good auctioneer will call out to you to ensure you know you are not the highest bidder. If in doubt, just raise your hand again and the auctioneer will let you know. They are used to this so keep track of what the auctioneer is doing to ensure you don't miss out on a lot. Most of the time, auctioneers refer to the highest bidder by description, but I've seen cases where someone didn't realise that the auctioneer was repeatedly telling them they were the under bidder. This was very frustrating for the auctioneer and annoying for the would-be buyer who lost out on a lot they thought they had won.

Determined bidders

There's a technique which dealers use to warn off other buyers. It's keeping their hand in the air during the bidding process. Other buyers will see this and know they're up against someone who is prepared to outbid everyone else.

Silver sporting-theme toastrack, 2006. CH.

It's only ever backfired once when an auctioneer decided to use this technique to deliberately up the bid. The auction house was left with a fake bid (bouncing a bid against the wall, see p33) and had alienated a good buyer. But in short, this method ensures the buyer gets the lot and at a good price because there is no competition from other bidders.

What happens if I...?

There is an age-old fear of all novice auction goers – one wrong move and you have won a lot you didn't want. But if you do any of the following, you will not have been seen as bidding. So please don't worry if you:
- Sneeze
- Scratch your head without making eye contact with the auctioneer
- Stretch without making eye contact with the auctioneer
- Blink or wink. These will be seen as nervous gestures, not bids
- Lift a leg

Auctioneers are experienced in what is and what is not a bidding gesture. If one does make a mistake, however, just shout, 'no!'. I did that when an auctioneer took my £15 bid as a £20 bid when there were two different bidders at the same time. I was only prepared to pay £15. Had I been prepared to pay £20, I wouldn't have said anything.

Bidding

Be confident, be clear and win that lot. But also know when to stop. If an auctioneer wants a higher bid than you're prepared to pay, just shake your head when they look at you for more money. That way, they know to move on. I am encouraged to bid for lots the auctioneers think I might want because they know what I've bought in the past and they want to make sure I don't miss out. I just smile and shake my head if a lot doesn't appeal.

Like many buyers, you might decide to increase your bid having previously either shaken your head or just stopped bidding. Just make a clear gesture to the auctioneer so they know you are back in the fray.

When to bid

I am never the first bidder unless no one else comes in and I really want that particular lot. In this case, I wait for the auctioneer to lower their starting bid.

It can go from £100 to £20 if you're lucky. Some auctioneers try it on or start at either the reserve or the estimate. Others just see what the room will pay and drop the price if no one bids. By bidding too soon, you could end up paying over the odds. Just sit back and wait. I also don't start bidding if there are already two bidders fighting for a lot. The auctioneer will let them bid first before taking on a new bidder so they retain the momentum. I step in once the second bidder has faded. There is less competition that way. It also means the auctioneer isn't so distracted by too many bidders that they miss your final bid.

How to lower the increments

There are no universal set increments when it comes to the auction world. Each house will have its own style with bids under £20 increasing in anything from £1, £2 or £5. Or up to £100, there are 'patterned increments' (£2-£5-£8-£10) or straight £5 and £10 increments. There are also auction houses that offer other prices. Get to know how they work, especially when leaving commission bids (see p78) so your bid is a viable one. Ask before bidding if you don't know the auction house. It is worth shouting out another option e.g. £125 instead of £130 or £150 after a £120 bid. Not all auctioneers will agree but most will. I've only ever seen one auctioneer turn this down, but the saleroom was buzzing so he didn't need to take compromise bids. Most auctioneers just want as high a price as possible so are flexible, particularly when selling lots worth thousands where £500 increments can be taken when the bidding starts to slow down.

Just remember the buyer's premium and VAT on the premium (see p26).

The winning bidder

When you have won your first lot, the auctioneer will either ask for your name, paddle or registration number. Simply hold up your paddle or card and they'll write it down or ask you to read it out. If you need to give your name, just give your surname unless it's a common one, in which case, give your first name as well. After that, the auctioneer should recognise you for subsequent lots. But be prepared to identify yourself again, especially at larger auctions when the auctioneers change around to keep the energy going or to sell their specialist area. Regulars will get recognised very quickly. Just listen to your name or number to ensure it's right when they call it out.

Chapter 13

Collecting Goods, Including Paying, Packaging and Delivery

Y OU DON'T have to stay to the end of the auction to collect your goods. I'd actually advise paying for them as soon as you've finished bidding so you don't get stuck in the huge queue at the end of the sale.

Paying for your lots

You should have checked payment methods before the auction (see p48) and come prepared. If not, just check at the desk when you get there but expect to be charged extra if using a credit card (generally around 2-2.5% extra). If paying by cheque, the auction house will normally wait for the cheque to clear before allowing you to collect lots so they can guarantee being paid. Otherwise, you'll be given a receipt which you have to take to one of the porters who will collect your goods for you. You cannot just collect them yourself without a porter being involved as it could look like you're trying to steal lots. Just be patient.

Packing your lots

Too many salerooms don't provide enough packaging – or any at all. Depending what you're buying, it's worth bringing your own. I always take blankets with me when buying paintings or furniture so they won't get damaged on the way home. I also take bags of clean newspaper and bubble wrap to protect against breakages. Most auction houses will have some boxes but these are rationed and available to the first people to ask so take your own and look after your goods.

Not all auction houses have great security and dealers have been known to swap goods during the auction itself when the staff are watching the saleroom, not the viewing rooms or lots. Check folios and job lots before leaving the auction houses after paying for them and check that you're collecting everything for which you paid. Speak to the auctioneer if not.

COMMON TRICKS

There's nothing more frustrating than bidding for a job lot, only to discover that the piece you wanted isn't in the lot when you collect your goods. If you're lucky, you can prove this and make a fuss at the time. Check all lots carefully before leaving the auction house and when the porter is still there. Swapping or stealing part lots is a common trick and can be hard to prove, especially after you've left the building. Create a fuss and demand to see the auctioneer who lotted the goods. They should have adequate records to show which client sold what. The lot labels don't just have the lot number but the seller's code and, apart from the largest job lots, that could help to show the veracity of your claim. Did the seller put the missing item into the auction, was it catalogued or in the auctioneer's notes?

Another common trick concerns folios of pictures. Some dealers will swap all of the good ones either just before the auction, or even during the auction when security can often be lax outside the saleroom itself. Auction rooms spread over several rooms on several floors and with too many unwatched exit points can be a nightmare. All of the better pictures can end up in the one folio which wasn't as good when catalogued, or at the start of the viewing and which is sold for less than the lots where buyers expected to see the better pictures. Again, check the folios before leaving and demand a refund if the choice items are missing and what's left isn't worth what you just paid. Demand to speak to the auctioneer who catalogued the lot and even insist that they contact the original owner who can verify what was submitted.

There can be problems but just check that you collect what you actually paid for and create a fuss if not, even stipulate that the owner/MD of the auction house is called and let them know that this is not the end of the matter. Basically, the louder the fuss (I don't mean shout), the more quickly the situation will be resolved. If it's not dealt with properly, report them (see p97) and boycott the auction house. If they don't look after their clients and their money, don't give them any more of it. Certainly don't sell at an auction house which doesn't take such theft seriously or protect other people's investments.

Shippers and removal firms

The trouble with auctions is that there are often too many bargains to resist. It's fine if you have a large van or are buying smaller objects, but there will be times when you won't be able to fit all of your buys in your vehicle. In some cases, careful repacking is all that's needed. Some auction houses will charge you extra if you want to collect the goods the next day, others won't but it's worth finding out. However, if you've bought something which simply won't fit into your car, don't worry about it, just ask around and see who can deliver it for you. Some auction houses either have their own service or regular removal firms whom they can recommend but these might not be the best or cheapest option. Again, ask the porters as they know who has the best – and worst – reputations. Shippers and removal firms frequent many auctions so speak to the drivers and see what they're charging and whether you like them or not. Cheap can be cheap for a reason. I also check the parking lots whenever I arrive at an auction both for viewings and sales to see who's a regular and what shape their vans are in. I won't trust my lots to anyone who can't even look after their own van, especially if rust spots will let in rain water.

With the advent of the internet and auction houses selling live on eBay (see p81), many have in-house firms and their vans tend to be newer and better looking than many other firms as they're an advertising tool. This does influence me when buying goods which can get damaged en route if they get wet. I once had a mattress ruined in a house move when my goods were left in an old van overnight and it leaked – something I wouldn't want to happen if buying vintage clothes, paintings, furniture or fabrics. It might be an obvious thing to say but many people panic if they realise that their impulse bid for an amazing bargain necessitates both extra costs and planning. Relax, just ask around, check the vans and – as with everything – speak to the porters. Above all, spend that bit extra on insurance so, if things do go wrong, you're covered.

Don't forget to warn the removal men about stairs or winding staircases before agreeing a price or they could charge you extra.

Exports

If buying to send abroad, speak to shippers in advance to get their costs and book them. This might be vague pre-auction as you can't guarantee getting everything you want, but it's worth knowing that the shippers are available to collect what you want. Shippers are easy to find:

• Recommendations. Porters, auction houses (many will have links to shippers), antique dealers. Look for cards on the counters at auction houses
• Adverts in the antiques press e.g. *The Antiques Trade Gazette*
• Local telephone directory. But recommendations are best

If you're going to buy larger items or need removal firms or shippers regularly, ask about a loyalty discount and always factor extra costs such as removal firms into your profit margins when buying or selling.

Official bodies

Always check that your shipper or removal firm are fully insured. This might cost extra but will be worth it for peace of mind. Some excellent firms might not belong to official bodies so it's worth asking as, in the case of a dispute, you can go to them for advice:

- BIFA – British International Freight Association (www.bifa.org or 020 8844 2266)
- FIATA – Swiss-based International Federation of Freight Forwarders Associations (www.fiata.com)
- The Removals Industry Ombudsman – Only those who have agreed to join its scheme are covered, including members of the National Guild of Removers and Storers and the National Register of Approved Removers (ROARS) (www.removalsombudsman.org.uk, 01442 891736 or write to them at Chess Chambers, 2, Broadway Court, Chesham, Bucks, HP5 1EG)

Late-Eighteenth Century mahogany, Dutch bureau with floral marquetry, estimate £5-6,000. I'd expect to see it at fairs for £12-15,000, or more. Ask the auction house to recommend a good removal firm who will wrap it carefully so it arrives safely. It's worth paying more for a better, safer service, especially when buying quality goods. **LW.**

CHAPTER 14

STAYING IN TOUCH MAILING LISTS AND NEWSLETTERS

MANY SALEROOMS now offer mailing lists and e-mail newsletters as a way of encouraging loyalty and promoting sales. It's always worth signing up to these to keep an eye on the market. It's free but just double check that this data will not be sold elsewhere.

They will e-mail you newsletters with the dates of their sales and many also have a link to their catalogues (often before the catalogue has been printed) which enables you to see what's coming up. It's also a good way to keep an eye on the market to see if some items are out of fashion or too many of them are available, helping you to decide what will be cheap but for the right reason. Out of fashion goods might never reach their old prices but popular goods which happen to be inundating that particular market, can offer bargain buys as too many will drive down the price at auction. Be careful in case everyone's selling something because they've heard there are problems with it. Use your judgement or speak to the auction house for advice if you have a friendly auctioneer or porter there. This can be down to an error in a price guide. One price guide author mistakenly valued a common china figure at £750 instead of £32 and dealers bought as many of them as possible at its real value, believing that they had a bargain – then flooded the market when they realised their mistake.

Some auction houses post catalogues for free and others charge for this. It's worth signing up to the free ones and consider paying for the service if you'd buy the catalogue anyway. It's a good way to see what your regular or good auction houses are selling and for how much.

I also sign up for internet services such as Artfact (www.artfact.com) which sends a monthly e-mail link to auction sites and their catalogues, mainly US-based ones, but it's useful to gauge the overseas market. Remember to add Customs charges and shipping costs if intending to buy from US or other non-

EU countries. Check that the auction houses will either send goods abroad or co-operate with shippers you would otherwise have to organise yourself. Overseas markets can be very useful, especially as high value goods in the UK can be very cheap in the US and vice versa.

Sign up to newsletters and e-mails so you know what's coming up at auctions or you could miss out on choice lots such as this German Historimus Humpen.

CHAPTER 15

Your Rights

WHEN it comes to auctions, it is a case of buyer beware – or that's what they want you to think. But you do have rights, even if they can be difficult to enforce if the auction house wishes to be uncooperative.

What to do

If buying a lot which is no longer complete (i.e. pieces stolen or broken), it's best to state your claim before leaving the auction house to ensure that they don't think you're lying or mistaken. They could believe that you've just changed your mind and want your money back. Check all lots before taking them away and make a fuss there and then if possible. If you don't notice in time, make a formal complaint in writing, either hand-delivered or sent recorded delivery and demand either full reimbursement if returning all of the goods or a percentage of your money back. If the best piece of a job lot is missing, consider returning the whole lot as they will base the value on the average price per lot. If the auction house won't provide any reimbursement and do not handle your case to your satisfaction, report them to the Society of Fine Arts Auctioneers*. Don't use them again unless the bargains really are too good to resist (and you're willing to risk further problems because of this). But don't sell through them as their security is obviously too lax.

If a piece has been damaged between the viewing and the end of the auction, try to get your money back but don't expect it unless the auction house themselves have dropped it, in which case, expect a full refund.

If the auction house has posted your goods and they've arrived damaged because of poor packaging, take plenty of pictures of the pieces and packaging and make a complaint in writing, demanding your money back. In this case, the auction house might take its time but it has to compensate you as the inferior packaging is their fault. Keep the packaging in case they're awkward and refuse to settle until they see it. They'll have expected you to have thrown it away and will try to use this to avoid payment. The photos will enforce your

---

* The Society of Fine Arts Auctioneers can be contacted via www.sofaa.org, 01483 225891 or write to SOFAA, London Road, Send, Woking, Surrey, GU23 7LN.

case but keep the packaging as a safety net.

You realise (or were told) afterwards that the auctioneer deliberately forced you to pay more by bouncing bids against the wall. You have no rights as you continued to bid, thereby agreeing to pay the higher price.

You drop your pieces on the way back and they're ruined. If you paid by credit card, speak to the credit card company as you might be insured. If not, check your house insurance but, as it's en route, it might not be insured depending on your insurance and if antiques over a certain price are covered.

Legal protection

Your rights as a buyer are encompassed by The Sale of Goods Act, 1979, which states that goods must match their description (i.e. sold as described, so a George II sideboard must date from that era and not be 'in the style of') and must suit the purpose for which they were sold. The auction house should refund you if they breach the Act. However, you might need to involve Trading Standards or even the police to try to get a refund or have action taken against an auction house. Ultimately, demand your rights but create a paper trail so you have everything in writing should this go to court. And, if you have problems with an auction house deliberately lying about goods (e.g. selling them as something which they're not, be it from a particular era or a certain make – or just a plain old fake),

This 1880 doll will appeal to the traditional doll market but also look at job lots of more modern dolls that the auctioneer is liable to overlook – the nostalgia market is huge, especially with Susan Brewer's two new books on British dolls of the 1950s and 1960s bringing much-needed knowledge to the market. **TH.**

tell other would-be buyers and sellers so they don't get caught out. Hit the auction house where it hurts – their reputation and pocket. Just be prepared to prove what you say.

Case Study

An auction house sold goods as being made by certain potteries such as Wade, Royal Doulton and Carlton Ware. They weren't. Some were fake and others were not made by the pottery named. These false descriptions led to them being investigated by the police and, eventually, shut down. Whilst buyers did get their fingers burnt and not all got their money back, by informing the authorities, they ensured that other people were protected. If you get ripped off, start by telling Trading Standards and then warn other dealers or buyers.

Maximise your profits by buying for your market. This map of Middlesex will fetch more there than elsewhere in the country so buy from a different area and sell locally for maximum profits – taking petrol prices into account. You can even buy at one auction and sell at another to take advantage of the reversed 'coals to Newcastle' effect. **SW.**

CHAPTER 16

IDEAS FOR WHERE TO MAKE YOUR PROFIT

OPTIONS, together with their pros and cons, are listed on p152 and they offer alternatives to selling through auction. In brief, depending on what you have bought, your lifestyle and needs, they are:

- Antiques fairs
- Specialist antiques or other fairs such as conventions (for books, movie posters etc)
- Antiques centres
- Antiques and general markets

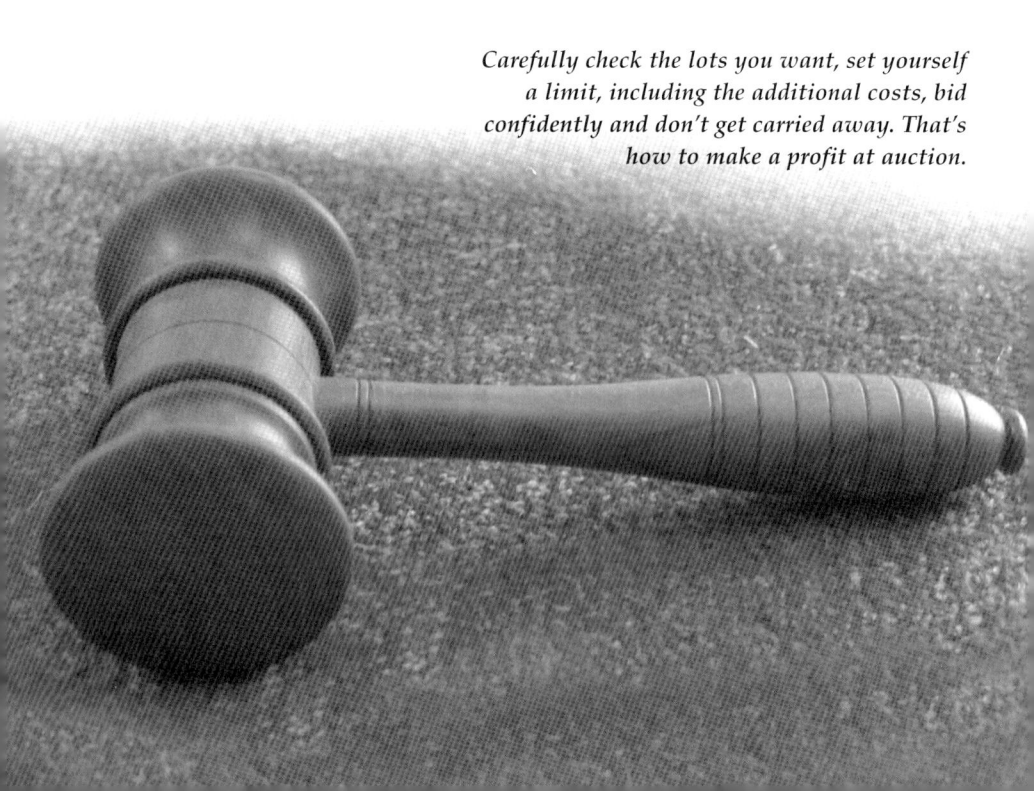

Carefully check the lots you want, set yourself a limit, including the additional costs, bid confidently and don't get carried away. That's how to make a profit at auction.

- Specialist auctions
- Internet auctions, such as eBay
- Your own website (try to get links to other sites, including antiques and collectables sites)
- Car boot sales*
- For sale ads in specialist newspapers and magazines such as fan magazines and the collecting press

---

* For advice on buying and selling at car boots, including a county-based directory, read *How to Profit from Car Boot Sales* by Fiona Shoop (published by Remember When).

Choosing the right auction house is essential. This is part of my old Wade collection which I sold through what used to be Phillips, (now Bonhams) which was the perfect choice for these particular pieces. BN.

SECTION THREE
SELLING AT AUCTION

Chapter 1

Why Sell at Auction?

THERE are many reasons to sell at auction but the main one, of course, is to make a profit. These are some of the advantages of auction sales:

- They attract an international audience (e.g. through the internet) and serious collectors
- Auctions do not have a set price (unlike fairs) which means prices can go above their estimate and the true market value can be determined – as long as the right buyers know about it
- They are good for realising the true market price for those rarer or more unusual pieces which can be hard to price yourself
- The cataloguing is done by experts (in most cases) for specialist sales. They will highlights the important facts to attract buyers, resulting in higher prices
- Specialist sales mean that the right buyers know about your rarer goods so higher prices are generally achieved
- Unlike antiques fairs, buyers have limited time so can't rely on seeing your goods at the next fair. Pressure on buyers increases sales
- Auctions are physically easier to sell at than antiques fairs. You take in your lots, then it's up to the auctioneer to organise everything. No early mornings, stall rent or packing goods at the end of the day
- There is no direct selling. Let others do the work
- Payment is received within four weeks (sometimes on the day itself, depending on the auction house) so you know what money you'll be receiving
- Larger goods can be sold more easily. Space and transport is always a consideration at antiques fairs, and eBay sales where the 'buyer collects' option can lessen the price achieved
- You benefit from easy record-keeping for tax purposes or when dealing with an inheritance and other benefactors. Paperwork stops accusations (see p157)
- What better place to get rid of unwanted goods or stock which isn't selling? You'll make money and clear space. You might make a loss on your goods but

at least you'll have cash to spend on items with more appeal. Then you can start making a profit again
- Auction houses can set up the advertising and marketing to ensure a good turnout for your more unusual pieces. This is also particularly useful if you have pieces which are great bargains for buyers – but means less money for you. These include dinner and tea services (unless spectacular) and run-of-the-mill goods like Wade Whimsies and Beatrix Potter figures by Beswick and Royal Albert (unless rare versions)

Selling rare goods

It's worth saying that not everyone knows that what they have is rare. A quick look at *The Antiques Roadshow* will tell you that. Conversely, some people think their common goods are worth a fortune – and that's where the auctioneer comes in. In theory. I'm saying more about how to find the right auctioneer in the next chapter (see p110) but the most obvious way to get the right price for choice items is to put them in specialist auctions where the serious buyers go.

A large Arts and Crafts copper bowl by Newlyn. A perfect auction piece which would attract fierce competition in the saleroom. WW.

This pair of Victorian claret jugs attracted fierce competition at a specialist jewellery and silver sale. The glass was from a Stourbridge maker, presumed to be Stevens and Williams, because of the quality workmanship and style, and the silver mounts were by Charles Edwards, 1883. DN.

Specialist sales

Specialist sales (see p42) are great for selling rarer items, but if your Edwardian violin or diamond ring isn't anything special, then they won't reach their full potential if sold amongst the elite of their type – a specialist musical instrument sale or top-of-the-range jewellery sale. Instead, consider selling them in a general sale where they won't seem so ordinary, will have more appeal and fetch better prices. Speak to your friendly auctioneer for advice. At these sort of auctions, job lots are fantastic for buyers but not sellers as people are after more unusual items so will hold onto their money for more exciting items. Your more ordinary items (I hate to say common, but that's what they are) will bomb. Choose your sales carefully.

I have sold through several specialist sales where I know that the rarer or more collectable pieces will make more money because the serious buyers are aware of them. I earn more in this competitive environment than selling through antiques fairs – even specialist antiques fairs – where the pressure

This Birmingham Guild of Handicraft Arts and Crafts lamp is best suited to a specialist Arts and Crafts sale to attract the most interest. WW.

isn't the same as at auctions which allow no second chances. The buyers don't have the opportunity to have a quick look round and see if they can get it cheaper elsewhere but have to decide to commit there and then.

What can't be sold

In the old days, before health and safety was an issue, you could sell virtually anything at auction. This is no longer the case and these are some of the main items you cannot sell at auction:

• **Furniture with soft coverings** which do not have fire retardant labels. Or the auction house must accept that they are designer collectables. Check that they understand what you're selling before transporting it in case they won't accept your lot
• **Tripod or five-legged chairs**, even ones intended for doctors to use during surgery. The ruling is aimed at ensuring chairs sold are fit for purpose and won't tilt over, for example
• **Stuffed animals and birds**. These are a contentious issue so speak to your auction house before submitting. Red squirrels and other threatened species must have been stuffed at least 50 years previously and you are expected to have the paperwork to prove it. Unfortunately not all auction houses follow this rule and not all auctioneers recognise threatened birds unless very obvious such as the humming bird
• **Ivory**. If 'worked' (i.e. carved, not an elephant's tusk) it must date to at least June, 1947. If you can't prove that it was made before that date, salerooms

won't sell it unless you can get an Article 10 permit from DEFRA
- **Elephants' tusks**. These cannot be sold, regardless of age
- **Tortoiseshell**. Unless dated not later than June 1947

You are also not allowed to sell any of the above at antiques fairs. Some dealers do and they are breaking the law. Always ask for proof of age before buying ivory goods in case you wish to resell them at a later date.

Stuffed endangered birds and animals are not allowed to be sold at auction unless you can prove that they were killed at least 50 years ago. These birds are safe to sell but a red squirrel without documentation to prove its age could not be sold. WW.

CHAPTER 2

How to Choose the Right Auction House

ONE OF the most frequent questions I'm asked is 'how do I find the right auction house'. It's often not as simple as basic geography, although it's worth looking at the auction directory in section five (see p189). You might even need to sell at more than one auction house, depending on what you're selling. The following should be taken into consideration:

- Do you like the auctioneer you met? If not or you didn't trust them, don't use this auction house
- Has the auction house got a good reputation? Speak to the trade and see what they think of it. Some auctions have been sued for 'losing' goods or failing to pay for sold lots and the trade will generally know about this. If they have a bad track record, avoid them
- Advertising. If they don't bother with this, why should you bother to go? If you are selling specialist goods, look at the relevant specialist auctions but also remember that many auction houses have specialist sales, as well as general ones
- Commission rates. Is their commission competitive, especially if there are equally good auction houses nearby?
- What other charges do they have? Are these competitive or justified by superior advertising?
- What's their cataloguing like? Don't be afraid to ask to see their latest catalogue to give you an idea of the descriptions, quality and estimates used
- How many days do they have for viewings? Some only have viewings on the day of the sale which reduces your chances, especially if they only use village halls or similar venues. Personally, I wouldn't sell my goods at a saleroom with less than two days' worth of viewings
- I would expect proper salerooms to have security measures in place but not the village halls and other non-official venues. If in doubt, ask. They won't think that you're intending to rob them but, if they won't allay your fears, don't sell through them

Auctioneers

Not all auctioneers are equal. Try to avoid newly qualified ones or ones who have only recently become the resident specialist unless they can prove their devotion to their subject. This might not seem fair, but you've got to think of your own interests. I've seen auctions where the cataloguing was done by two 'experts' and you really could see the difference. It is your money so act in your own interests and work with experienced or very knowledgeable valuers whose work you can check before selling – exactly as you would do with a builder, for example. Don't be afraid to ask questions. Experienced auctioneers love showing their expertise:

- What do you think it will go for? Look for hesitation or lack of eye contact
- Can you tell me more about it? Another way of judging their expertise. See how much detail they provide e.g. dates, makers, history. Not just what's on the backstamp
- Ask about its chances. Do they come up often? Again, find out what they know. If you discover they have others in the auction, hold it back for another time

I've worked as a consultant to Phillips (now Bonhams) because they had a gap in their knowledge-base which I could fill and I'd rather an auction house call in an outside expert than not admit a weakness in subject area. Don't be afraid to ask if they'll call in an expert if they don't have one already. Don't use them if not or you could lose money.

George Kidner, one of my favourite auctioneers, performing an appraisal. When choosing an auction house, make sure you feel comfortable with the auctioneer's personality and knowledge.

It doesn't have to be a choice between general and specialist sales but general and better quality general auctions. Gorringes hold regular sales at one of their Lewes salerooms but also have a bigger sale at their other saleroom in the town (seen here), attracting more interesting lots such as the Royal Doulton Lambeth Ware vases at the top left of this photo. Dealers come from several counties to buy here and competition is fierce.

GENERAL AUCTIONS

If you are selling general lots which don't need specialist auctions or buyers, look at general auctions. I always recommend speaking to two or three auction houses so you get a feel for their expertise and likeability. I know one auctioneer who knows his business but is so obnoxious and disdainful about some of his clients and lots that I wouldn't sell through him. An auctioneer should be acting in your interest, not theirs and discretion is also an important factor. I don't care if they like their clients but I certainly don't want to know if not. By speaking to more than one, you get a chance to see who you like and also listen to different information about your lot. Some items are easier to value than others. For instance, most Royal Doulton figures are easy to estimate as they come up so often but others, such as studio pottery or silver coffeepots are less predictable. As with selling through estate agents, don't be swayed by the highest estimate alone unless they can back it up with figures. When did they sell the last one and for how much? Check all of the questions asked at the beginning of this chapter after looking at the directory and then make a decision. You might even want to try more than one auction house if you're intending to sell on a regular basis so you can check out their cataloguing to decide which to use more frequently.

Ultimately, when it comes to general auctions, look at the questions to ask, a combination of location and commission rates can often be a deciding factor.

This 1960s Beatles dress benefited from being sold with other Beatles goods, including some original sketches by John Lennon, at a specialist entertainment sale with a Beatles section.

Catalogues

These vary between auction houses. Weekly or fortnightly sales often just have printed A4 sheets of paper instead of the glossy catalogues used by specialist or better sales. These vary between £1 and over £20 but I'd always recommend purchasing a catalogue both as a seller and a buyer. As a seller at one of the bigger auctions, you will automatically be sent a glossy catalogue. But you'll normally have to buy you own at those more regular sales with printed A4 catalogues. It's worth doing so for record keeping. I'll provide more details of the cataloguing process in chapter five (see p124) but, at this stage, you just need to look at them to study form. I bought a 'tall china vase' for £32 and sold what should have been described as 'a late-Nineteenth Century Majolica vase with pierced flared rim and looped handles, with flower decoration (12")' for £500. That's why I never sold through that auction house. Detail and expertise are vital when it comes to making a profit.

Specialist sales

How can you tell if your goods are better suited to a specialist sale than a general one?
- They need real expertise. This is especially true of harder to value goods such as ancient and Oriental, books and ephemera
- They are more appealing to knowledgeable buyers or need an international market
- They would fetch more money amongst similar goods and might otherwise risk going unnoticed at a general auction or not attract monied buyers
- They would benefit from the increased marketing which is used for specialist auctions

Chapter 3

Negotiating Better Commission Rates – and Other Vital Questions

ONE WAY to make money is to pay less of it to the auction house. If selling regularly through a saleroom, selling a high value lot or lots, or selling several lots, ask for a discount from their commission rate. Most auction houses will agree to this unless there is a lot of extra work involved, or the numerous goods are not expected to fetch much money, relatively speaking (e.g. estate auctions, see section four, p143).

Getting a discount

Before you sign a sale agreement, ask about their commission rate (see p26). This can be standard or have graduating levels, depending on the estimated sales figures. Ask for a discount, explaining why, but never say what rate you want to pay. That way, you could get a better commission rate than expected. At the last five auction houses through which I've sold, all but one gave me a discount and all of the discounts were larger than expected. I got a third off but had only been expecting half that, if anything. It's always worth asking, especially if they're not the only auction house in town or the only specialist in that field. You could always hold back some lots to see how they do and take them to a rival auction house who might be more willing to discount their rate. Just ask nicely – but as though you expect them to say yes. You won't be the first to ask.

One auction house reduced their commission rate by 50%, although I did agree to catalogue the goods for them. This worked in my favour as I got the exact descriptions I wanted and could choose what went in each lot, ensuring far higher profits, especially at such a good rate. If you're an expert in your field or selling your collection, it might be worth offering to catalogue your goods for a higher discount.

When selling a collection or several goods, don't be afraid to negotiate a better commission as there's always another auction house who will offer you one if your initial choice doesn't. Getting a discount off the standard commission rate is not a question of acting as a Lady or a Tramp but of making bigger profits.

OTHER COSTS

Don't forget to ask about other costs such as:

• Minimum commission rate. Some auction houses have a minimum commission rate which can vary hugely per saleroom. This means that if your lot sells for £20 and the commission rate is 10%, they won't deduct £2 (plus VAT on the £2) but the minimum amount which, if £10 for example, means that you only get £10. If the rate is £60 and your lot only fetches £50, you won't get a penny – and might even be charged extra if insurance costs and lottage are involved

• Lottage. Some auction houses charge a lottage (fee) for entering goods into auction. This can be as little as £1 but, if selling goods estimated to sell for £5 or under, £1 lottage, plus commission and VAT on the commission, as well as insurance costs (if any) can negate any profit and a car boot sale might prove a better option

- Insurance. Some salerooms charge insurance for lots. This can be around 1% which does add up and cut into profits but is worth taking out (if not already compulsory) as this guarantees payment if your goods are broken prior to the auction. This is normally up to cost of the the reserve, not the estimate, but at least you won't lose everything
- Storage. Some auction houses will only hold onto bought or sold lots for 24-48 hours after the auction (others a bit longer) and you will be charged for every extra day they have to store your lots – and they'll charge you per lot

Minimum Commission Rates

If selling several lots or if you're a regular, ask the auction house to remove this charge. I haven't paid a minimum commission charge for a long time because I ask not to and that has saved me thousands of pounds over the years. I also don't pay lottage when selling goods because I ask not to.

BUYERS AND SHIPPERS

Ask what sort of buyers they have so you can assess if it's the right auction for your goods. Also ask about shippers, as regular shippers are a good indication of a strong international market which increases your sales opportunities.

PHOTOS

Some auction houses expect you to pay if featuring your images in their catalogue. It's up to you whether you agree but, for better lots, it's worth it as they will attract more buyers and could be featured in newspaper advertising, as well as the catalogue, attracting buyers who might not normally use that saleroom. Others don't charge and you won't know photos are being included in their catalogue until you get it. Most auction houses now take photos of most lots because of internet catalogues and live auctions on eBay (see p81) where buyers expect to see pictures of lots before deciding if to buy them. I've seen one auction which even tries to charge for a photo on their website catalogue and this can really add up. In that case, I certainly wouldn't pay – or sell through such a greedy auction house. These days, I would expect website catalogue photos not just to be free but to be done automatically for most, if not all, lots. Whilst it takes time, it's in the auction house's interest to attract as wide an audience as possible.

A picture says a thousand words which is why you want an auction house which takes photos of their lots, especially for their website catalogue. This Victorian picture is easily understood when seen but harder to imagine with just words. CH.

SALE DATES AND CHOICES

Ask which is the best sale for your lots. If you can afford to hold on, there might be a more suitable sale in a couple of months or more, for example 'entertainment' for Beatles-related china or a Christmas wine sale for vintage wines. It's worth taking their advice if you don't need the money urgently but do ensure that you know exactly what is being sold and when. It's also worth being aware of seasonal needs. Never sell lots on days with important sporting fixtures as you won't get as many potential buyers. Be wary too of selling during the summer season where the antiques world 'dies' (mid-June-September) as many dealers won't be around or many reduce their buying during the quiet season. Pre-Christmas sales are great for toys and other specialist sales when buyers are looking for presents or 'practical' goods such as vintage wines.

Catalogues

I'll be talking about this in more detail in chapter five (see p124) but always ask about cataloguing before you leave your lots. They aren't all vital but it just ensures that your questions are answered:

Know your sales. If selling general goods, a glossy catalogued sale isn't necessarily needed but better items, such as this "Nineteenth Century parquetry lady's sewing table with drawer and sliding silk bag', would do better if photographed in a glossy catalogue where the image shows just how desirable they are, much more so than a description on its own. SW.

- What sort of catalogues will they create? Are they A4 paper, glossy outside with paper inside or full glossy?
- When will the descriptions be ready for you to see – pre- or post-printing? This is important as it means you might not be able to change the cataloguing before other people see it. If this concerns you, ask if they could e-mail/send you the descriptions first. If they refuse without a good reason (e.g. timeframe), this might not be the best auction house for you
- Will the catalogues be available on-line? This will increase buyers, especially if they also do live auctions through eBay or other sources, including their own website
- Will you be sent a free catalogue? This might not be done automatically for non-glossy versions, so ask to have one. You will have a record of the sale through your personal paperwork, but it's useful to have the catalogue to see what else is being sold, especially if they're selling similar or identical lots or you want to sell through them in future and want to check their overall expertise

This charming painting of **The Young Fruit Sellers** *by the Italian artist Antonio Paoletti (1834-1912) uses people as objects in a still life, rather than portraits, so will have more appeal than solemn-faced strangers hanging on a wall. It sold for £11,000. As the artist died in 1912, if the buyer can afford to wait until the centenary of his death, they can capitalise on renewed interest to maximise their profits. LW.*

Chapter 4

Should You Set Reserves?

THIS is not such an obvious answer as it might seem and depends on what you're selling and why. If selling to clear space or 'dump stock' or you just don't want the goods back and they're not high value, don't set a reserve. If they're high value, set a realistic one on the low-side.

What is a Reserve?

This is the lowest price at which you agree to sell your goods. Or is it? Beware the letters A.D. or the words 'auctioneer's discretion' which gives the auctioneer the right to sell your goods for under this price, usually 10% less (£90 for a £100 reserve) but it can be more, and there's nothing you can do about it as you agreed. Do what I do and refuse to agree to this term, unless you just want to clear the item. That way, you know exactly what's the lowest price you've agreed to take.

Reasons for setting reserves

Some auction houses won't sell goods under a certain level based on their estimates so this might be a moot point (but ask the question). Otherwise, set a reserve if:

• You want to protect your own interests and ensure that your lots are not sold for under a specific sum (but see 'What is a reserve')
• You want to protect yourself from a quiet day at the auction. You can always sell the lot elsewhere, but you could see a £100 lot sold for £20 if the auction isn't busy that day or the right buyers aren't around
• Your lots are high value and a reserve re-enforces this with the auctioneer
• You know the market value better than the auctioneer, especially for lesser-known items such a studio pottery

- The auctioneer is not the most compelling person on the podium and you want to ensure that they start at a realistic point. If they start too low and don't have a natural auctioneering energy, trying to up the price might be a struggle. A reserve forces them to start slightly higher which can push the price to an acceptable level
- You just want to. It's your right

I've worked on many TV shows where they try not to set reserves to guarantee sales, often at the expense of the contributor. I always set them to protect the seller. It also helps to determine market value better. I'd rather not sell a lot than give it away for a silly price. Of course, if I just want to get rid of something which is not high value, I don't bother with reserves.

How to set reserves

The majority of auction houses write estimates in their catalogues or sales particulars. Sometimes, when a lot of goods are being sold, figures are not set at the time but when cataloguing. The first time you see the estimates is when you see the catalogue or pre-catalogue details. At this point (if not done when giving the goods to the auction house), set the reserve. There are basic rules for setting reserves:

- Never set the reserve higher than the lower estimate e.g. at £150 for a £150-200 lot – unless you believe that the auctioneer is wrong. In which case, be prepared to argue with them or withdraw your lots (see p126). Setting a reserve which the auctioneer deems 'too high' can incur costs if the lot doesn't sell (see the next page)
- Be realistic and set the reserve at or preferably, under, the lower estimate to get the right figure. By setting it slightly too high (e.g. lower estimate), you could be forcing the auctioneer to start the bidding too high which means you might not even get a starting bid or the necessary impetus to get to the right amount. For a £100-150 estimate, I'd set a £75-80 reserve
- Know your auction house's bidding increments. If they go in £20s after £300, don't set a £330 reserve. They might not think to tell you until it's too late and you could have lost the sale. Whereas a £320 reserve could have got it (not applicable if you've agreed to the auctioneer's discretion, see p120)
- Speak to the auctioneer for their advice if you trust them to act in your interests and not their own

If you are selling a mid to high-value lot, set a reserve instead of sitting on the edge of your seat and praying that it will sell for what you need (or more). This tapestry-backed prie dieu chair with finials was knelt on for praying.

AUCTION TERMS

Some auction houses might try to charge you if the goods don't sell because they don't meet your reserve price if this is higher than the estimate or else higher than they recommended. Or just because they didn't sell. This is a clever trick to try to get novices not to set reserves. Just ask them to remove this term, I do. You could end up losing money otherwise.

If they won't agree and you're not setting ridiculous reserves, this might not be the right auction house for you. These charges can be as much as 8%, plus VAT, of the estimated price. I would never agree to this. Just speak to the auction house and reach an agreement before signing the contract – or sell your goods elsewhere.

REASONS FOR NOT SETTING RESERVES

There are very valid reasons:

• The market value is indeterminate and setting reserves with an exaggerated estimate could lose you sales, especially if the auction room is lethargic and a bidding impetus can't be gained

- You don't want the goods back – especially for job lots or large items for which you no longer have the space
- The goods are low value

CONCLUSION

When selling my own goods, I always set reserves unless selling to clear space when moving or 'dumping stock' when I never want to see things again. I'll make up any losses with gains on other lots and that's how most dealers work, judging each lot on its own merits. I always set reserves for items over £50 whether selling for myself, other people or an estate as it protects those involved. And that's what reserves are, a form of protection against a quiet day at the auction house. After all, you can always sell the goods another time and, if necessary, at another auction house. In short, the decision whether to set a reserve is down to you. Don't be intimidated into selling at an auction house where the auctioneer is trying to force you to accept a very low reserve or no reserve at all. Just find another saleroom.

This Jomaz lion is a beautiful quality piece by Joseph Mazer and highly collectable. A few stones are missing but these can be found at specialist suppliers or ask a friendly dealer if they have any spare to sell.

CHAPTER 5

Protecting Your Interests

AN AUCTIONEER is working for an auction house, not for you and their needs don't always match yours. To them, it's numbers. To you, it could be your mortgage or a much-needed holiday. Don't be afraid to question what they're doing as there could actually be a good reason for it, they might realise that they've made a mistake or you might need to do something to look after your own interests.

Job lots

If you are submitting several items to auction, the auctioneer could decide to put some or all of them into a job lot. You do not have to agree to this if you don't want to. I once had a valuer stick two Deco platters worth £120 and £180

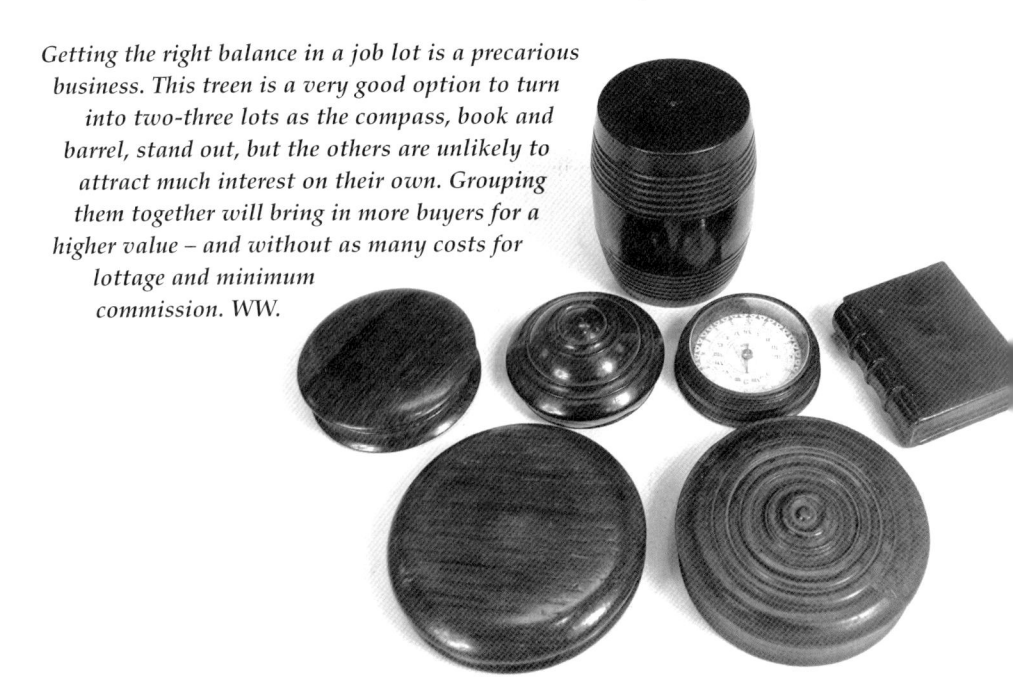

Getting the right balance in a job lot is a precarious business. This treen is a very good option to turn into two-three lots as the compass, book and barrel, stand out, but the others are unlikely to attract much interest on their own. Grouping them together will bring in more buyers for a higher value – and without as many costs for lottage and minimum commission. WW.

each into a box full of other items and told him to take them out. These are your items and you do not have to agree to anything, so don't be afraid to voice your opinions but back them up with information if possible. In my case, I mentioned the value, makes and period to support my views. Sometimes, auctioneers are very busy and will group goods together without thinking it through carefully enough. However, they might also have realised that several lower value goods will sell better and, if there are lottage fees and minimum commissions involved, will cost you less this way. Ask them to explain their choice. You can always ask them to split the lots into a smaller group and some individual pieces if you disagree.

I know one novice seller who had 400 sketches put into one folio and would have lost a fortune if he hadn't asked for my advice or ignored what the auctioneer recommended. He reduced the folio, ensuring enough of interest was still left in it to attract buyers, and sold the rest another time. If he hadn't, he would have lost thousands of pounds. A job lot that large devalues the goods, making it look as though they're worth so little, they have to be sold in such large numbers. Far better to have around 50 mixed quality sketches in the folio than 400 and, time allowing, enter them in different auctions.

Catalogue descriptions

These will either be sent to you (by post or e-mail) before they go into the catalogue or once the catalogue is in the public domain. The former is easier because it gives you the opportunity to change the description. If you're not happy, speak to the auctioneer and talk through your concerns. If, for example, you're selling an autograph album, say which names you want mentioned. I've had stunning Art Deco figures catalogued without the period being noted. This would have lost me a lot of money, as would a low valuation based on the auctioneer's ignorance of the subject matter if I hadn't complained. If you are submitting a lot of goods at once, you won't have the chance to agree to descriptions when you sign the sales agreement and these are the more problematic areas. If in doubt, discuss.

In an ideal world, you can tell the auctioneer what you want included in the catalogue when you submit lots but accept that they will have to fit descriptions to their house style e.g. teapot and cover (instead of lid). This is not possible when submitting several lots at once.

However, when the description is already catalogued and these have been printed and/or e-mailed, you can't change them. If they are liable to lose you money, you only have one real option to protect your interests – pull the lots.

This pair of Mabel Lucie Attwell Sam and Sara figures by Wade are worth around £100-150 in today's market. If they were catalogued as a 'pair of Wade dogs', I'd ask the auctioneer to change the description or, if they refuse, pull the lot. What's worth money here is the Mabel Lucie Attwell name so check that the cataloguing mentions the money-making names for maximum profits.

PULLING LOTS

This is a last-case scenario but it is essential where you would lose a significant amount of money by not doing so. Whilst some auction houses get annoyed if you do this (I've had one auctioneer actually throw books at me), most accept that it's your right to do so and you can still sell through them in future without embarrassment.

Pulling Lots
Withdrawing lots from sale is known as pulling lots.

EXAMPLES OF WHEN TO PULL LOTS

I've had to pull a surprising number of lots in the last few years and not just for myself but to help other people when asked. This is down to:

- Poor groupings which could lose you a fortune
- Bad descriptions liable to lose you money
- Too low an estimate which devalues your goods

Poor Groupings

The 400-piece folio and the two Art Deco platters being thrown in amongst job lots are good examples of where poor groupings will devalue your goods, losing you money. Depending on the description and whether there are any photos either in the catalogue or online at this point, you can always choose just to remove certain items and leave the rest in. I've done this several times and then either sold the choice items in a future sale with a better description (and estimate) or sold them at another auction house.

Bad Descriptions

Not everyone can attend auction viewings or sales, especially in these days of internet catalogues. Therefore, the descriptions are vital for maximum profits. If they simply don't show the goods to their advantage (make, name or important era missing or just inaccurately described), they won't reach their potential. I was selling some one-off Wade prototypes worth £300-500 each and a stunning 1939 Wade Grebe signed by Faust Lang worth £1,000-1,500. The latter was grouped with other items. They were described as 'Whimsies' and 'several birds' respectively with ridiculously low estimates which wouldn't have warned anyone that these were fantastic lots for collectors. I had put a lot of goods into the auction but knew I did not have that many Whimsies so asked the auction house to pull the lots until I could see them. The five lots included a rare Alphabet train (worth £400), the prototypes and other goods MIB (mint in box) whose boxes quite clearly showed that they

Correct cataloguing is vital if you want to make money. One saleroom described all Wade animals as 'Whimsies', including this Bernie and Poo ornament which is worth £30-50 instead of the 50p-£3 most Whimsies are worth. Pull lots which are badly catalogued if you don't want to lose money.

weren't Whimsies at all but which the valuer used as a basic description for all Wade animals, regardless of accuracy. If I hadn't taken action, this would have lost me thousands. The 'set' of birds also included two Wade Connoisseur birds (worth £150 each) and a rare 1950s Wade tree with bluebirds (worth £500-700). The estimate for the bird lot was £100-200 – for all of them (true value: £1,800-2,500). If it can happen to me, it can happen to anyone.

How to pull lots

It is very simple. If you were sent a pre-printed description, speak to the auctioneer to express your concerns and, if they fail to remedy the problem, either ask to pull your lots or put it in writing. You don't even have to say why you want to withdraw them if you'd rather not. Remember, it's your money you're protecting, not theirs.

Charges for withdrawing lots

I've seen some Ts&Cs where they try to charge for withdrawing lots unless this is because of misattribution (e.g. wrongly described lots) or authenticity (e.g. questioning whether the item is genuine or not). In one case, the auction house has said that it will charge for lost:

• Commission and buyer's premium, plus VAT which would have been achieved based on the mid-estimate – e.g. fees based on a £125 sale for a £100-150 lot
• Expenses incurred e.g. photography, storage, insurance etc. The 'etc' is a huge concern as these are unspecified fees which to you're expected to agree. Personally, I wouldn't sell through any auction house which had so much detail and then an added etc. In this case, I wondered how often sellers had withdrawn their goods – and why

However, if the auction house has misdescribed your goods, including putting an unrealistically low estimate on them and they are not prepared to change them, then argue about this fee as this counts as misattribution, albeit not quite in the way they are expecting the term to be used. I have never been charged a fee for withdrawing lots, despite pulling tens of thousands of pounds worth of lots because of poor descriptions and/or estimates.

CHAPTER 6

WHAT HAPPENS TO UNSOLD LOTS?

I GET ASKED this question a lot, particularly by people who have read the small print in the Ts&Cs and are worried that they might end up being charged for their lots not selling. Firstly, this charge is rarely imposed and only then if the client insisted on setting reserves deemed too high by the auction house (even if the auction house had undervalued the goods). But, generally, the charge is only made if the seller was particularly awkward. What I do when setting reserves at a slightly higher level than the auctioneer suggests (if they suggested any reserves) is to ask them not to impose this non-sale charge. Get them to cross it out in the contract if preferred. No one's ever refused this instruction or charged me for goods which haven't sold, even if I do set slightly higher reserves than suggested – normally when selling for someone else so their interests are protected or when I know the area better than the auctioneer.

AFTER THE SALE

Not all of your goods have sold. So what happens next? If the lot almost reached its reserve, or the auctioneer's lowest acceptable price (e.g. £200 on a £400 lot, depending on the saleroom), then the auctioneer, with your permission, can re-offer the item to the lowest bidder at the price they bid. This happens a lot on daytime TV shows and is a legitimate sales device. It isn't ideal but at least you get a sale.

Some buyers offer to purchase unsold lots after the auction and the auctioneer can choose to contact you with that offer (not all will do so if the offer is deemed too low). You can then decide if to sell it that way. I've even been offered unsold lots by auctioneers who know that they would appeal to me when I haven't attended the auction or put in a bid. I get them at the reserve price or my highest offer, if the seller agrees or the auctioneer has discretionary rights. Regulars do get these opportunities. The seller's rights are still protected and, as the vendor, you have the right to refuse to drop your price. If the buyer offers the reserve price after the auction, the auction house won't consult you but will accept your pre-agreed reserve price at that stage.

And if there are no post-sale offers?

If your lot had no reserve and couldn't attract any bidders or it didn't meet your reserve, you have two options:

- Collect your goods and either keep them or try to sell them elsewhere
- Leave the lots in for the next auction

Collecting lots

Some auctions, such as those in village halls and not a saleroom, will demand that you collect your goods within a specific timeframe (perhaps on the night of the sale or the following day) and return them nearer the time of the next sale as they don't have storage facilities. Others will expect you to collect unsold lots which are not being re-entered for sale within a week or 28 days of the sale. If you fail to do so, you will be charged storage fees and this will be made clear in the Ts&Cs. Not all auction houses will arrange for goods to be sent back to you by post so you will have to collect them yourself. Bear this in mind when choosing which auction house to use and what reserves, if any, to set.

Re-entering lots

If leaving the goods for the next auction, you will be expected either to sell them at a lower reserve or not to set a reserve at all. Depending on the goods and their estimate, I would be loathe to agree to enter any lots which previously had reserves with no reserves at all – if you set one initially, then they must be worth something so don't agree to sell them for a pittance unless you really want to get rid of them. Otherwise, take them to another auction house.

CHAPTER 7

WHEN AND HOW YOU GET PAID

PAYMENT terms will be written in the Ts&Cs of the sales contract which you signed when taking goods to auction. By signing them, you have agreed to this so make sure that you read them carefully as payment can vary hugely between auction houses and that could be a determining factor when deciding where and when to sell your belongings.

WHEN WILL YOU BE PAID?

There are several variations on this and the basic rule, from my experience, seems to be the bigger or better the auction house, the longer it takes to pay you:

- On the day of the auction or the day after. This is very rare but smaller auctions, often the village hall ones, do pay very quickly and in cash. This is particularly useful as you don't always know from where they actually operate
- A fortnight after the auction. Not that common
- Three weeks/21 days after the auction. Very common
- Four weeks after the auction. A month is a long time to wait to get your own money

---

Village Hall Auctions

I love buying from these but would never sell anywhere I didn't have an office address I can check out before trusting my belongings to people who might not be easy to find. I know one auction house which had four owners in about eight months. Others have been operating for years so ask around being selling your goods there.

How will you be paid?

Some auctions pay cash but this is very rare. The majority of salerooms pay by cheque which is generally posted to the seller, although some allow vendors to collect their cheques after the agreed period, usually three-four weeks. As it takes about five working days for cheques to clear and post is often slow, this means that it can take you almost six weeks to have the money in your account after an auction so this can be an important consideration when choosing an auction house. Read the Ts&Cs in the sale catalogue before committing yourself.

Deductions

When you are paid, any expenses will have been deducted and will be listed on the sales forms. Some auction houses will include the VAT with the commission and not list it separately. Check that the commission rate matches the agreed one and e-mail or visit the auction house immediately if not. Ensure that you have all the relevant paperwork in case there are problems, but most will resolve this immediately and either send extra cheques or ask you to return the previous one and send you a new one. In this case, go in person to swap cheques and avoid further delay.

Your cheque will be less the agreed fees which will be clearly stated in the sales form which comes with your cheque. Ask for the paperwork if you haven't received it automatically as you will need this for tax purposes (see p139) and to make sure that you have not been overcharged:

- Commission, plus VAT. Sometimes listed as one figure and not with separate VAT
- Minimum commission, plus VAT. If a minimum commission is set, this will be instead of a fixed commission rate for goods meeting (or under) that set figure (see p116)
- Lottage. If any (see p115)
- Insurance. If any
- Any fees for unsold lots not meeting reserves higher than the auctioneer's suggestion. But where possible, try to avoid this payment and, if the auction house refuses to remove this term, consider selling elsewhere
- If your lot sells for £100, this could leave you with a cheque for £86.25 (based on 10%, plus VAT commission (if VAT is 17.5%), 1% insurance and £1 lottage fees) or £80.37 with a 15% commission and identical fees. That's a lot of money – even more if you've had to pay extra charges, including photography. Too

many sellers forget this when receiving their payment and are disappointed, so estimate all costs before agreeing to sell your lots at that auction house. It's not always the case that the higher the fee, the better the saleroom.

It's worth hunting around for the best auction house. Higher commission isn't indicative of better service. Also look for those extra costs such as minimum commission. Don't forget to think in terms of buyers as well. This fox stirrup cup would sell better in a rural area than a city. WW.

Chapter 8
Your Rights

AUCTION houses can make mistakes. It is often the nature of these mistakes that help to determine your rights. Missing something rare is one of those unfortunate errors where the seller has no protection. But knowingly mis-representing lots is entirely different. It is also very hard to prove.

In most cases, your rights are strongest pre-auction where you have the right to set reserves, ask for the catalogue description to be changed (if not already printed) and withdraw lots if not. Complaining about cataloguing post-auction is too late, as in the case studies I have related here.

It is vital that you read the sales particulars and Ts&Cs of the auction house as, to an extent, you can refuse to agree to certain rules such as minimum commission (your case is stronger if you're a regular buyer or seller or selling a lot of goods), paying for unsold lots where the reserve is higher than the auction house suggested and paying for withdrawing lots. Once you sign your sales contract or don't address wrong or poor cataloguing, these rights are terminated.

Broken goods

One of the most common problems encountered by sellers is broken lots. They can be damaged by the auction house team or would-be buyers during viewings. They can even be stolen. What are your rights? If you are insured (that 1% charge) and the auction house breaks your item, they will pay you up to the value of your reserve or the lower end of the estimate, whichever is lower. It is more difficult to prove that goods were broken by buyers once it has been assigned to the auction house. Taking photos of everything you sell will help to protect your interests – include a newspaper of the day the goods were taken to the auction house as proof of date. This is not always practical if selling dozens of items.

Not all auction houses write condition reports (or accurate ones) but, if they do, then you can ask them to check this – if you are even aware of the damage before the auction. Not everyone admits to damaging goods so, where feasible, check your goods prior to the auction in the saleroom and bring any damage

Case Studies

A vendor recently sold a painting at auction for £2 million; having initially been told it would fetch £1,500. A cause for celebration? Yes – until they heard that it was actually worth £15-20 million. The Rembrandt self-portrait (24cm x 17cm / $9^1/_2$in x $6^1/_2$in) of the artist as a laughing young man was even entitled *The Young Rembrandt as Democrates* but, as the vendor couldn't supply a provenance or prove that it was an authentic Rembrandt, the auction house wouldn't attribute it to the artist and set a £1,500 estimate on it. As the seller agreed to that estimate and didn't ask the auction house to do research, they have no comeback and cannot legally hold the auction house responsible. However, I would be very disappointed that the auction house did not do their own research as such a find would have made their reputation, which the adverse publicity did not.

A less obvious case concerned a cracked glass claret jug, sold in an unrelated box with the name of a designer on it. When the shabby 'Nineteenth Century French' jug, estimated at £200 sold for £220,000, the auction house initially thought that the interest was in the box. However, it had not realised that this was one of the 'holy grails' of Islamic art, an Eleventh Century rock crystal water jug, one of only six made (the last one being sold at auction in 1862 where it was bought by the Victoria & Albert Museum). The rare Egyptian artefact was actually worth £5 million, according to an expert in that field. The seller would have no case against the auction house.

These are worst-case auction scenarios but, if you feel that what you have is something special, get a second opinion, even a third. In the case of the Rembrandt, I would have taken it to an auction house with a reputation for selling the artist and asked their advice. Hindsight can be a costly mistake.

to the attention of the auctioneer or porter. If insured, demand your money based on the previous condition and then they will own the damaged lots and can sell them – for less than their original estimate if the damage is bad, or they can just accept the loss.

If you are selling a painting or other item which is put in a precarious position such as on the floor, under lots which people might want to lean closer to see and could risk putting their feet through your painting, ask the porter to move the lot to a safer location.

Ultimately, it's your burden to prove breakages occurred after you handed in the lots and before the sale. Put everything in writing should the case go to court if the auction house fails to take proper measures to protect your lots or reimburse you.

Stolen goods

Theft does happen, even at the best auction houses. If this is only discovered after the auction when the lot has been sold, it becomes the buyer's responsibility and you will be paid in full. If the auction house tries to tell you differently, threaten legal action as the goods were in their protection and you should not be held responsible. If the theft is discovered before the auction, if you are insured, you will get paid the reserve price or the lower end of the estimate, whichever is lower. If you are not insured, expect to have to argue but it is the auction house's responsibility to protect your goods. Threaten them with legal action but also mention negative publicity as they will not want the local press (which attracts buyers) or the antiques press (especially *The Antiques Trade Gazette*) to be aware of any problems with security. Such threats normally see a quick resolution but you probably won't be able to trade there again. With such lax security, would you want to?

Lost lots

All salerooms are different, but many are chaotic and some lose goods because of this. Put any requests for the missing goods in writing so you have a proof for a judge if it should go to court. This helps them to find the goods quicker or to pay out for their failure to safeguard your goods. If the latter, they will then own the lots and can sell them when they find them, keeping the proceeds.

When I worked for *Antiques & Collectables* magazine, I had far too many letters from readers saying that they'd sent in or left goods at, salerooms that had subsequently been misplaced and, in most cases, the auction house refused to admit that they'd ever had them. If sending in items for valuation or sale, post them by special delivery which means that they're insured up to a certain value (pay for more insurance if necessary) and that the auction house has to sign to accept delivery. Enclose a note stating what's in the parcel so you have a record of what was sent. If there is a discrepancy between your details and what's in the package, they will ring you immediately. Failure to do so means that they accept that what you have written regarding the contents is true, so you have proof of delivery and goods. This is useful should they ever deny receiving the goods.

If leaving goods behind, do the same thing. If the auction house doesn't give you a form to say what has been left and when, have your own details prepared before you go and get them to sign it. This is essential to prevent problems of denial.

Be persistent. I contacted one auction house half a dozen times before they 'found' the picture they'd collected. I would never sell through them again because of this lack of care. If you're not persistent, you could lose out. But put everything in writing and either hand-deliver or, better still, send letters recorded delivery so they have to sign for it and you can prove receipt.

Get the name of the auction house's owner or Managing Director, especially if part of a larger chain. Write to them, copying in the manager of the auction house you were dealing with, but make sure they know you mean business and go above the head of anyone who has tried to fob you off. If you make a fuss, you're more likely to get what you want. If you're quiet and ask nicely, once, you'll probably not see your goods again. This is not theft (in most cases), just lazy, disorganised practice.

The hardest position is when you've left goods to be valued with an auctioneer who has since retired and your goods can't be found. Demand that they contact the auctioneer. This is generally not a case of theft but the auction houses don't know the 'filing system' of the old valuer and need their help finding your goods. Again, make a fuss in writing (not in person) so they have an incentive to discover exactly where your goods have been stored. It's not an easy situation but can be resolved with patience and persistence. Never get personal, never be libellous (i.e. mention theft) but let them know that you expect them to do their job, be professional and find your missing goods. With the right paperwork already in place, you can, at least, prove receipt.

Hidden goods

Auction houses often use every available space to sell goods during viewings and auctions, even cupboards which they're selling. Not all buyers can find these lots but the auctioneer and porters know where they are. This is acceptable business practice, but there are illegal methods as well. Including not putting the goods on display or correctly descibing them so they don't seem worth seeing. This is illegal and, looking at the catalogue pre-sale and either withdrawing the lots or demanding a change of wording (if not already printed) could have protected the seller. In this case, if they found out, they would have a case against the auction house.

Dealers often hide choice lots during viewings so other buyers don't see them. This is unethical but the auction house cannot be held responsible unless they participated.

CONCLUSION

Your rights are strongest before the sale. Afterwards, if you discover that the auction house had knowingly misdescribed your goods, you have a case but it will be difficult to prove. This is why it's essential to speak to more than one auction house and check catalogues before the sale. But, if your goods are broken or stolen, you shouldn't lose out, so be persistent and demand your rights. Just expect it to take some time and then hit the auction house where it hurts by taking your business elsewhere. Tell everyone what happened to you so they also take their business elsewhere. Nothing libellous or slanderous, just that your goods were lost/broken and the auction house refused to take responsibility.

Set aside money to pax your tax bill so you don't have to hunt around for it. Nineteeth Century Majolica game pie dish. CH.

CHAPTER 9

TAX MATTERS

TAX NEEDN'T be taxing if you're prepared, and auctions make life easier as they come with paperwork. Keep a record of everything you buy and sell, plus your expenses (e.g. stationery, paper, wrapping, bags and petrol) at the end of every auction so your accounts are stress-free.

WHO NEEDS TO PAY TAX?

Not everyone involved in buying and selling through auctions needs to pay tax:

• If doing so as a business (e.g. as an antique dealer or house clearance), you will need to pay tax (and the self-employed part of the self-assessment form)
• If selling goods, not as a business, but earning more than £9,600 than they cost you originally or were worth when you were given them, you will need to pay Capital Gains Tax (CGT) which needs a self-assessment form
• If you just buy goods for yourself or as gifts, you do not need to pay tax
• If you sell the odd thing because you're moving home or just feel like a change, and those goods do not total more than £6,000, you do not need to pay CGT*

SELF-EMPLOYED RESPONSIBILITIES

If you are buying or selling through auctions as a business, you have three months before you need to register as self-employed – even if you already have a PAYE job. Failure to do so could incur fines and, in extreme cases, could even mean prison for defrauding the tax office. Tax inspectors are very interested in the antiques world and visit antiques fairs and centres to catch people who don't pay tax, even writing down car registration numbers in car parks at fairs. In the areas where you have to register as a second-hand dealer if selling via auctions, antiques fairs and car boots etc (see p191); you must also be registered to pay tax as they already have a record of what you're doing so you will be caught out. Register with your local tax office and ensure that you fill in the self-employed part of the self-assessment form. This is a separate

* Tax year 2008-09 figures.

Self-assessment Details

Whether you're running a business (i.e. self-employed) or paying Capital Gains Tax, you will have to register to pay your tax by self-assessment. This is very easy:
- Ring 0845 915 4515
- Register on the tax website – ww.hmrc.gov.uk and click through to self-assessment/self-employment

It is your responsibility to ensure that you receive the tax return form and file it on time. Ring or go to your local tax office to collect the form if necessary.

document and, from experience, they often forget to send it out with the main form so double check early and ask for one to be posted or collect it, if necessary.

CAPITAL GAINS TAX

This is complicated and the Government website (www.hmrc.gov.uk) does not really explain it properly. Basically:

- Annual exemption for individuals. If you earn under £9,600 in profits (for the tax year 2008-09, this rate will increase for subsequent years), you do not have to pay CGT
- Chattels exemption. If the individual item or set you are selling is worth under £6,000, you do not need to pay CGT

If you are self-employed and sell goods at auction as part of this business, they do not come under the CGT ruling but the less generous self-employment rules. But it's not worth trying to cheat the system because the taxman does visit antiques venues on a regular basis and you could get caught. In my opinion, this needs reviewing as the self-employed on lower incomes end up paying more than those who are exempt under the CGT rule.

RECORDS

Even if just buying at auction, always keep the records in case you decide to sell the goods later. For the self-employed, records relating to the business must be kept for five years and 10 months. Failure to do so could result in fines of £3,000. Apart from tax matters, it also shows you what you paid and allows you to assess both that particular auction and market patterns. Do some goods fare better at certain times of year? If so, use this information to make a higher profit.

VAT

If you are registered for VAT you can reclaim all of the VAT charges incurred at auction, including that on commission or buyer's premium. Keep all of your paperwork for this. Note, the taxable threshold for the 2008-09 tax year is £67,000 – not £67,000 in profits but in total.

Paper trail

Regardless of why you are using auctions, keep all of the paperwork to protect you should you need it, such as for tax checks or if you decide to sell your goods at a later date. I also keep all of the old catalogues where I've sold goods just out of interest and to keep track of what I've had over the years as, in some cases, I'll never find goods like them again.

If someone crosses your palm with silver, the taxman will expect some of that profit if you earn over a certain amount a year – even if you hold a full-time job and pay tax on that. Register as self-employed to avoid getting caught and fined – or worse.

What do you do when a loved one dies? It can feel overwhelming.

SECTION FOUR
Estate Auctions

Chapter 1

What Happens When Someone Dies? Estate Auctions

For many people, the first time they sell at auction is when a family member dies. This is a very distressing process and can be time-sensitive in cases where homes need to be cleared and sold. It is also bewildering as the language used by auctioneers is not always familiar, such as 'job lots', 'commission' and 'reserves'. To me, these words are commonplace but I know from experience that not everyone understands them and that was why my father asked me to be in charge of his estate when he was diagnosed with cancer. Afterwards, sitting around the kitchen table with my two sisters who had little or no auction experience, I realised that estate auctions as they are sometimes known (especially in the US) have their own issues. I hope that I can answer all of your questions here as I did for my own sisters. As you can see from the picture used to introduce this section, dad's estate might have had a few more things to clear than most people's but the questions I was asked and the choices I had to make, will be just as relevant for many of you.

The first thing I will say is do not sell to anyone who rings or turns up at your door. They do not have your interests in mind and, even if you know them, you won't get the most money or have the proper paperwork that you'll need for lawyers and the other heirs (if applicable). My advice is simple – never sell to the person who values your goods. After dad died, mum had a call from a dealer who'd known dad and said that he'd 'help her out' by buying his collections. He then tutted at her when she said they'd already gone to auction. We knew that, apart from being grossly insensitive, he would have ripped us off. No decent person would ever behave that way. An auction protected us from such people and we knew that those valuing the goods had no vested interest. I was in sole charge of a huge and varied series of collections and also had the protection of paperwork so that my own actions were clear for the legal and tax side, as well as the other heirs.

Paper trail

It might seem like an odd thing to have said but the auctions allowed me to show exactly what I was up to and also provided a record of dad's collections, which had been such an important part of his life. They also showed what each item or job lot was worth, according to the auctioneer. I was able to contest the prices if needed and to set reserves. A dealer coming in would have paid one price and we'd always have wondered what we'd missed and if we'd made a mistake. An auction gives you peace of mind and a permanent record, especially if you're not just selling for yourself but other heirs and it is also important that you do right by your loved one. So never feel rushed or bullied into doing anything but take your time and, if necessary, ask for help.

First things first

Before you start thinking about auctions, not all deaths are expected. When someone dies, money should not be your first thought. Take the time to grieve and to find out from a lawyer where you stand. Some estates are more complicated than others; some have specific bequests where goods have to be found and given to named people, whilst others have even more complications. Has the person who died even left a will? First step, speak to their lawyer. Don't let anyone take anything until you have established what you are allowed to do.

Probate

Probate gets more complicated the more the estate's worth, especially if it includes a property. In some cases, absolutely nothing can be removed from the home until probate is granted – that's when you're given the go-ahead to start sorting out and disposing of the estate after an estimate of its value, for tax purposes, is settled. You might need to bring in an auctioneer to help value the goods, depending on what type of belongings make up the estate. In an ideal world, specific items or whole collections will be bequeathed in the will so there are no squabbles, especially where common-law partnerships, especially gay partnerships, are concerned. This has caused a lot of heartache amongst collectors who don't have the proper paperwork in place so, when one dies unexpectedly, the other's assets aren't protected, especially when family members haven't approved of the relationship.

Your lawyer can advise you when you can start clearing and selling the estate. To avoid problems, don't do anything before getting the legal go-ahead

It can be hard to know where to start, especially if you have to sort out the belongings of an avid collector. First, wait until your lawyer tells you that you can start removing anything, even items mentioned in a will. But you can at least begin organising things into groups for heirs, selling, charity and rubbish. After a death, it gives you something to focus on and gives you back a sense of control, plus a chance to relive happy memories. This used to be our dining room.

and ask for the permission to be given in writing, especially if there are several heirs. This stops any unjust accusations, as well as protecting you from probate infringement.

Is it worth anything?

The reality is that, if you don't have a background in antiques and collectables, you probably won't know what's worth money. It might be an idea before anything gets divided between family members, to bring in an auctioneer to do a valuation with the intention of selling through them if you feel comfortable with them (see p110). Again, it's not a pleasant thought, but some people might want a possession because it's worth something, not because it has sentimental value. To avoid any accusations, get goods valued. What some families have done is allow relatives and friends to take what they want

ESTATE AUCTIONS 147

Where There's a Will

If you're a collector, ensure that you leave a will clarifying exactly who gets what so there are no complications when you're gone. Even include photos like this small collection of treen and other goods so there's no confusion.

Even if you're not a collector, it's important to leave a will to protect the interests of those you love.

to an equal value so no one feels anyone has taken advantage or not got enough. Some people want money and not belongings (no space, not their style, don't want the memories etc) and this can be taken into account when the estate is sold at auction. For example, Aunt Jane got the £2,000 painting and cousin Ed didn't take anything so Aunt Jane had £2,000 debited from her final cut when the estate was shared out. Just think ahead and make sure everyone agrees to prevent future issues. Money and greed isn't worth losing a family over. In my business and as a journalist, I've heard so many horror stories that it's worth urging everyone to take a deep breath and start talking before any upsets occur.

What next?

Once the family and other heirs have taken what they want in an open fashion with everything recorded for the lawyer and executor, then is the time to start organising dispersing the estate, including taking goods to auction. Remember, this is not an easy time and people cope differently. I know that it really helped me to sort out dad's estate and I felt that it was helping him, not just the other benefactors; whilst my sisters found it too distressing to sort through his life's passion and mum had to empty the rest of the house prior to selling it. Everyone will behave differently and there's no right or wrong way but do make sure everyone agrees on what's being done so no one can make a fuss later or be hurt that they didn't have time to get something which would mean a lot at a later date, when the grief has settled.

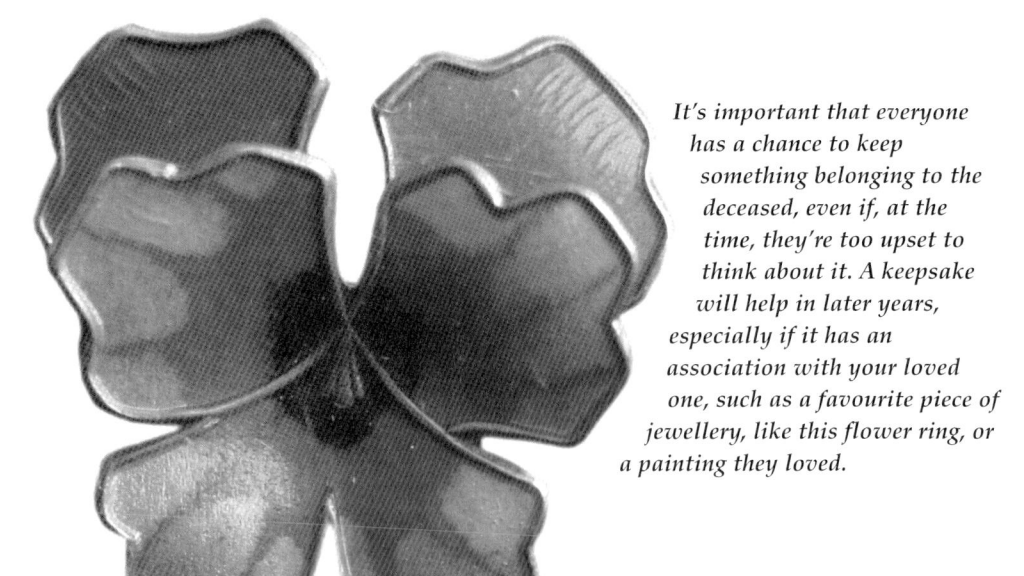

It's important that everyone has a chance to keep something belonging to the deceased, even if, at the time, they're too upset to think about it. A keepsake will help in later years, especially if it has an association with your loved one, such as a favourite piece of jewellery, like this flower ring, or a painting they loved.

CHAPTER 2

WHY SELL AT AUCTION?

AUCTIONS are not suitable for all estates as not everything will realise the most money or, to be honest, be auction material. Other possibilities include:

- eBay
- Antique dealers
- Specialist dealers
- House clearance firms
- Car boot sales
- Charity shops
- Recycling and the rubbish tip

I will be covering all of these in more detail but the obvious reason to sell at auction is to make money. It is also a good way of clearing a lot of items via job lots.

What's not auction material

This is subjective and I'd advise that you let the auctioneer see everything before sorting goods into piles for auctions, specialist dealers, house clearance, charity shops, recycling etc. Let the auctioneer see everything, including crockery, glass and crystal, cutlery, kitchen goods (kitchenalia e.g. old storage jars and bowls etc), books and even clothes if vintage. Otherwise, as a very basic rule of thumb – but only after the auctioneer has seen everything, just in case there are unexpected gems – these are the types of goods which are probably not auctionable:

- Clothes. Unless vintage or designer. Don't forget to go through all pockets in case money or jewellery etc has been left there
- Modern crockery and cutlery. Again, unless designer
- Personal paperwork. But go through everything in case share certificates

Job Lots

The term given to several items being sold in one go or 'lot'. This is used for lower value items or smaller collections. Job lots are very much aimed at the dealer market and can be very profitable or just a cheap way of getting more than one item. To be honest, many of these are fit only for the bin but there can be some decent pieces in there.

Speak to your auctioneer if you want to know why particular objects were grouped together. If you're not happy with their reasons, you can always pull the lots (see p174) or ask them to split them into smaller job lots. The main advantage is that you often stand more chance of selling the goods that way, vital if clearing items is a consideration. Some of dad's collection was sold in job lots of five boxes. That's a huge amount, but the reality was that interest in his unusual objects, which he loved and gave him years of happiness, was limited (especially as many were in poor condition) and none of the family wanted to store them.

Another advantage is that you only pay one set of commission/lottage instead of paying per item. Vital in cases where minimum commission starts at £10 (see p116).

---

and bank or pension statements are there as your lawyer will need them

- Computers and very modern gadgets. But older computing goods and mobile phones can be worth money e.g. Atari and some early mobile phones. Most auctioneers wouldn't recognise their value, so check the internet before selling or disposing of them to get an idea of sale values. Sell on eBay or specialist modern gadget sales if there are any (the market is getting there)

STORAGE SOLUTION

You might want to consider putting everything into storage. This has several benefits:

- Goods not left in an empty house. No more security worries
- Allows time to sort through things. Especially if no one has time to go

Not everything is suitable for auction so consider doing a car boot sale. Give high volume goods such as paperbacks to charity shops or look at the other options on p152. It depends on your own circumstances, not just whether you have space for unwanted goods but if you have time to sell them yourself. This is how the room on p142 looked after weeks of sorting through what was worth selling, what we wanted to read ourselves and what should go to charity.

through everything quickly or the benefactors are abroad and want to see the goods or help dispose of the assets
• Allows you time to grieve
• You live far from the home involved and don't have the time to commute.
• Allows you to organise everything closer to home so more control, less stress
• Allows you to test an auction house before committing everything to them. Some auction houses will sell everything in one sale because of their own storage demands which might not be in your interests
• Allows you to dribble goods through auction, realising more money, even allowing for storage costs

Whilst there are costs involved (these vary hugely per area and size of units), these will be deducted from the estate and, as long as all benefactors and executors agree, this is a very good option to consider. It certainly made a huge difference to us once we decided to store dad's goods and I would recommend it as an option if the house has to be cleared or would otherwise be left empty which is a security risk.

Pros and cons of other options

Depending on what you're selling, there might be other options to maximise profit and ease. This is a very difficult period and time has to be a factor, especially if you need to sell the house or there are several heirs, some of whom are pushing for a fast conclusion because of their needs – such as paying off medical expenses or funeral bills.

eBay

Pros

- Lower fees compared to auctions
- International market
- Good option for goods, such as some modern collectables and modern gadgets, which don't always do well at auction
- Most things sell on eBay, especially goods you might have given for free to charity shops

Cons

- Can be intimidating if you're not used to it, especially when grieving
- Time consuming
- It helps to know what you're selling to describe them for maximum profits
- You have to pack and post the goods which takes time, especially if you work during the day

Antique Dealers

Pros

- They'll buy most collectable goods

Cons

- They won't pay the full market value as they need to take their own profit into account
- Not all dealers are honest and you could get ripped off very easily, especially when grieving
- Never leave a dealer unattended in your house as a tiny percentage have been known to steal

Specialist Dealers e.g. record dealers and paperback book dealers

PROS ☑
- Good options for goods which don't have an easy market elsewhere
- Great to profit from paperback and mass-produced hardback books which would otherwise go to charity shops
- Look for specialist book dealers as well e.g. crime fiction, cookery book etc for maximum profits
- Space-consuming or heavy goods will be taken in one go – often, the dealer will even collect them straight from the house

CONS ☒
- Particularly for record dealers, do your research first so you don't inadvertently get ripped off (buy record price guides)
- Never leave a dealer unattended in your house as a tiny percentage have been known to steal goods

House Clearance Firms

PROS ☑
- They can take everything, including furniture and pay you for doing so. Saves having to pay for and load skips for unwanted washing machines, sofas etc

CONS ☒
- Some firms actually try to charge for collecting your goods and then selling them on for a profit, especially when you're particularly vulnerable
- They can be quite fussy and some no longer take everything, only wanting choice items – which you can probably sell for more at auction
- They often refuse to take furniture such as sofas which don't have fire retardant labels

Car Boot Sales

PROS ☑
- Make money from ordinary, household objects, clothes and books instead of giving them away for free
- Low pitch rent, around £6-10 and only half a day's work
- Can always give unsold goods to charity shops afterwards if desired
- All-weather venues (Hardstanding, undercover) operate even in bad weather

Cons
- Can be upsetting to sell loved one's goods and see other people handling them
- Can be cancelled due to bad weather after you've geared yourself up to do it

Charity Shops

Pros
- Get rid of unwanted clutter and help a charity
- It's a lovely way of other people benefiting from your loved one's cherished belongings e.g. books or shoes

Cons
- You're giving away part of your inheritance and it can add up, especially for books and designer/vintage clothes
- Some charity shops have become unpleasantly snobbish and can reject your 'gift' at a time of grief, causing great upset
- Not many of them collect goods so you'll need to be able to cart everything to the charity shop yourself, parking nearby can be difficult so take that into account when deciding who benefits

Recycling/Rubbish Tip

Pros
- No one buys old encyclopaedias or out of date travel guides so recycle them instead
- Throw away unwanted goods – and let go

Cons
- No profit. Sell books to dealers or give them to charity instead

Antique dealers

I've been an antique dealer since 1982 and I would never, ever recommend anyone selling to an antique dealer after a loved one has died as you are opening yourself up to being taken advantage of and to regretting it when the grief has lessened. It might seem an easy option and the person might seem pleasant but they're running a business. Go for auctions instead. Obviously, if this is a long-term family friend, you might want to discuss your concerns with them but the person who values the goods should have your interests in mind, not theirs. I personally would never buy from anyone at this time as they are liable to regret it afterwards, apart from never buying what I've valued. I always recommend good auction houses when people ask for my help under these circumstances and after I have valued goods so they know what to expect but I don't buy them.

Never let a 'knocker' into your home. They are the bane of the antiques world and come knocking, uninvited at the door, especially after reading

Car Boot Sales

Car boot sales can be a good option to dispose of non-auctionable goods such as normal clothes, paperbacks and household goods. But it could be upsetting if selling very personal items as people can make thoughtless comments and it can be hard watching a loved one's goods being handled or bought by strangers, especially if you're not used to car boots. But car boots can also be a lot of fun if you are up to it and surprisingly profitable.

Car boots are enjoyable under the right circumstances but think carefully about whether you will be able to watch strangers handling your loved one's belongings.

obituary columns. They have been known to steal goods when left unattended, as well as paying a pittance for profitable goods. A common trick is to pay more for a worthless piece to lull you into a false sense of security, and then value worthwhile goods at a low price. Often, they'll pay £5 for an ornament worth £500+, promising to return to pay £150 for that large, worthless bit of furniture – and you'll never see them again. Don't trust anybody who calls without an appointment. No decent antique dealer or auctioneer behaves that way. Nor do good dealers put notices through doors saying that they are 'in your area today' and offering to buy 'broken pieces of jewellery'. Those are common knocker tricks. Just don't let them in. It's a good reason not to put an obituary or notice of a funeral in your local paper. We didn't publish anything until after the house had been emptied.

Pros and cons of auctions

Auctions are very useful but, as you can see from the previous pages, they're not the only option. There will be times when auctions are not suitable or you might choose to mix auctions with other options such as car boot sales and charity shops (e.g. old but not vintage or designer clothes) or specialist dealers (especially for records or hardback books). It depends on the nature of the estate and the wishes of the heirs.

Pros ☑

There are many advantages to selling at auction. But always speak to more than one auction house so you have options and can choose the one which you trust or with better commission rates:

- All you have to do is pack everything
- Someone else does the cataloguing and works out values
- They sell it for you
- You don't have strangers in the house apart from the auctioneer and people collecting the lots to go to auction if there's too much for you to take – vital at a time of loss when not all 'dealers' are trustworthy or you don't want strangers around
- You don't have to do any paperwork apart from signing the sales contract (and making a personal note of what's going to auction)
- In the event of a dispute between heirs (it happens), the auction house's paperwork will show what's gone to auction and record all monies being paid out (see p169)

Separating the sellable from everything else is one of the reasons why a good auction house can be so helpful. If your loved one got a bit carried away, it can be hard to tell what anything is actually worth. But you could lose money if you assume it's all worthless and give it to a charity shop or throw everything away which are common mistakes to make when people are grieving.

- The auction won't happen that week so you have time to breathe and decide between you all what you want to keep
- If you are keeping goods from the estate, the auctioneer can act as an independent valuer so there's no fighting and the value of your chosen items can be deducted from your share of the estate if that's the way everyone wants to work. Everyone then feels they've been treated equally
- You have a record of what your loved one owned. It might not seem much now but, when everything's over, it's proof that that they existed, especially if selling their collection and that will mean a lot to you or other members of the family over the years
- No one has to handle cash. Prevents accusations and someone having to be responsible. Peace of mind is vital at such a time for all concerned, especially as people can be forgetful when grieving. The paper trail also stops any concerns over how much was really raised
- You make more money than when selling direct to dealers and have the peace of mind that goes with it
- You don't have to attend the auction so, unlike selling at fairs and car boots, don't see people handling your loved one's belongings
- Other people get to enjoy what your loved one owned – which will appeal to collectors as others will get pleasure from their prized collections

CONS

- You have to wait for your money, especially if the goods are being sold over more than one auction (see p163)
- If selling a collection, it's advisable to sell it over several auctions so the market isn't saturated and to allow collectors a chance to afford several lots

- Selling too much in one go will devalue the collection
- Some valuers will try to take advantage of your situation and either undervalue your goods in the catalogues or try to get you to sell the 'less valuable' lots to a 'friendly' dealer instead of at auction. Whilst rare, it does happen and, when grieving, you might not spot it. That's why it's vital to speak to more than one auction house

Should you go to the auction?

This is a hard one. Personally, I would advise against it as you might get upset at seeing your loved one's goods out of context or being handled by strangers in a sterile environment. Plus, not everyone will like what's being sold and will say so, not realising how hurtful that can be. I would recommend taking a lot of photos before anything is moved or packed and saying goodbye to them, and your memories, where they belong, at home. But keep the catalogue as a reminder and a record because it's not just about money but possessions and memories.

Always try to keep a photographic record when clearing an estate, not just for yourself but for those who, for whatever reason, couldn't be there. This is how the dining room seen on p146 looked just before the removal men arrived to take it to auction. By this stage, everything had been carefully wrapped and put into boxes but you can also hire removal firms who will do this for you if it's simply too much to do it yourself. When someone dies, there is a lot to organise so accept help when you need it.

One more thing

When I was packing dad's estate, I was flooded with memories. When he'd bought certain things, how much he loved some rather disgusting cherubs (not the best quality), when he'd hung some paintings. I wasn't prepared for so many thoughts at a very difficult time but I knew how vital it would be for all of us to have something from his collection so those memories wouldn't evaporate when the goods were sold. I kept something back for all of us, not because of their value, but because I knew how important it would be to have something that dad had touched and loved when everything had been sold and the painful grief eased. At the time, not everyone wanted something but I knew that they would regret this later and, being in charge of the auction as dad had asked, I also felt that it was my responsibility.

Being in charge of an estate auction is a huge burden – often too much so. If you are dying or your loved one has died, please don't let anyone be in the position I was in but sell the collections beforehand or, if you can't do so, arrange for two people to dispose of the estate so no one feels overwhelmed by it. I was so lucky that mum was there but she also had to pack the family house at the same time. There is a lot of work involved in packing and sorting collections and, in an ideal world, several heirs should be there, not just for the practical work like dusting and packing but to agree how to sell the estate and to share the memories. It is a difficult time but kindness and generosity makes it less so. If you or your family can't actually be there to help the person in charge, ring, offer verbal help or just support but don't let them feel alone, especially as it's also your inheritance and you should want to have a say in its disposal and know what's happening and when. Otherwise you could forfeit the right to complain or might not realise you want something until it's too late.

CHAPTER 3

Choosing the Right Auction or Auctions for Your Needs

FOR MOST of you, this won't be a huge issue. It is harder for those selling collections or specialist items. If the estate is relatively small or doesn't have a specialist element (e.g. a collection or you're selling the stock of a dealer), look at the directory at the back of the book and choose your nearest two or three auctions and, if you have time, visit them. Otherwise ring them. Personally, I'd visit them to see the state of their premises. Even if they don't have a sale that week, you can look at old catalogues or see what items are on display ready for the next auction. Some will have framed press releases showing their recent successes. This will help you to gauge what quality of goods they sell. It might be too upmarket or not quite quality enough to suit what you're selling. You need to match

Look at old catalogues to see if the auction house is suitable for what you're selling if it's specialist. This seller was in charge of clearing a family's estate and opted for one of the local auction house's better sales instead of the more regular ones. That way, he attracted more interest for his family's goods which were reflected in their hammer price. If only he'd known to negotiate commission rates, he could have earnt more money for the estate.

buyers to your goods so bear this in mind and see what you think of the auctioneer. In most cases, a general auctioneer will be your contact as they can value across the range. If you don't like them, just ask about commission rates and how regularly they hold auctions. You don't have to give them your contact details but just get the information to compare rates – and to use as a bargaining tool with another auction house in the vicinity to lower the other saleroom's commission.

SPECIALIST AUCTIONS

If you are selling the estate of a collector or dealer, it needn't feel so overwhelming if the auction world is new to you. After all, they probably bought and or sold through favourite auctions and either mentioned them to you or have the paperwork naming which salerooms they used. This also makes things easier as the auction house will already know what sort of things you're trying to sell and will have an established market, especially if you're disposing of a coherent collection. Most auction houses will be able to handle goods from general dealers. Just go with the one or ones you like. Otherwise, concentrate on what they're selling. Let's look at books:

Several auction houses such as Bloomsbury Auctions (see p213) and Dominic Winters (p203) have a good, solid reputation and very successful specialist book sales. Others, such as Cheffins (p193) also have book specialists and can sell more general goods as well. Speak to auction houses and see what their specialist areas or auctioneers are. If your loved one had a good book collection, save these for a specialist book auction where the right valuer will ensure that they are accurately described and where discerning buyers already go. Don't waste blue and white china and Oriental goods in a general sale but ensure that they get specialist valuations or your estate could lose out. The proper

Protect the estate by choosing your auction carefully. This set of Winnie the Pooh books, including first editions, is better suited to a specialist book sale than a general sale as the expert auctioneer will know what they should fetch and the serious book buyers will know about the sale.

description is vital for maximum profit which is why it's essential that you find the right auction house. Whilst Vectis (see p196) is the most well-known of the toy sales, Cheffins also has toy sales, sometimes as part of a broader, good quality sale but the serious buyers will know about it. More so than just a few toys mingled with other lots at more general sales.

Do your homework, speak to the trade and ask the auction houses about their specialist areas. Look at the *Antiques Trade Gazette* (available from larger fairs, some newsagents and www.antiquestradegazette.com) to see what sales are coming up. It will probably be too late to submit lots for those advertised auctions but your goods can go into their next one. It's just a good way to see who does what.

Late Entries

Never agree to let your goods be entered as 'late lots' where they get a sheet of paper inserted into catalogues. These are far too easy to miss and not the right way to sell your goods. Ensure that they are only ever mentioned in the main catalogue and not an easily dropped piece of paper.

SPECIALIST OR GENERAL?

Again, it depends on what you're selling. Top quality jewellery will do well in the jewellery section of good quality general auctions but don't sell any in normal general auctions where a few bits of jewellery are clumped together. Go for the monthly (or every other month) auction, not weekly or fortnightly which are lesser quality ones. But, if you're selling general goods, these more regular sales are perfectly suited to your needs where goods can be outclassed and, therefore, devalued, in the better quality auctions. The auctioneer will help you as they want to ensure that their auctions do the best they can and retain their reputation. If you have time, go to one of their auctions, otherwise, ask to see previous catalogues so you can gauge the quality for yourself and don't be rushed by deadlines. There will always be another auction.

WHICH IS THE RIGHT AUCTION?

Specialist goods benefit from specialist auctions. Look around and read the

It is unlikely that a general auctioneer will know how to value lots such as these ancient Islamic glass bottles. In this case, you need an auction house with a specialist glass department or an ancient goods valuer and then wait to sell them in an auction with similar items to attract maximum buyers and higher values.

antiques press (see p187) to see which auctions specialise in what. Also consider better quality general auctions which group lots into sections so all of the paintings or jewellery are sold together instead of everything being mixed up. This is an indicator not just of quality but of different auctioneers with specialist interests. The same auctioneers might have more than one saleroom in town (e.g. Gorringes in Lewes, see p226) and keep their better lots for their higher quality auction, while more general goods sell at their more regular one. This is a very good option as it means that one good auction house can handle everything for you and you don't have to worry about getting lots to different auctions.

It is a matter of personal choice but try to choose a good quality auction house whose sales are not too regular so dealers don't get bored going but feel they must go or they'd miss out. However, for run of-the-mill goods, general weekly or fortnightly auctions are absolutely fine.

How many auction houses should you use?

It depends on what you're selling and how specialist the auction house is. Ideally, it's easier to use just one at this difficult time when you want things to

𝓑e 𝒮ecurity 𝒞onscious

Don't give anyone your details or agree to let anyone other than the auctioneer help you to 'value' the lots. Very few people are actually this helpful without an ulterior motive. I never agree to value what I buy, but don't let anyone see your inheritance as it could be a security risk. That's why selling at auction is often the best option.

When my father died, my main concern, as the person in charge of selling his collections at auction, was to get them out of the house as people knew what he collected and I didn't want everything being in an empty house for too long. When dealers started ringing asking to 'help' us dispose of his estate, everything had already been sent to auction so we didn't have to worry about break-ins. Sadly, you do need to be aware of security when a well-known collector dies or an obituary or death notice is printed in the local paper. I deliberately didn't write about dad's death in the antiques press until the house had been cleared for just this reason.

be as easy as possible but there could be a reason not to, such as they specialise only in military goods, toys, books etc and you need a more general auction for other items. I like Cheffins in Cambridge which has several specialist departments and offers regular sales and a better quality, less frequent auction, including specialist areas. This allowed us to sell across the range, separating the lesser quality goods from the choice ones and selling good quality ephemera. We sold one photo for over £700, showing how vital specialist auctioneers are when it comes to selling quality goods at auction. This would probably not have been noticed at a more general sale which is one of the reasons I opted for an auction house with quality specialists.

Speak to two or three auction houses and then decide what to do based on your own needs, including convenience. If you have a lot of goods to transport, using one auction house could save on costs but, if there is a lot of it, consider splitting the goods so the market won't be

This Sylvac tortoise would appeal to general dealers as well as Sylvac specialists and collectors, so either sell it at a general auction or one of the better, less regular auctions held by a local auction house.

inundated. Storage is a huge issue at auction houses and they could put goods into bigger job lots, thereby devaluing them, because they need the room. In dad's case, I used three auction houses as he had so many items, one auction house proved disappointing and sales took place over a year to give us the best chance for maximum returns. Other estates are not quite so unmanageable and can be sold in a single auction or one general and one specialist one. Let the auction house be your guide and, if necessary, rent a storage unit (safer than an empty house if your loved one lived on their own) and gradually sell their collection over several auctions for maximum returns.

SHOULD YOU REALLY SPLIT COLLECTIONS?

If it's a small but choice collection and belonged to a well-known collector, then sell it together and ask the auctioneer if it should be sold as the 'collection of xxxx'. That would attract buyers and maximise your inheritance. Otherwise, a vast collection is often too much for the market to handle in one go, especially if there's more than one example of higher value items. You need competition for highest profits, especially these days, when there's limited money around, so sell over several auctions, allowing collectors and dealers to save up and buy more. You'll make more money that way.

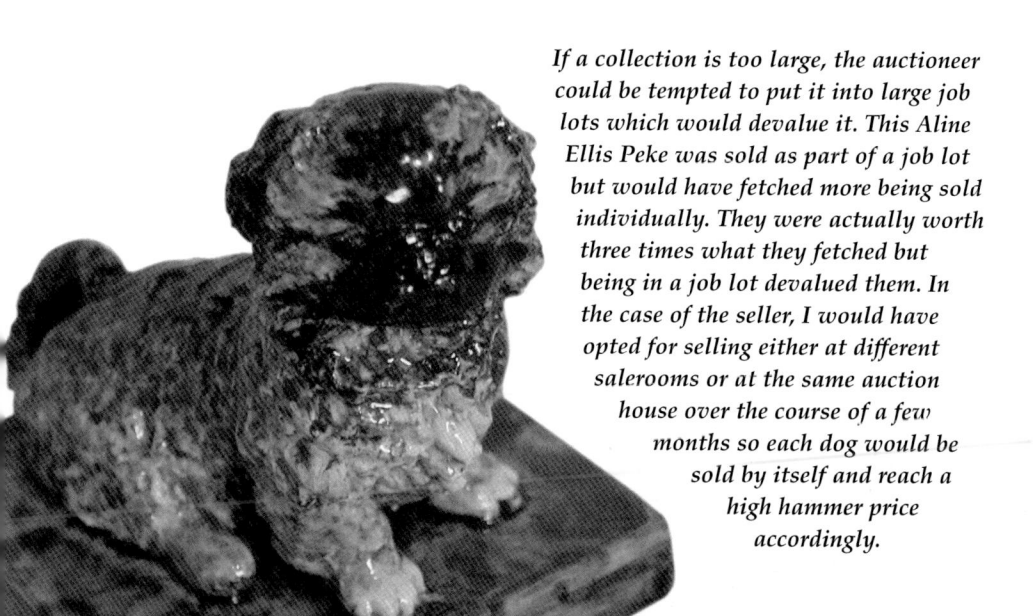

If a collection is too large, the auctioneer could be tempted to put it into large job lots which would devalue it. This Aline Ellis Peke was sold as part of a job lot but would have fetched more being sold individually. They were actually worth three times what they fetched but being in a job lot devalued them. In the case of the seller, I would have opted for selling either at different salerooms or at the same auction house over the course of a few months so each dog would be sold by itself and reach a high hammer price accordingly.

House sales – a good idea?

If you are selling a lot of goods, the auction house might ask you to consider selling the goods in the house. One of my favourite ever sales was a house sale by Cheffins in Cambridgeshire but I would never agree to one myself and certainly didn't want to do so when selling dad's estate. No matter how organised the auction house, you can never watch anyone all the time which means some goods might be stolen. You are also showing people what's available in a house which is no longer lived in during the viewing period.

If you're selling the house afterwards, you need to consider extra costs such as new carpets after hundreds of people (if you're lucky) have been through it, plus the lawn will get crushed by visitors, cars or a marquee if you need one. There's a lot to consider but, when grieving, make your life as easy as possible. Let the auction house use their own saleroom and keep strangers away from your loved one's home. I really do believe, apart from the practical considerations, that it would be too upsetting. That said, I would never recommend a house sale at any time because of the safety aspect, despite loving attending them as a buyer.

Letting go is one of the hardest aspects of estate auctions. This Nineteenth Century ebonised and amboyna veneered stereoscopic postcard viewer was one of my dad's favourite pieces but, whilst beautiful, it was also cumbersome and none of the family wanted to keep it so we sold it – but set a good reserve. It is tempting to hold onto everything but not always practical. CH.

CHAPTER 4
Probate and Other Legalities

IN A PERFECT world, everyone will leave a will. Collectors really must do so to protect their heirs. There are awful scenarios when two people collect together, one dies and the other can't prove how much they put into the collection financially, so a family member gets the lot. At the moment, if a collector dies and leaves no will but there is a spouse and children, their spouse will inherit £125,000 and the rest is left in trust for the children – even including the house (if not included in the £125,000). So, if you haven't written a will already, do so as soon as possible to spare everyone else a messy situation.

When writing your will, it's a good idea to name who gets certain pieces and then take a photo of the items to leave with your will. This means everyone knows exactly which pieces were left to whom so there can't be any disagreements or misunderstandings. This is a great tip for collectors or anyone leaving a will so people get exactly what they wanted them to have, with no confusion. Some people put labels on the bottom of pieces but these have been known to be swapped.

The following advice is based on a will being in place. Firstly, the solicitor will either read the will to the heirs or send them a copy. It is essential that

---

Choosing Executors

Choose the most responsible people as executors but don't forget that lawyers will charge for the time they spend helping an estate and these fees will come from the estate itself. Acting independently, a lawyer or non-inheriting executor is ideally placed to deal with matters calmly and without bias or self-interest.

Don't forget to tell someone that they're named as your executor so it's not a shock when it's too late to do anything. Update your will if the executor dies or your own circumstances change.

people know who the family solicitor is or, where there are no family splits, where the will is kept. The executors will then be placed in charge of the estate and every decision must be run past them, including who disposes of the estate at auction.

Probate

Unless your lawyer tells you otherwise, absolutely no goods must be removed from the home until probate has been granted. This is when the estate has been valued for tax purposes. This is often done by the valuer of the auction house (where you're intending to sell the estate if the house itself is not included) an independent valuer, including an estate agent or the person in charge of disposing of the estate at auction. Your lawyer can advise you how this works and even suggest people to ask for valuations.

You can invite auctioneers in to consider selling the estate before probate has been granted or before you have been given permission to remove goods. Even family members cannot remove items mentioned in the will at this time or items which they wish to keep. You can't even start taking goods to charity shops during this period as it could be considered theft or an attempt to defraud the government (probate being a form of tax).

Once probate has been granted or your lawyer says that you can remove goods (this can be prior to probate being granted), you can start taking goods to auction.

Allocating responsibilities

The heirs need to decide who will be responsible for the auctions. Ideally, this should be the work of two people to relieve the burden as it can be exhausting, especially when you are grieving. This does not have to be an executor but can be the heirs who best understand how auctions work or are interested in or knowledgeable about the collection, if one is involved. Or it could be the person who lives closest or who has the most spare time. Ideally, everyone should help pack the estate once the auction house has been signed up as it is very tiring and time-consuming. Some auction houses will be able to help with packing but this can cost extra and, if there are a lot of goods, it's easier to have everything packed before people come to collect the goods.

I would suggest that everyone agrees exactly how they wish to proceed to avoid upset later. The person or people in charge of the sales should let the others know which auction houses are being used and why; when the auctions are and then send details of the lots so everyone feels involved. However, only those dealing with the auction house and the executors should be speaking to them. This is to avoid the old 'too many chefs' cliché, especially as you need the auction house on side and not feeling like they're getting too many conflicting instructions. The paperwork should always be addressed to the main executor and not the person dealing with the auction house (to avoid conflict) apart from the sales particulars when the heir in charge of the auction needs to see that the inheritance has been catalogued or lotted properly. All paperwork involving money must go to the executor and the person signing the goods to the saleroom must do so on behalf of the estate and not just in their own name – this avoids any problems.

Setting up a bank account

If selling an estate through auction or even selling an inherited house, it is advisable to set up a separate bank account in the name of 'the estate of xxx'. This avoids not only potential accusations but also shows the taxman that everything is above board. Cheques from the auction house should be made payable to this account and not to the person dealing with them or the executor. Again, this avoids any possible problems. It also allows cheques to be paid for expenses such as hiring removal firms to take the goods to auction or paying for storage. Everything comes out of a central fund and not anyone's pockets which might not be reimbursed. You can close the old bank account of the deceased and move it to this account to help with the necessary expenditure of disposing of the estate. Only the two executors can access the account and you might wish to set up a system where both (if two) have to sign for any expenditure to avoid accusations and for everyone's peace of mind. Ask the bank what paperwork, including the will and Certificate of Death, they need to set up this account.

Sales particulars and catalogues

The sales particulars are often e-mailed to people selling goods at auction. These can then be forwarded to the other heirs and executors or printed off and posted if they don't have computers. Always ask for enough catalogues so no one feels left out and so everyone has a record of their loved one's collections or belongings. This will not seem so important at the time but will help later on, especially after the first stage of grieving when memories feel more important as everything has gone and the immediate grief has changed.

If withdrawing lots or any problems

If you have any problems with the auction house, let the other heirs know what decision you're taking ahead of time, explaining why. This stops any concerns or confusion and they have the chance to ask questions before you do anything. It also means that they feel involved as they might feel useless or even that they're letting you or their loved one down by not being involved. In my case, I sent clear e-mails saying exactly why I was concerned about some cataloguing and giving examples of how it should have been catalogued, stating that, if I didn't take action, we stood to lose thousands. It just makes everything clearer and, auctions are not everyone's world; not everyone understand their intricacies so it is vital to explain exactly why you are doing something unexpected if it is necessary to take action.

Storage

If you have decided to put goods into storage to sell over time or to give you space to decide what to do, don't forget to let everyone know exactly what's been sent where to avoid any mis-understanding.

Dealing with Loss

Everyone deals with loss differently. You expect a family to come together to grieve but the opposite is often true with families driven apart by greed or long-held grievances. By establishing clear communication and a very clear paper trail, you will avoid many of the pitfalls I hear about on my shows. Auctions provide the relevant paperwork for you so everyone can see what was sold, where and for how much so there can be no accusations of theft.

The results

Details of what the lots fetched will be posted to you after the sale and before you receive a cheque. Send a copy to all of the heirs as amounts deducted, including commission, will also be listed. Interested parties will then have a record of what money is going into the estate's account and can see everything tallies at the end (don't forget to send them copies of any expenditure as well). This is one of the best parts of selling an estate as you see favourite items recorded, alongside what they made.

Chapter 5

How to Get Lots to Auction

Auction houses are generally very helpful when it comes to clearing estates. As you are often clearing a whole house, you will probably have to deal with removal firms and the auction house will either arrange for one of their regular firms to be sent or give you their contact details. In both these cases, you will probably get a discount from their normal rate if you mention the auction house.

Packing up

Packing up a loved one's possessions is a very painful process as memories will often be overwhelming so expect it to take longer than normal and try to get everyone involved for support. Use old newspapers and boxes which are

Packing up a house can be a messy business. Take a change of clothes with you if you're liable to get dirty so you don't go home feeling and looking worse than you have to as it can make you feel even more distressed.

free from supermarkets (as they recycle them, it's a good idea to ask for some to be saved for you; banana boxes with lids are always antique dealers' favourites). Otherwise, arrange to buy some from the removal firm – far cheaper than most self-storage units. Take as many photos as you can pre-packing, not just as a record should anything get broken or go missing (it does happen, unfortunately) but for your own memories later.

If dealing with more than one auction house, note the name of the relevant one on the side of the box and store them in separate rooms or areas so there won't be any confusion.

Collection day

Ensure all items are easily accessible and access is clear. Then it is a case of either offering to help load the removal van or simply take a back seat. But be prepared to make lots of cups of tea. These firms are used to dealing with antiques so you don't have to worry that furniture won't be wrapped properly or your loved one's goods will be treated disrespectfully. That's also why it's best to go with the auction house's recommended firm.

Paperwork and payment

The auction house will have given them paperwork or you'll have been sent it in the post to sign and give to the removal firm. Either the auction house will deduct the pre-agreed delivery charges from your account after the sale or you will have to pay on the day of collection, usually in cash. Just ensure that you have agreed a figure upfront and get the paperwork relating to payment to give to the executor for the records as this will be deducted from the estate and won't be your financial responsibility. Don't forget to tip and add this gratuity to the paperwork.

Smaller estates

Smaller amounts of personal possessions can be driven to the auction house but I'm assuming that many of the estates will include furniture unless the deceased didn't live alone. In some cases, the auctioneer will actually turn up in an estate car or small van and collect the goods themselves. Don't forget to get more than one set of paperwork if they come more than once and add any extras to the general description e.g. 'photograph of a Victorian woman in five frames' added to the more general 'collection of books'. It just leaves you a paper trail should the extras get misplaced at the auction house.

Chapter 6

Protecting the Interests of the Estate

WHEN selling an estate through auction, many of the points I've made about selling at auction in the previous section are relevant but you're lucky, you get to blame an entire estate and not sound demanding in your own right. This means that the auction house can't argue with you or try to get you to change your mind, especially when they are in the wrong over valuations or inadequately described/misdescribed lots.

General points

As with selling your own goods at auction, try to get the best possible commission rate. Never say what you want to pay but let the auction house give you a rate – it's probably better than you would have requested (e.g. going from 15% to 10%, instead of 12^1/$_2$%). But, with an estate, you are more likely to get the auction house to waive the minimum commission charge and the unsold lots' charge (if the reserve is set higher than the auctioneer's recommendation) as you're generally selling more lots than people normally do. This especially applies if selling over more than one sale, and you can blame any necessary essential higher reserves on the rest of the heirs. They can't argue with that.

Job lots and catalogues

Obviously, because you are selling more items, you should expect more and larger job lots (see p150). You don't always have to agree to this and can ask to be there at cataloguing (which not all auction houses will like) or that you see the descriptions before they're in the catalogue, if possible. You are working on behalf of other heirs so will feel a greater sense of responsibility than if you were selling for yourself. If you really don't like how it's been catalogued or feel that it's not in the interests of the estate, speak to the

This steam engine was part of a specialist sale and was catalogued perfectly to ensure maximum profits and to reflect the auction house's own expertise. DN.

auctioneer and explain why. This is easier to do if you have auction experience but, if not, ask for help. You can also speak to friendly antique dealers and ask what they would do in your situation. Remember, you're not alone as there are good people in the trade who just want everyone to get the best out of it and enjoy the experience. If you're not happy and the auctioneer isn't being co-operative, do what I do and withdraw the lots.

Pulling lots

You can pull (withdraw) lots if you're not happy with the descriptions, grouping or valuation. The goods belong to the estate, not the auction house so stress that you're working for an estate and they want to withdraw these lots. You might need to pull lots for the next auction as well if they haven't been catalogued or if you feel the auctioneer will not act in your interest after you've pulled lots. Sadly, it does happen but let the auction house, not just the auctioneer, know exactly why you're pulling lots if their behaviour has not been acceptable. Remember, it is not the only auction house around and there are

Pulled Lot

When I sold dad's estate, I withdrew one lot when I saw that it was catalogued as 11 files of autographs. No names mentioned at all – no George IV, Victoria, Peel, Palmerston, Laurence Olivier, Garibaldi, Wilberforce. It's the worst cataloguing I've ever seen – all with an estimate of £200-400 for hundreds of signatures. To those not attending the auction, this description, along with the valuation, meant that this was an unimportant lot, not worth considering so competition was limited to those who took the time to attend the viewing and actually look through each of the 11 ring binders. It was potentially disastrous for us as sellers but great for the buyers who would have had an absolute bargain. I did the only thing I could and pulled that lot (and several others), writing to the rest of the estate and executors with examples of what I'd have expected to see in the catalogue so they could see exactly why I was so concerned. I then sold just a handful of those signatures elsewhere, with each of the prominent names mentioned in the catalogue, and achieved £330 for those few autographs. The estate would have lost thousands of pounds if I hadn't withdrawn that lot. I was just grateful that I'd spent time going through everything before it went to auction so knew that those files were of far greater interest than their cataloguing suggested. That's why it's so important to read the catalogue descriptions when they come to you and not just trust the auctioneer to act in your interest, no matter how reputable the auction house.

others who will help to sell your lots and not only listen to your concerns but catalogue the goods properly, making both you and them more money. They will help arrange collection if the goods are too large to go into your car. Don't be embarrassed to withdraw lots as you are quite rightly protecting an estate and your loved one's memory. It's a hard job but should be done properly so you don't have any regrets later. Withdrawing lots can sometimes be the only option and often means you'll make a lot more money elsewhere.

WHY DO AUCTIONEERS NOT ALWAYS CATALOGUE PROPERLY?

Some auctioneers are superb and catalogue expertly, others lack this expertise and are too general or too specialist, not always recognising better goods and others, let's face it, are lazy. You can see this in the cataloguing if you take the time to look at catalogues prior to committing your lots to auction. However, you can get caught out when auctioneers move on and a new person starts. Sometimes, they take their time to get established and this inexperience or feeling their way shows in their cataloguing. Some auction houses just have very basic cataloguing so it's an art form that has to be learnt. Others are corrupt or just unpleasant, deliberately writing poor descriptions so only their 'friends' know the lots are better than described and profit from this. Mostly, though, bad cataloguing is down to ignorance. I knew a lovely auctioneer who just didn't know a particular artist whose work rarely came to market and they catalogued accordingly, not for a rare painting but one with no form. It's a skill and I loved cataloguing for what was then Phillips (now Bonhams) because I knew the subject area very well and that's why I worked there as a consultant. Bottom line, if you're not happy, sell it elsewhere.

Setting reserves

I talked about setting reserves in the last section (see p120) but it can be different when selling on behalf of an estate. You want to protect the interests of the estate by ensuring that the lots don't sell for a pittance

Take the time to find the right auction for the belongings. These postcards of Scott's expedition are best suited to a specialist ephemera auction, as part of a small collection of postcards. ESS.

but you also don't want to get left with unwanted goods. In many cases, the heirs get together to decide who wants what (after any items mentioned in the will have been distributed), sometimes deducting the value of what they've taken from their share of the estate, based on the valuation by the auctioneer. Everything else goes to auction. This suggests that, for whatever reason, none of you wanted it so, if you set too high a reserve, you could be stuck with something you didn't want. Hopefully, you'll have a helpful auctioneer and can discuss your situation with them. Some auction houses try not to set reserves so they get a higher rate of sold lots but that's not in your interests. Look at what's being sold and for how much and determine what gets reserves based on that. Do you share your loved one's interest in spiritualist paintings? (This was a Victorian favourite where mediums claimed that a spirit was drawing an image through them). Don't set a reserve if they're worth £75 or under but, if estimated at £100-150, set a reserve of somewhere between £60-75 if you really don't want those lots in your house.

It really is a question of being guided by the value and content of each lot, but sometimes, sentimentality means that you don't mind getting something back or want to protect that old American rocking chair so set the reserve accordingly, again, not too high but a realistic level – that chair worth £200-300? Set £120-150 as a reserve.

LETTING GO

The hardest part of estate auctions is letting go. Don't put overly high reserves on your lots so people have to pay more for your memories as you don't want to keep everything. If you're not sure about whether you can part with an item, speak to the other heirs and ask to keep it for a bit longer, selling it on behalf of the estate at a later date when things are less painful and you can bear to let go. You don't have to sell everything at once, just accept that no one is what they own but keep some things for their sentimental value. If you think you'll regret selling something, keep it for now. You'll regret it otherwise.

UNSOLD LOTS

Some lots might not sell because they either didn't reach the reserve or there was no interest in the room. You have three options here:

• Leave them in for the next auction. Remove or lower the reserve if you have one and the auctioneer will automatically lower the estimate

Set sensible reserves so your lots sell and you don't make the auctioneer struggle by setting them too high. They need to build up momentum. This tortoiseshell tea caddy was worth £400-600 and sold for £640. I'd have recommended a £340/350 reserve based on this as setting the reserve at the lower estimate can prevent momentum and lose you sales. LW.

• Remove the lot and sell it elsewhere. Depends on the size and weight of the item. It might benefit from a different area and fresh buyers, but it will cost money to move if it's a large piece of furniture. Take all extra costs into account
• Keep it. Talk to the rest of the estate and see if anyone wants to keep it

There is no right answer here. It depends on what the lots are, your needs and the practicalities involved. Our favourite rocking chair didn't sell the first time but we had all decided not to keep it for practical reasons. It was best to leave it at the saleroom to sell at the next auction with a slightly lower reserve and estimate.

Testing the water

If you have time, you can just sell a few lots at a couple of different auctions to see how they work. Take a few choice items, enough to tempt the auction house and buyers and see what they make of it and how you enjoy working with them. Selling an estate is a very personal and difficult business so you want an auction house that treats not just you but the deceased and their belongings with respect. The perfect auctioneer is out there; just take the time to find them.

CHAPTER 7

GETTING PAID AND PAYING TAX

AS OUTLINED previously (see p169), the cheques from the auction house should be made payable to 'the estate of xxx' or some other pre-agreed name with a special bank account set up. Depending when the auction house pays up (see p131), these will be posted after the sales particulars have been received. Not all auction houses send a second copy of these particulars, especially if you have sold several pages of goods through them. Photocopy the sales results and send copies to all of the heirs and executors for their records, keeping a set for yourself.

COSTS

Don't forget that the final total from the auction house will be less costs including:

• Commission rate, plus VAT on the commission e.g. £10 + £1.75 on a 10% commission if a lot sells for £100 (depending on the rate of VAT)
• Minimum commission – if any – as an estate, you can negotiate for this extra charge to be removed. If this is applicable, this over-rides the commission rate should the lot sell for under the starting point for minimum commission e.g. a £50 item where the minimum commission is £30 a lot, means the estate will have £30 + VAT deducted from the £50, but not an additional commission charge
• Lottage. Entry fee per lot, if applicable. Again, you should try to get this waived when you sign the sale agreement if selling on behalf of an estate
• Insurance. If any
• Photography fees. If any (see p116)

TAX MATTERS

If, when the costs are deducted, including any storage, packaging or removal fees, the value of goods for each heir is under £9,600 (for the 2008-09 tax year), you will not have to pay any Capital Gains Tax (CGT). Otherwise, each heir will need to pay CGT so speak to your local tax office and arrange to be sent a self-assessment form with a separate form for CGT. If they forget to send this extra form, don't forget to chase it up as you will be fined for late submission and the tax office not sending the right forms is not an allowable excuse for submitting a late tax return. Speak to your lawyer or accountant for more details about tax relating to inherited goods.

Don't give the tax office an excuse to hunt you down, speak to them about registering to pay tax if you inherit more than the official allowance. Ask the tax office or your lawyer for advice, if necessary.

Chapter 8
Conclusion

WHEN SELLING on behalf of an estate or part of an estate where someone else is in charge, make sure the paperwork is in place and that everyone is kept informed all the way through, including which auctions are being chosen and why and, especially, if lots are withdrawn, including why and where they are now. It's a difficult responsibility but it helps if everyone knows what's going on so everyone's interests are protected. And don't forget all the charges, including your own responsibilities for declaring tax.

What I would add, from my own experience, is that disposing of an estate is a very painful job and should never be one person's responsibility. More than that, it is not about getting rid of goods but about distributing the belongings, the memories of someone you loved so take your time, don't let anyone rush you, especially an auction house and, please, take care of yourself and remember to keep something back, even a valueless trinket as, whilst similar items can probably be bought again, memories can't and, if you sell everything, you will regret it. That's why I kept things back for all of us so we'd always have something that dad had cherished and, when the grief has eased, that's when they will really matter.

Just ensure that all of the paperwork is in place to avoid problems later – and never dispose of or distribute any goods until either probate has been granted or the lawyer confirms that you may start clearing the estate.

Good Luck.

SECTION FIVE

INFORMATION AND AUCTION DIRECTORY

Regency mahogany and ebony inlaid knife box, est £2,000-3,000.

Glossary

Apostle spoons: Teaspoons with figures of the Apostles topping the shafts. Often sold in boxed sets.
Appraisal: Valuation by an auctioneer.
Auctioneer's discretion: The seller agrees that the auctioneer can sell their goods below their reserve, generally 10% under the reserve price but not always specified. Also listed as A.D. on paperwork. N.B. I never agree to this.

Backstamp: The factory mark on the base of a piece, most often used for china but also used for other types of goods including glass.
Bisque: Rough, unglazed white porcelain.
Buyer's premium: A fee on top of the hammer price, generally about 10-15%, plus VAT on this fee.

Catalogue: List of lots being sold at auction, sometimes with images and presented either in plain, typed form or in glossy, bound format.
Caveat Emptor: Buyer beware.
Chintz: Flowery decorations.
Commission: A fee based on the hammer price that the seller has to pay to the auction house, generally about 10-15%, plus VAT on this fee.
Commission bid: Absentee attempt to buy a lot, confirmed in writing.
Cover: Lid.
Crazing: Cracks in the glaze of china but not the china itself. If this crazing is too regular, it suggests that the item is a fake and is designed to look older than it is through the presence of crazing.
Cuttings: Autographs cut from the bottom of letters or autograph books. Also refers to articles cut from newspapers and magazines, often stuck into scrapbooks and sold as ephemera.

Die-cast: Generally referring to toys such as Corgi cars, it's the method by which the metal figures are moulded. It can also refer to plastic but this is used less often.

Embossed: Relief work, moulded ornamentation.
Epergnes: Vases arranged in branches to form an extravagant centrepiece.
Ephemera: Card and paper goods not meant for long-term possession, e.g. letters, postcards, diaries, wine labels and packaging.

Estate auctions: Sales of goods belonging to the deceased.
Etching: Print.

Figural: Shaped, not just as a figure (human or animal) but a variety of shapes.
F&G: Framed and glazed, pictures which have been framed with a glass front.
Folio: Collection of non-framed art sold in a lot, generally referring to sketches, loose watercolours and etchings and often sold in a folder.

Gavel: The auctioneer's hammer.

Hallmark: The markings on gold, silver and platinum used to determine quality, age and assay (hallmark) office.
Hammer price: The price at which the lot sells (highest bid if the reserve is met) – but not the price paid which will be increased by extras such as the buyer's premium, VAT on the premium and, if necessary, VAT on the final bid.

Inlaid: Material such as different woods inserted or embedded in an item.

Art comes in a variety of forms and it helps to understand what the auction catalogue means when using terms such as F&G, folios, etchings and studies or you could end up buying a mass-produced, unsigned print thinking that it's an original painting. But don't be fooled into thinking prints aren't worth much; look for hand-signed (not printed signatures) and/or numbered ones.

Lion passant: Lion in a walking position, a mark seen on silver and gold hallmarks or heraldic material.
Lion rampant: Lion raised on its hind legs, a mark seen on silver and gold hallmarks or heraldic material.
Lithograph: Print.
Lot: Goods being sold in auction, either in individual goes or with several in one go (job lots).
Lottage: Entry fee charged by some auction houses for submitting lots to auction.
Loupe: Eyeglass used to magnify things, especially used by the silver, gold and jewellery dealers.

Marquetry: Goods with inlay detail, most often used for different woods (often in a pattern) but can also refer to ivory and metal.
Mint: Perfect.
MIB: Mint in box i.e. still in its original box and in perfect (mint) condition.

Nef: Centrepiece, generally made of silver and in the shape of a ship. Once designed as a drinking vessel but, later designed to hold the host's cutlery.
Nicked: Chipped.

Paddle: Bidder's device, ranges from a wooden bat (paddle) to a piece of card which has your registration number on it (see Register).
Parquetry: Blocks of wood used for decoration.
Pepper caster: Pepper pot.
Primary market: Retail shops, not auctions, antiques shops, fairs, centres or second-hand dealers which count as secondary market.
Pulling lots: Withdrawing items for sale, this can be done by the seller or the auction house if there is a problem with the lot (e.g. they discover it's fake or there is confusion over the ownership).

Register, to: To give your details to the auction house so you can buy there.
Registration Act: Legal obligation to register as a second-hand dealer if selling in certain regions as a business or on a regular basis (see p191).
Reserve: The lowest price at which you agree to sell a lot.
Reticello: Latticework decoration.
Ringer: Fake created by joining an older part of an item to a more recent part (e.g. old, hallmarked base of a coffeepot to a modern top).

Saleroom: Either another name for an auction house or the room in which the sale is conducted.

Salt cellar: Open dish in which salt was served, often in a glass liner to prevent the salt from corroding the metal dish.
Second: Imperfect item.
Secondary market: Second-hand goods being sold e.g. at auctions, antiques shops, fairs, centres or second-hand dealers.
Sketch: Study for a painting, generally pen & ink, pencil or watercolour on paper.

Vendor: The seller.
Vestas: Matchboxes, often metal and sometimes figural.

Wrong leg, the: When the person bidding on behalf of the commission bidder is the underbidder but cannot increase their bid to reach the price set by the bidder as they would be bidding against themselves (they are on the 'wrong leg' of the bidding process).

Bronze group 'Restraining the Horse' by Nikolai Ivanovich Lieberich (1882-83). Estimated to fetch £1,200-1,800 it went for £2,400 at a particularly buoyant auction at Gorringes' North St saleroom in Lewes.

Publications and Websites

THERE are a number of antiques publications, some of which also have auction listings. Magazines and newspapers include:

Antiques Diary – www.antiquesdiaryonline.co.uk or ring to subscribe, 01425 280340

Antiques Info – www.antiques-info.com or ring to subscribe, 01843 862069

Antiques Trade Gazette – ww.antiquestradegazette.com or ring to subscribe, 020 7420 6601

Apollo – www.apollo-magazine.com or ring to subscribe, 01795 592884

BBC Homes and Antiques – www.homesandantiques.com or ring to subscribe, 01795 414740

Collect It! – www.collectit.info or ring to subscribe, 01778 392460

Don't miss out on must-buy lots such as this Newlyn copper teaset. Make sure you know what's going on in the auction world. WW.

Websites

www.antiquestradegazette.com
www.artfact.com
www.auctionhammer.co.uk
www.governmentauctionsuk.com
www.invaluable.com
www.the-saleroom.com (part of *Antiques Trade Gazette*)
www.ukauctioneers.co.uk

Recommended reading

Bannister, Judith (ed.), *British Silver Hallmarks* (W. Foulsham & Co. Ltd)
Bradbury, Frederick, *Bradbury's Book of Hallmarks* (J. W. Northend Ltd)
Danckert, Ludwig, *Dictionary of European Porcelain* (NAG Press)
Godden, Geoffrey A., *The Encyclopaedia of British Pottery and Porcelain Marks* (Barrie & Jenkins). N.B., Known as *Godden's* in the trade
Shoop, Fiona, *How to Deal in Antiques* (How To Books, 4th Edition, 2009)
Shoop, Fiona, *How to Profit from Car Boot Sales* (Remember When)
Yates-Owen, Eric and Fournier, Robert, *British Studio Potters Marks* (A & C Black)

Auction Directory

AUCTIONS vary hugely from proper auction houses with several days of viewings to village halls with evening auctions which only have viewings that afternoon. In each case, both quality and expertise also vary hugely. The following directory is divided into counties. Please note, inclusion in these listings is not necessarily a recommendation but this directory has been assembled to give as full listings as possible.

Whilst compiling this directory, I noticed that several auction houses offered to buy goods with cash directly from sellers. Whilst I am sure most of this is perfectly legitimate, I personally would never advise doing so. Never sell to the person valuing

Not all auctions take place in salerooms. Some auction houses use larger venues such as hotels, racecourses and showgrounds. There are also auctions in people's own houses, such as this superb one-off auction in Fowlmere run by Cambridge-based Cheffins. It's great for buyers, as it's more interesting than a saleroom and you get to see how goods look in a more natural setting – though I'd never want strangers traipsing through my house. I'd always worry just what went home with them, no matter how good the auction house and its staff. It's why I'd never recommend anyone doing a house sale, even when selling an estate (see p166). CH.

your goods, be it an auction house employee on behalf of themselves or their auction house (or an antiques dealer). Their job in that situation is to think of their profit margins, not your needs. Instead, either sell the goods via their auctions or, if you don't feel comfortable, sell through another auction house. Anyone with a vested interest is not working in your interest.

Offices versus Salerooms

Not all auction houses have salerooms in the areas listed. Some, such as Bonhams, also have offices where they value goods and arrange for them to be sold at one of their salerooms. In this case, ask them to arrange transportation.

Other auction houses have small offices but rent space at large venues such as hotels, racecourses and showgrounds. In these cases, where possible, I have listed their office address so you know where to take goods for valuations. Never sell at an auction house where you don't have a full address to see where your goods or money have been taken.

Choose your saleroom carefully, this extravagant San Demos armchair, part of a suite, and The Beatles guitar would be out of place in a traditional, country auction and the prices achieved would reflect that.

Registration Acts

The whole of Scotland and 10 other areas are covered by Registration Acts where dealers, even occasional ones, need to register with Trading Standards before selling in these areas at antiques fairs, centres, car boot sales and to be a regular seller at auctions. However, you do not need to register to buy at auctions in these places, as long as you are not intending to sell in any of the areas listed:
- Scotland – The whole of Scotland is covered by a Registration Act, whilst some cities, such as Glasgow also have their own registration requirements. Ask before selling regularly at auctions
- Greater Manchester
- Hereford City
- Humberside
- Kent
- Lancashire
- Merseyside
- Newcastle
- Worcester City
- Yorkshire (North)
- Yorkshire (South)

Sotheby's

Sotheby's is a superb auction house but I have chosen not to list the regional offices for the simple reason that the minimum threshold for which they will accept a lot is £3,000. All goods worth £3,000+ are sent to their New Bond St saleroom in London to be sold. However, if you do have goods suitable for them, please ring 020 7293 5000 for details of your local office or representative. Please note, it is £3,000 per lot, not for a whole collection of goods.

ABERDEENSHIRE

Anyone selling at auction or other antiques venues or car boot sales in Scotland on a regular basis needs to register with Trading Standards to comply with the Registration Act

John Milne Fine Art Auctioneers
9, North Silver St
ABERDEEN
01224 639336
www.johnmilne-auctioneers.com

Thainstone Specialist Auctions
Thainstone Centre
INVERURIE
01467 623700
www.goanm.co.uk/tsa

ANGUS

Anyone selling at auction or other antiques venues or car boot sales in Scotland on a regular basis needs to register with Trading Standards to comply with the Registration Act

Taylors Auction Rooms
Panmure Row
MONTROSE
01674 672775
www.scotlands-treasures.co.uk/taylors-auctions/

AVON

See Bristol or Somerset. N.B. Bath is now in Somerset

AYRSHIRE

Anyone selling at auction or other antiques venues or car boot sales in Scotland on a regular basis needs to register with Trading Standards to comply with the Registration Act

Thomas R. Callan
22, Smith St
AYR
01292 267681 / 0800 037 8000
www.trcallan.com

BEDFORDSHIRE

W. & H. Peacock
26, Newnham St
BEDFORD
01234 266366
www.peacockauction.co.uk

Sheffield Railwayana Auctions
4, The Glebe
CLAPHAM, BEDFORD
Sales also held in Derby and, for larger objects, at other venues
01234 325341
www.sheffieldrailwayana.co.uk

Piano Auctions Ltd
Malting Farmhouse
CARDINGTON
01234 831742
Sales in central London
www.pianoauctions.co.uk

Charles Ross Auctioneers
The Old Town Hall Salerooms
WOBURN
01525 290502
www.charles-ross.co.uk

BERKSHIRE

Edwards & Elliott
32, High St
ASCOT
01334 876363
www.edwardsandelliott.co.uk

Simpson's Auctions
New Hall, Broadmoor Rd
WALTHAM ST LAWRENCE, Nr MAIDENHEAD
01344 481292

Dreweatts
Donnington Priory Salerooms
DONNINGTON / NEWBURY
Formerly known as Dreweatt Neate
01635 553553
www.dnfa.co.uk

Law Fine Art
Ash Cottage, Ashmore Green Rd

ASHMORE GREEN, NEWBURY
01635 860033

Special Auction Services
First Floor, Kennetholme, Bath Rd
MIDGHAM, READING
0118 971 2949
www.specialauctionservices.com

Thimbleby & Shorland
Market House, 31, Great Knollys St
READING
0118 950 8611
www.tsauction.co.uk

Martin & Pole
The Auction House, 10, Milton Rd
WOKINGHAM
0118 979 0460
www.martinpole.co.uk

BRISTOL

Bristol is now a unitary council
Clevedon Salerooms
The Auction Centre, Kenn Rd, Kenn
CLEVEDON, BRISTOL
01934 830111
www.clevedon-salerooms.co.uk

Dreweatts
Baynton Rd
ASHTON, BRISTOL
0117 953 1603 / 0117 953 0803
www.dnfa.co.uk

Dreweatts
The Apsley Rd Saleroom, St John's Place
Apsley Rd
CLIFTON, BRISTOL
0117 973 7201
www.dnfa.co.uk

BUCKINGHAMSHIRE

Amersham Auction Rooms
125, Station Rd
AMERSHAM
Formerly known as Pretty & Ellis
01494 729292 / 08700 460606

www.amershamauctionrooms.co.uk

Old Amersham Auctions
British Legion Hall, Whieldon St
OLD AMERSHAM
Office address: 2, School Lane, Old Amersham
01494 722758
www.old-amersham-auctions.co.uk

Bourne End Auction Rooms Ltd
Station Approach
BOURNE END
01628 531500
www.bourneendauctionrooms.com

Dickins Auctioneers Ltd
The Claydon Saleroom, Calvert Rd
MIDDLE CLAYDON, BUCKINGHAM
01296 714434
www.dickinsauctioneers.com

Auction at Denham
Denham Memorial Hall, Village Rd
DENHAM
01753 646138

Bosleys Military Auctioneers
The Old Royal Military College, Remnantz
MARLOW
01682 488188
www.bosleys.co.uk

CAMBRIDGESHIRE

Bonhams
17, Emmanuel Rd
CAMBRIDGE
Regional office
01223 366523
www.bonhams.com

Cheffins Fine Art Auctioneers
Clifton House, 1-2, Clifton Rd
CAMBRIDGE
01223 213343
www.cheffins.co.uk

Blyth & Co.
7-9, Market Place

ELY
01353 668320
www.blyths.com

Burwell Auctions
The Church Hall, High St
SOHAM, ELY
01353 727100

Rowley Fine Art Auctioneers & Valuers
8, Downham Rd
ELY
01353 653020
www.rowleyfineart.com

Goldsmiths
15, Market Place
OUNDLE, PETERBOROUGH
01832 272349
www.ukpropertyshop.co.uk/estate-agents/goldsmiths-50062.shtml

Southams
8, Market Place
OUNDLE, PETERBOROUGH
01832 273565
www.southams.com

Hyperion Auctions
The Salerooms, Station Rd
ST IVES
01480 464140
www.hyperionauctions.co.uk

W. & H. Peacock
75, New St
ST NEOTS
01480 474550

Willingham Auctions
25, High St
WILLINGHAM
01954 261252
www.willinghamauctions.com

Clifford Cross Auctions Ltd
Chase Auction Halls, Chapel Rd
WISBECH
01945 583398

Grounds & Co.
2, Nene Quay
WISBECH
01945 585041
www.grounds.co.uk/auction.html

Maxey & Sons
Auction Hall, Cattle Market Chase
WISBECH
Possibly the loudest auction website; mute volume if viewing at work
01945 583123 (office) / 584609 (auction hall)
www.maxeyandson.co.uk

CARDIFF

Anthemion Auctions
15, Norwich Rd
CARDIFF
029 2047 2444
www.anthemionauctions.com

Bonhams
7-8, Park Place
CARDIFF
Regional office
029 2072 7980
www.bonhams.com

CARMARTHENSHIRE

Peter Francis Fine Art Auctioneer
19, King St
CARMARTHEN
01267 233456
www.peterfrancis.co.uk

Terry Thomas & Co.
2, St Marys St
CARMARTHEN
01267 253865
www.terrythomas.co.uk

Country Leisuresport of Wales
10, Old Rd
LLANELLI
01554 771655 / 077 2153 0684 (sale day only)
Specialists in sporting goods, including fishing tackle. Sales held at the British Legion Club
www.countryleisuresport.co.uk

Welsh Country Auctions
2, Carmarthen Rd
CROSSHANDS, Nr LLANELLI
01269 844428
www.welshcountryauctions.co.uk

Jones & Llewellyn
Llandeilo Auction Rooms, Station Rd
LLANDEILO
01558 823430

Clee, Thompkinson & Francis
Ty Ocsiwn Tywi, Tywi Auction House
LLANDOVERY
01550 720440 / 01269 591884
www.ctf-uk.com/furniture.html

CEREDIGION

Stephen Jones & Co.
The Auction Rooms, Henllan
LLANDYSUL
01559 371541

CHESHIRE

Patrick Cheyne
38, Hale Rd
ALTRINCHAM
0161 941 4879

John Arnold & Co. (W. Bradshaw)
Central Salerooms, 15, Station Rd
CHEADLE HULME
0161 485 2777

Bonhams
New House, 150, Christleton Rd
CHESTER
01244 313936
www.bonhams.com

Byrne's Fine Art Auctioneers
Pullman House, The Sidings, Chester St
SALTNEY, CHESTER
01244 681311
www.byrnesauctioneers.co.uk

Adam Partridge Auctioneers & Valuers
1, Bank Place, Tommy's Lane

CONGLETON
*The saleroom is The Gate Hall, Chain & Gate,
North Rd, Macclesfield*
01260 274603 (office) / 078 1543 1158 (saleroom)
www.adampartridge.co.uk

Whittaker & Biggs
Brown St Auction Rooms, Brown St
CONGLETON
01260 279858
www.whittakerandbiggs.co.uk/auction.html

H. & H. Classic Auctions
Whitegate Farm, Hatton Lane
HATTON
Specialists in classic cars
01925 730630

Frank R. Marshall & Co.
Marshall House, Church Hill
KNUTSFORD
01565 653284
www.frankmarshall.co.uk

Peter Wilson Fine Art Auctioneers Ltd
Victoria Gallery, Market St
NANTWICH
01270 623878
www.peterwilson.co.uk

Andrew Hilditch & Son
Hanover House, 1a, The Square
SANDBACH
01270 767246 / 01270 762048

STOCKPORT
See Greater Manchester (p204)

Wright Manley
Beeston Castle Salerooms
TARPORLEY
01829 262150
www.wrightmanley.co.uk

Lloyd Cameron & Partners
The Milner Institute, Runcorn Rd
MOORE, WARRINGTON
Postal address only (not for consultations)

8, Buckfast Court, Runcorn, WA7 1QJ
01928 579796
www.lloydcameron.co.uk

Maxwells of Wilmslow
133a Woodford Rd
WOODFORD
0161 439 5182
www.maxwells-auctioneers.co.uk

CONWY AND COLWYN

Rogers Jones Co.
33, Abergele Rd
COLWYN BAY
01492 532176
www.rogersjones.co.uk

CORNWALL

Kivells
8, Belle Vue
BUDE
01288 359999
www.kivells.com/auctions

Mill House Auctions Ltd
Trannack Mill House, Coverack Bridges
HELSTON
01326 565183

Jefferys
5, Fore St
LOSTWITHIEL
01208 871947 / 871948
www.jefferysauctions.co.uk

Bonhams
Cornubia Hall, Eastcliffe Rd
PAR
01726 814047
www.bonhams.com

W. H. Lane & Son
Jubilee House, Queen St
PENZANCE
01736 361447
www.whlaneauctioneersandvaluers.co.uk

David Lay

The Penzance Auction House
ALVERTON, PENZANCE
01736 361414
www.davidlay.co.uk

Donald Weekes
3, Market Place
ST COLUMB
01637 880525
www.donaldweekes.co.uk/auctions.asp

Lodge & Thomas Auctioneers
58, Lemon St
TRURO
01872 272722
www.lodgeandthomas.co.uk/chattels.htm

Truro Auction Centre
Triplet Business Centre,
Poldice Valley
Nr CHACEWATER, TRURO
01209 822266

Lambrays Auction Rooms
Polmorla Walk Galleries,
The Platt
WADEBRIDGE
01208 813593

COUNTY DURHAM

Addisons Auctioneers
The Auction Rooms, Staindrop Rd
BARNARD CASTLE
01833 690545
www.addisons-auctioneers.co.uk

Thomas Watson
The Gallery Saleroom, Northumberland St
DARLINGTON
01325 462559
www.thomaswatson.com

Vectis Auctions Ltd
Fleck Way
THORNABY, STOCKTON-ON-TEES
Specialist toy auctioneers
01642 750616
www.vectis.co.uk

CUMBRIA

Furness Auctions Ltd
The Auction House, School St
BARROW-IN-FURNESS
01229 432220
www.furnessauctions.co.uk

Bonhams
48, Cecil St
CARLISLE
Regional office
01228 542422
www.bonhams.com

Cumbria Auction Rooms
The Auction Centre, Rosehills
CARLISLE
01228 640927
www.borderway.com/index.php?id=furnitur
e_fine_art

Thomson, Roddick & Medcalf
Coleridge House, Shaddongate
CARLISLE
01228 528939
www.thomsonroddick.com/auction

Mitchells Fine Art Auctioneers
The Furniture Hall, 47, Station Rd
COCKERMOUTH
01900 827800
www.mitchellsfineart.com

Kendal Auction Rooms (North West Auctions Ltd)
The Auction Mart, Appleby Rd
KENDAL
01539 733770
www.kendalauctionrooms.co.uk

James Thompson Fine Art Auctioneers
64, Main St
KIRKBY LONSDALE
01524 271555
www.jthompson-auctioneers.co.uk

Penrith Farmers' & Kidd's PLC
Skirsgill Salerooms
PENRITH
01768 890781
www.pfkauctions.co.uk

Howard Whitaker
The Central Auction Galleries, Brogden St
ULVERSTON
01229 581010

DENBIGHSHIRE

Aqueduct Auctioneers
The Methodist Chapel, Holyhead Rd
FRONCYSYLLTE, LLANGOLLEN
01691 774567
www.aqueductauctions.co.uk

DERBYSHIRE

Fidler-Taylor & Co.
The Derbyshire Saleroom, Buxton Rd (A6)
BAKEWELL
01629 580228 / 01335 346246
www.fidler-taylor.co.uk

Bamfords Ltd
The Derby Auction House, Chequers Rd
Off Pendragon Island
DERBY
01332 210000
www.bamfords-auctions.co.uk

Hansons Auctioneers & Valuers Ltd
36, Main St
ETWALL
01283 733988
www.hansonsauctioneers.co.uk

Bamfords
The Old Picture Palace, 133, Dale Rd
MATLOCK
01629 57460
www.bamfords-auctions.co.uk

DEVON

Rendells Auctioneers
Stonepark Saleroom, Stonepark
ASHBURTON
01364 653017
www.rendellsfineart.co.uk

Gunter's Auctions
74, Newport Rd
BARNSTAPLE
01271 325958 / 07787 900725
www.barnstapleauctions.com
www.guntersauctions.co.uk

Torridge Auctions
The Lion Store, 19, Barnstaple St
EAST-THE-WATER, BIDEFORD
01237 471955
www.torridgeauctions.co.uk

S. J. Hales Auctioneers
Tracey House, Newton Rd
BOVEY TRACEY
01626 836684
www.sjhales.com

Palmers Whitton and Laing Auctions
The Sale Room, Victoria Place
BUDLEIGH SALTERTON
01392 252621
www.whittonandlaing.com/auctions.html

The Dartmoor Auctioneer
Highbury
CHAGFORD
Auction held at The Jubilee Hall in Chagford and other venues
01647 432415
www.lotsaway.co.uk

Oaks & Partners
The Old Tannery, Exeter Rd
CULLOMPTON
01884 35848
www.invaluable.com/oaksandpartners/

Bearne's
St Edmund's Court, Okehampton St
EXETER
01392 207000
www.bearnes.co.uk

Hampton & Littlewood Auctioneers & Valuers
The Auction Rooms, Alphin Brook Rd
ALPHINGTON, EXETER
01392 413100

www.hamptonandlittlewood.co.uk

Queens Road Auctions
9, Queens Rd
ST THOMAS, EXETER
01392 256256
www.queensroadauctions.com

Whitton & Laing
32, Okehampton St
EXETER
01392 252621
www.whittonandlaing.com/auctions.html

Martin Spencer-Thomas Auctioneers & Valuers
Bicton St Auction Rooms, Bicton St
EXMOUTH
01395 267403
www.martinspencerthomas.co.uk

Kivells
Stanhope House
HOLSWORTHY
01409 253275
www.kivells.com/auctions

Bonhams
Dowell St
HONITON
01404 41872
www.bonhams.com

Greenslade Taylor Hunt
111, High St
HONITON
01404 46222
www.gth.net/auctions

Michael J. Bowman
6, Haccombe House
Nr NETHERTON, NEWTON ABBOT
01626 872890
www.invaluable.com/bowman

Okehampton Auctions
Unit 4a, Fatherford Farm, Exeter Rd
OKEHAMPTON
01837 55592
www.okehamptonauctions.co.uk

Philip G. Pyle
The Bridge Auction Rooms, 15, Market St
HATHERLEIGHT, OKEHAMPTON
01837 810756

Beesleys
262, Torquay Rd
PAIGNTON
01803 522222

Eric Distin
New Rd
CALLINGTON, PLYMOUTH
01579 383322
www.ericdistin.co.uk

Eldreds
1, Belliver Way
ROBOROUGH, PLYMOUTH
01752 721199
www.eldreds.net

The Plymouth Auction Rooms
Unit 359, Faraday Mill Trade Park
CATTEDOWN, PLYMOUTH
01752 254740
www.plymouthauctions.co.uk

Shobrook Auctions Ltd
20, Western Approach
PLYMOUTH
01752 663341
www.shobrook.co.uk/antique_auctions

Lyme Bay Auction Galleries
Harepath Rd
SEATON
01297 22453
www.lymebayauction.co.uk

Potbury's
High St
SIDMOUTH
01395 515555
www.potburys.co.uk

John D. Fleming
The Savoy
SOUTH MOLTON
01769 574888

Stannary Gallery Auctioneers
The Stannary Gallery, Drake Rd
TAVISTOCK
01822 617800

Chilcotts
The Chilcott School Saleroom, St Peter St
TIVERTON
01884 250020
www.chilcottsoftiverton.co.uk

Greenslade Taylor Hunt
5, Fore St
TIVERTON
01884 243000
www.gth.net/auctions

West of England Auctions
3, Warren Rd
TORQUAY
01803 211266 / 212286
www.west-of-england-auctions.com

DORSET

Blandford Auction Rooms
1a, Alfred St
BLANDFORD FORUM
01258 452454

Dalkeith Auctions
Dalkeith Hall, Dalkeith Steps, 81, Old Christchurch Rd
BOURNEMOUTH
01202 292905
www.dalkeithauctions.co.uk

House & Son
11-14 Lansdowne House, Christchurch Rd
The Lansdowne
BOURNEMOUTH
01202 298044
www.houseandson.com

Ridoetts
177, Holdenhurst Rd
BOURNEMOUTH
01202 555686

The Auction House of Bridport

The Auction House, 1, St Michael's
Trading Estate
BRIDPORT
The Saleroom is in Tannery Rd, off West St
01308 459400
www.bridportauctionhouse.com

William Morey & Sons
Unit 3, Pymore Mills Estate
PYMORE, BRIDPORT
01308 422078

Bulstrodes
Auction Rooms, 13, Stour Rd
CHRISTCHURCH
01202 482244
www.bulstrodes.co.uk

Duke's
The Dorchester Fine Art Salerooms
Weymouth Ave
DORCHESTER
01305 265080
www.dukes-auctions.com

Duke's Grove Auctions
The Grove
DORCHESTER
01305 257444
www.dukes-auctions.com

Greenslade Taylor Hunt
Westgate House, 45 High West Street
DORCHESTER
01305 268786
www.gth.net/auctions

Davey & Davey Auctioneers
The Poole Salerooms, 13, St Peters Rd
PARKSTONE, POOLE
01202 748567
www.daveyanddavey.com

Semley Auctioneers
Station Rd
SEMLEY, SHAFTESBURY
01747 855122
www.semleyauctioneers.com

Charterhouse Auctioneers
The Long St Salerooms, Long St
SHERBORNE
01935 812277
www.charterhouse-auctions.co.uk

Onslows
The Coach House, Manor Rd
STOURPAINE
01258 488838
www.onslows.co.uk

Cottees Auctions Ltd
The Market, East St
WAREHAM
01929 552826
www.cottees.co.uk

George Kidner Auctioneers
8, West Borough
WIMBORNE
01202 842900
www.georgekidner.co.uk

DUMFRIESSHIRE

Anyone selling at auction or other antiques venues or car boot sales in Scotland on a regular basis needs to register with Trading Standards to comply with the Registration Act

Thomson, Roddick & Medcalf
Auction Centre, Irongray Rd
DUMFRIES
01387 721635
www.thomsonroddick.com/auctions

DUNDEE

Anyone selling at auction or other antiques venues or car boot sales in Scotland on a regular basis needs to register with Trading Standards to comply with the Registration Act

Curr & Dewar Auctioneers
Unit E, 6, North Isla St
DUNDEE
01382 833974
www.curranddewar.com

EDINBURGH

Anyone selling at auction or other antiques venues or car boot sales in Scotland on a regular basis needs to register with Trading Standards to comply with the Registration Act

Bonhams
22, Queen St
EDINBURGH
0131 225 2266
www.bonhams.com

Lyon & Turnball
33, Broughton Place
EDINBURGH
0131 557 8844
www.lyonandturnball.com

Ramsay Cornish Auctioneers
15-17, Jane St
EDINBURGH
0131 553 7000
www.ramsaycornish.com

Shapes Auctioneers
Bankhead Ave
SIGHTHILL, EDINBURGH
0131 453 3222
www.shapesauctioneers.co.uk

Thomson, Roddick & Medcalf
The Auction Centre, Carnethie St
ROSEWELL, EDINBURGH
0131 440 2448
www.thomsonroddick.com/auction

ESSEX

Brentwood Antique Auctions
45, North Rd
BRENTWOOD
01277 224599
www.brentwoodantiqueauction.co.uk

Cooper Hirst Auctions
Victoria Rd
CHELMSFORD
070 5350 6696

Chelmsford Auction Rooms (R. L. & S. H. Rowland)
42, Mildmay Rd
CHELMSFORD
01245 354251
www.chelmsfordauctionrooms.co.uk

Reeman Dansie Auctions (incorporating Kingsford Auctions)
8, Wyncolls Rd, Severalls Business Park
COLCHESTER
01206 754754
www.reemans.com

Stanfords Auctioneers
The Livestock Market, Wyncolls Rd
Off Severalls Lane
COLCHESTER
01206 842156
www.stanfords-auctions.co.uk

Mullucks Wells (incorporating Trembath Welch)
Fine Art Auctions, The Old Town Hall
GREAT DUNMOW
01371 873014
www.mullucks.co.uk

Stour Valley Auctions
23, Station Rd
DOVERCOURT, Nr HARWICH
01255 241785

Plaistow Auctions
Unit 1, 62-70 Fowler Rd
Hainault Industrial Estate
ILFORD
020 8500 5110
www.plaistowauctions.net

Chalkwell Auctions
The Arlington Rooms, London Rd
LEIGH-ON-SEA
01702 710383
www.ridgeweb.co.uk/chalkwell_auctions.htm

Leigh Auction Rooms
88-90, Pall Mall
LEIGH-ON-SEA
01702 477051

Stacey's Auctioneers & Valuers
Entered under Rochford (see below)

Boningtons Valuers & Auctioneers
Ambrose House
LOUGHTON
020 8508 4800
www.boningtons.com

Stacey's Auctioneers & Valuers'
The Freight House, Bradley Way (saleroom address only)
ROCHFORD
Office address: 959, London Rd, Leigh-on-Sea
01702 475614 / 01702 545655 (auction day only)
www.staceyauctioneers.com

Saffron Walden Auctions
1, Market St
SAFFRON WALDEN
01799 513281

Sworders Fine Art Auctioneers
14, Cambridge Rd
STANSTED MOUNTFITCHET
01279 817778
www.sworder.co.uk

Chapel & Chapel
499-503, London Rd
WESTCLIFF-ON-SEA
01702 343734

FIFE

Anyone selling at auction or other antiques venues or car boot sales in Scotland on a regular basis needs to register with Trading Standards to comply with the Registration Act

East Central Auctions
Castleblair Lane
DUNFERMLINE
01383 727434

M. D. Auction Co.
Unit 15-17, Smeaton Industrial Estate
Hayfield Rd
KIRKCALDY

01592 640969

Pine Lodge Auctions & Interiors
Pine Lodge, Cuper Rd
LADYBANK
01337 832895

FLINTSHIRE

Dodds Property World (K. Hugh Dodd & Partners)
Victoria Auction Galleries, 9, Chester St
MOLD, CLWYD
Antiques & collectables, as well as a property auction house
01352 755705
www.door-key.com/auction.html

GLAMORGAN

Pontypridd Auctions Ltd
39a, Cefn Lane
GLYNCOCH, PONTYPRIDD
01443 403764
www.pontypriddauctions.com

GLASGOW

Anyone selling at auction or other antiques venues or car boot sales in Scotland on a regular basis needs to register with Trading Standards to comply with the Registration Act. Those trading in Glasgow will also need additional registration as it is covered by its own Act

Bonhams
176, Vincent St
GLASGOW
Regional office
0141 223 8866
www.bonhams.com

Collins & Paterson Auctioneers
141, West Regent St
GLASGOW
0141 229 1326
www.cp-auctioneers.co.uk

Great Western Auctions Ltd
1291, Dumbarton Rd

GLASGOW
0141 954 1500
www.greatwesternauctions.com

McTear's & Co. Ltd
Meiklewood Gate, 31, Meiklewood Rd
GLASGOW
General auctioneers and whisky specialists
0141 810 2880
www.mctears.co.uk

GLOUCESTERSHIRE

Humberts (incorporating Tayler & Fletcher)
London House, High St
BOURTON-ON-THE-WATER
01451 821666
www.humberts.co.uk

The Cotswold Auction Company
Chapel Walk Saleroom
Chapel Walk
CHELTENHAM
01242 256363
www.cotswoldauction.co.uk

Humberts (including Tayler & Fletcher)
Pitville Pump Room
CHELTENHAM
01451 821666
www.humberts.co.uk

Mallams
Grosvenor Galleries, 26, Grosvenor St
CHELTENHAM
01242 235712
www.mallams.co.uk

The Cotswold Auction Company
The Coach House, Swan Yard
9-13 West Market Place
CIRENCESTER
01285 642420
www.cotswoldauction.co.uk

Fraser Glennie & Partners
The Coach House
UPPER SIDDINGTON, CIRENCESTER
01285 659677
www.fraser-glennie.co.uk

Moore, Allen and Innocent
The Norcote Salerooms, Burford Rd
NORCOTE, CIRENCESTER
01285 646050
www.mooreallen.co.uk

Specialised Postcard Auctions
Corinium Galleries, 25, Gloucester St
CIRENCESTER
01285 659057

The Cotswold Auction Company
St Barnabus Church Hall, Stroud Rd
GLOUCESTER
Address used in sale week only
01452 521177 / 077 7411 1716 (sale week only)
www.cotswoldauction.co.uk

Mews Auctions
Unit 36a, The Mews, Brook St
MITCHELDEAN
01594 544769

Smiths Newent Auction Rooms
16, Broad St
NEWENT
01531 820767
www.smithsnewentauctions.co.uk

Simon Chorley
Prinknash Abbey Park
PRINKNASH
01452 344499
www.simonchorley.com

Dominic Winter Book Auctions
Mallard House, Broadway Lane
SOUTH CERNEY
01285 860006
www.dominic-winter.co.uk

Stroud Auctions Ltd
The Old Barn, The Bear of Rodborough
RODBOROUGH COMMON, STROUD
01453 873800
www.stroudauctions.co.uk

Graham Singer Auctioneers
5, Warren Business Park

KNOCKDOWN, TETBURY
01454 238600
www.grahamsinger.com/auctions

Bonhams
22a, Long St
TETBURY
Regional office
01666 502200
www.bonhams.com

G. W. Railwayana Auctions Ltd
25, Jubilee Drive
BREDON, TEWKESBURY
Auctions held at venues, including Pershore High School
01684 773487 / 01386 421324
www.gwra.co.uk

Tewkesbury Auction Rooms
1-2, Church St
TEWKESBURY
01684 299907
www.tewkesburyauctions.com

Wotton Auction Rooms
Tabernacle Rd
WOTTON-UNDER-EDGE
01453 844733
www.wottonauctionrooms.co.uk

GRAMPIAN AND MORAYSHIRE

Anyone selling at auction or other antiques venues or car boot sales in Scotland on a regular basis needs to register with Trading Standards to comply with the Registration Act

Cluny Auctions
44, Commercial Rd
BUCKIE, MORAY
01542 833318
www.clunyauctions.co.uk

Elgin Auction Centre (Aberdeen & Northern Marts)
New Elgin Rd
ELGIN, MORAY
01343 547047
www.goanm.co.uk/anmarts

Forres Saleroom
Tytler St
FORRES, MORAY
01309 672422

GREATER MANCHESTER

Anyone selling at auction or other antiques venues or car boot sales in Greater Manchester on a regular basis needs to register with Trading Standards to comply with the Registration Act

Simon Charles Auctioneers & Valuers
The Auction Centre, Nile St, Guide Bridge
ASHTON-UNDER-LYNE
0161 339 9449
Specialises in vintage wine, classic cars, diamonds and antique furniture
www.simoncharles-auctioneers.co.uk

Bonhams
The Stables, 213, Ashley Rd
HALE
Regional office
0161 927 3822
www.bonhams.com

Capes Dunn
The Auction Galleries, 38, Charles St
Off Princes St
MANCHESTER
0161 273 1911

Prestwich Auctions
Masonic Hall, Hospital Rd
SWINTON, MANCHESTER
0774 886 0711

A. F. Brock & Co. Ltd
Acton Court Hotel, Buxton Rd
STOCKPORT
Office address: 269 London Rd, Hazel Grove, Stockport
0161 456 5050
www.afbrock.co.uk

Philip Davies & Sons
The Auction Centre, Hammond Ave
Whitehill Industrial Estate
STOCKPORT

0161 429 0300
www.pdsauctioneers.co.uk

Eric Gill & Co. Ltd
22, Clapgate
ROMILEY, STOCKPORT
0161 285 4850

MOS Auctioneers & Valuers
Unit 2, Newby Rd
Newby Rd Industrial Estate
HAZEL GROVE, STOCKPORT
0161 484 0444

Riverside Auction Centre
Unit 19a, Chadkirk Industrial Estate
Vale Rd, Off Otterspool Rd
ROMILEY, STOCKPORT
0161 449 7999
www.riversideauctions.co.uk

GWYNEDD

R. G. Jones (Farmers Mart)
Livestock Market, Bala Rd
DOLGELLAU
01341 422334

HAMPSHIRE

Hampshire Auctions
Andover Saleroom, 41a, London St
ANDOVER
01264 364820
www.hampshireauctions.com

Manor House Auctions
Heckfield Memorial Hall, Church Lane
HECKFIELD
*Office address: 5, Crossborough Gardens
Crossborough Hill, Basingstoke*
01256 841300
www.manorhouseauctions.co.uk

George Kidner Auctioneers
The Lymington Saleroom, Emsworth Rd
LYMINGTON
01590 670070
www.georgekidner.co.uk

Green Lane Auctions
Lyndhurst Community Centre
LYNDHURST
023 8039 7216
http://homepage.ntlworld.com/green.lane.a
uction/updates.htm

S. R. Thomas (Odiham Auctions)
Unit 4, Priors Farm, West Green Rd
MATTINGLEY
01189 326824

Manor House Auctions
Odiham Baker Hall, Off King St
ODIHAM
*Office address: 5, Crossborough Gardens
Crossborough Hill, Basingstoke*
01256 841300
www.manorhouseauctions.co.uk

Jacobs & Hunt Fine Art Auctioneers Ltd
26, Lavant St
PETERSFIELD
01730 233933
www.jacobsandhunt.co.uk

D. M. Nesbit & Co.
7, Clarendon Rd
SOUTHSEA
023 9229 5568
www.nesbits.co.uk

Evans & Partridge
Agriculture House, High St
STOCKBRIDGE
01264 810702
www.evansandpartridge.co.uk

Bonhams
The Red House, Hyde St
WINCHESTER
Regional office
01962 862515
www.bonhams.com

Andrew Smith & Son
The Auction Rooms, Manor Farm
ITCHEN STOKE, Nr WINCHESTER
01962 735988
www.andrewsmithandson.com

Raw & Co.
Thornfield, Hurdle Way
COMPTON DOWN, WINCHESTER
01962 713663

HEREFORDSHIRE

Anyone selling at auction or other antiques venues or car boot sales in Hereford City on a regular basis needs to register with Trading Standards to comply with the Registration Act

Y. Gelli Book Auctions
Broad St
HAY-ON-WYE
01497 821179

Sunderlands
The Salerooms, Newmarket St
HEREFORD
01432 266894
www.sunderlandsfinearts.co.uk

Nigel Ward & Co.
The Border Property Centre
PONTRILAS, HEREFORD
01981 240140
www.nigel-ward.co.uk

John Goodwin
3-5 New St
LEDBURY
01531 634648
www.johngoodwin.co.uk/auctions.html

H. J. Pugh & Co.
Newmarket House, Market St
LEDBURY
01531 631122
www.hjpugh.com

Brightwells Fine Art Auctioneers & Valuers
Easters Court
LEOMINSTER
01568 611122
www.brightwells.com

Kingsland Auction Services
Shirlheath Saleroom
KINGSLAND, Nr LEOMINSTER

01568 708564

Morris Bricknell
Stroud House, 30, Gloucester Rd
ROSS-ON-WYE
01989 768320 / 077 1263 1566 (sale and viewing days only)
www.morrisbricknell.com/html/auctions.html

Williams, Watkins & Richards
Ross Auction Centre
ROSS-ON-WYE
01989 762225
www.williamsandwatkins.co.uk

HERTFORDSHIRE

Pippins Auctioneers
Hitchin Town Football Club, Fishponds Rd
HITCHIN
Office address: 31, Caxton Point, Caxton Way, Stevenage
01462 422966 / 077 1579 0305 (sale day only)
www.pippinsauctions.co.uk

Bayles Auctioneers
Nortonbury Farm, Northonbury Lane
LETCHWORTH
01462 894517

Harpenden Auctions
86, High St
REDBOURN
01582 500226 / 500722

Hertfordshire Auctions
Porters Wood Industrial Estate, Valley Rd
ST ALBANS
01727 846090 / 854662
www.hertsauctions.com

Tring Market Auctions
Brook St
TRING
01442 826446
www.tringmarketauctions.co.uk

Amwell Auctions
Function Rooms, Hertford Rugby Club
Hoe Lane

WARE
01920 871901

Ware Militaria Auctions
Function Rooms, Hertford Rugby Club
Hoe Lane
WARE
01920 871383
www.ware-militaria-auction.com

INVERNESSHIRE

Anyone selling at auction or other antiques venues or car boot sales in Scotland on a regular basis needs to register with Trading Standards to comply with the Registration Act

Frasers
8a, Harbour Rd
INVERNESS
01463 232395

ISLE OF MAN

Chrystals Auctions
The Mart, 4, Bowring Rd
RAMSEY
01624 815555
www.chrystalsauctions.com

ISLE OF WIGHT

Bonhams
Ryde Castle Hotel, Esplanade
RYDE
Regional valuations
01983 282228
www.bonhams.com

Ways
The Auction House, Garfield Rd
RYDE
01983 562255

Shanklin Auction Rooms
Island Auction Rooms, 79, Regent St
SHANKLIN
01983 863441
www.shanklinauctionrooms.co.uk

JERSEY

Bonhams
Royal Jersey Agricultural and Horticultural Showground
TRINITY
*Office address: Westaway Chambers, 39, Don St
St Helier*
01534 722241
www.bonhams.com

KENT

Anyone selling at auction or other antiques venues or car boot sales in Kent on a regular basis needs to register with Trading Standards to comply with the Registration Act

Parkinson Auctioneers
46, Beaver Rd
ASHFORD
01233 624426
www.parkinson-uk.com

Frederick Andrews Ltd
The Village Hall
BARHAM
*Office address: Duke Of Clarence Trading Estate
High Street, Bluetown, Sheerness*
01795 662741
www.frederickandrewsauctioneers.co.uk

Mervyn Carey
Twysden Cottage
BENENDEN
01580 240283

D. H. Allen
North House, Oakley Rd
BROMLEY
020 8462 1735

St Andrews Auction
St Andrews Church Hall, Burnt Ash Lane
BROMLEY
077 8854 5265

The Canterbury Auction Galleries
40, Station Rd West, Entrance from Kirby's Lane

CANTERBURY
01227 763337
www.thecanterburyauctiongalleries.com

Abbey Auction Rooms
1-3 Rhode St
CHATHAM
01634 817572
www.abbeyauctionrooms.co.uk

Kent Country Auctions
Chilham Village Hall
CHILHAM
Office address: 14, West St, Faversham
01795 590174 / 077 6671 4253
www.geocities.com/kentcountryauctions

Bentley's Fine Art Auctioneers
The Old Granary, Waterloo Rd
CRANBROOK
01580 715857
www.bentleysfineartauctioneers.co.uk

Humberts Fine Art (Incorporating Calcutt MacLean Standen Fine Art)
The Estate Office, Stone St
CRANBROOK
01580 713828
www.humberts.co.uk

Crayford Auction Rooms
Farm Buildings, Maiden Lane
CRAYFORD
01322 528680

Watermans Auction Rooms
Shellbank Lane, Manor Farm
Green Street Green
DARENTH
01474 700033
www.watermansauctionrooms.co.uk

Kent Country Auctions
14, West St
FAVERSHAM
01795 590174

Kent Auction Galleries Ltd
Unit C., Highfield Estate, Off Warren Rd
FOLKESTONE
01303 246810 / 01303 240808

www.kentauctiongalleriesltd.co.uk

Wealden Auction Galleries (Desmond Judd)
Colliers Green Rd
HEADCORN
070 5354 3471

Gordon Day & Partners
Bowens Yard, Park Corner
KNOCKHOLT
01959 533263
www.gordondayauctions.com

Lamberhurst Auctions
Forstal Farm, Goudhurst Rd
LAMBERHURST
01892 891200

Frederick Andrews Ltd
The Village Hall
LYMINGE
Office address: Duke Of Clarence Trading Estate High Street, Bluetown, Sheerness
01795 662741
www.frederickandrewsauctioneers.co.uk

Frederick Andrews Ltd
The Market Hall, Lockmeadow
MAIDSTONE
Office address: Duke Of Clarence Trading Estate High Street, Bluetown, Sheerness
Sales held alternate Thursdays with J. Stuart Watson
01795 662741
www.frederickandrewsauctioneers.co.uk

Clive Emson Auctioneers
Nimbus House, 20/20 Business Park.
Liphook Way
MAIDSTONE
Office address: Rocky Hill, London Road
0845 8500333
www.cliveemsonauctions.co.uk

B. J. Norris
The Quest, West St
HARRIETSHAM, Nr MAIDSTONE
01622 859515

J. Stuart Watson
The Market Hall, Lockmeadow

MAIDSTONE
Office address: Barker Rd, Maidstone
Sale held alternate Thursdays with Frederick Andrews Ltd
01622 692515

Peter S. Williams
The Market Hall, Lockmeadow
Office address: Orchard End, Maidstone Rd Sutton Valence, Maidstone
MAIDSTONE
01622 842350

Pettmans
52, Athelstan Rd
CLIFTONVILLE, MARGATE
01843 220234
www.pettmans.com

Orpington Sale Rooms
Unit 7, Tripes Farm, Chelsfield Lane
ORPINGTON
01689 896678
www.orpsalerooms.co.uk

Ibbett Mosely
Otford Village Memorial Hall
OTFORD
01732 456731
Office address: 125, High St, Sevenoaks
www.ibbettmosely.co.uk

Amhurst Auctions
375, High St
ROCHESTER
01634 815713

Medway Auction
23, High St
ROCHESTER
01634 847444

Pettmans
Sandwich Auction Room, The Drill Hall
The Quay
SANDWICH
01304 621000
www.sandwichauctionroom.com

Bonhams

13, Lime Tree Walk
SEVENOAKS
Regional office
01732 740310
www.bonhams.com

Hayton's Auctioneers & Valuers
The Drill Hall, Argyle Rd
SEVENOAKS
Office address: 3, Chesterfield Drive, Riverhead Sevenoaks
01732 457344 / 077 7843 3786 (sale day)
www.haytons-auctioneers.co.uk

Ibbett Mosely
125, High St
SEVENOAKS
01732 456731
www.ibbettmosely.co.uk

John M. Peyto & Co. Ltd
Highfield, The Coach House
Row Dow Lane, Otford Hills
SEVENOAKS
On-site plant machinery auction and tender sales
01959 524022

Frederick Andrews Ltd
Units 13/14, Duke of Clarence Trading Estate, High St
BLUETOWN, SHEERNESS
01795 662741
www.frederickandrewsauctioneers.co.uk

Five Arches Auction Rooms
Swanley Village Nursery, Swanley Village Rd
SWANLEY
01322 669090
www.fivearchesauctionrooms.co.uk

Lambert & Foster
Tenterden Auction Rooms, 102 High St
TENTERDEN
01580 762083
www.lambertandfoster.co.uk/auction te.asp

Dreweatts
The Auction Hall, The Pantiles
TUNBRIDGE WELLS
Formerly Bracketts Fine Art Auctioneers

01892 544500
www.dnfa.com

Bonhams
95-97, Tankerton Rd
WHITSTABLE
Regional office
01227 275007
www.bonhams.com

LANARKSHIRE

Anyone selling at auction or other antiques venues or car boot sales in Scotland on a regular basis needs to register with Trading Standards to comply with the Registration Act

Auction Rooms Bothwell
Unit C, Coalburn Rd
Fallside Industrial Estate
BOTHWELL
The sister saleroom to Auction Rooms Falkirk
01698 811744
www.auctionroomsbothwell.co.uk

Hamilton Auction Market (L.S. Smellie & Sons Ltd)
Hamilton Auction Market
4, Lower Auchingramont Rd
HAMILTON
01698 282007
www.hamiltonauctionmarket.com

LANCASHIRE

Anyone selling at auction or other antiques venues or car boot sales in Lancashire on a regular basis needs to register with Trading Standards to comply with the Registration Act

Tony & Sons Ltd
2-8 Lynwood Rd
BLACKBURN
01254 691748

Walton & Walton Auctioneers
Parker St Salerooms
Off Kingsway/Bank Parade
BURNLEY
01282 423247

www.waltonandwalton.co.uk

Charnock Auction House Ltd
South Exhibition Hall, Park Hall
CHARNOCK RICHARD
01257 450606
www.charnockauctions.com

Smythes
The Auction Galleries, 174, Victoria Rd West
CLEVELEYS
01253 852184
www.smythes.net

Silverwoods Auctioneers & Valuers
Clitheroe Auction Mart, Ribblesdale Centre
Lincoln Way
CLITHEROE
01200 423322
www.silverwoods.co.uk

James Thompson Fine Art Auctioneers
64, Main St
KIRKBY LONSDALE
01524 271555
www.jthompson-auctioneers.co.uk

Warren & Wignall Ltd
The Mill, Earnshaw Bridge
LEYLAND
01772 451430 / 453252
www.warrenandwignall.co.uk

Kingsway Auctions
The Galleries, Kingsway
ANSDELL, LYTHAM-ST-ANNES
01253 735442
www.kingswayauctions.co.uk

Henry Holden & Son Ltd
Central Salerooms, Towneley Rd
LONGRIDGE, PRESTON
01772 783274
www.henryholdenandson.co.uk

Longridge Auction Market (Daniel R. McCarthy)
Towneley Rd
LONGRIDGE, PRESTON
01772 784177

Central Auction Rooms
4, Baron St
ROCHDALE
01706 646298

SOUTHPORT
See Greater Manchester (p204)

Howarth & Belshaw
Auction Rooms, Unit 1, Eckersley Mill
Swan Meadow Rd
WIGAN
01942 826435

Wigan Auction Rooms
33, Dicconson St
WIGAN
01942 241484

LEICESTERSHIRE

Roy Green
15, The Nook
ANSTEY
0116 235 3009
www.roygreen.co.uk

Fallowell & Partners
Hermitage House, 7, Belvoir Rd
COALVILLE
01530 810033
www.machinlane.com/coalville.php

Churchgate Auctions Ltd
123, Scudamore Rd
LEICESTER
0116 287 4856
www.churchgateauctions.co.uk

Warner Auctions
52, Sanvey Gate
LEICESTER
0116 251 2510

Freckeltons
1, Leicester Rd
LOUGHBOROUGH
01509 214564

Bonhams
34, High St
MARKET HARBOROUGH
Regional office
01858 438900
www.bonhams.com

Gilding's Fine Art Auctioneers
64, Roman Way
MARKET HARBOROUGH
01858 410414
www.gildings.co.uk

Shouler & Son
County Auction Rooms, Kings Rd
MELTON MOWBRAY
01664 560181
www.shoulers.co.uk/auction-rooms.html

David Stanley Auctions
Stordon Grange
OSGATHORPE
Specialist tool auctions
01530 222320
www.davidstanley.com

Gadsbys Auctioneers
1, Tuxford Rd, Off Cannock St
THURMASTON
0116 246 1066

LINCOLNSHIRE

Eleys Auctions
Unit 8-11, Haven Business Park
Slippery Gowt Lane
BOSTON
01205 316600
www.eleys-auctions.co.uk

Martin Wright
17, Main Ridge West
BOSTON
01205 351200

Richardsons
Bourne Auction Rooms, Spalding Rd
BOURNE
01778 422686
www.richardsonsauctions.co.uk

Brown & Co. Auction Rooms
Old Courts Rd
BRIGG
01652 650172
www.brown-co.com

Drewery & Wheeldon
124, Trinity St
GAINSBOROUGH
01427 616436
www.dreweryandwheeldon.co.uk

Golding Young & Co.
Old Wharf Rd
GRANTHAM
Particularly loud website, mute your volume if browsing at work
01476 565118
www.goldingyoung.com

Marilyn Swain
North End Farm, Long St
FOSTON, GRANTHAM
01400 283377
www.marilynswainauctions.co.uk

Jackson, Green & Preston
41-45 Duncombe St
GRIMSBY
01472 311115
www.jacksongreenpreston.co.uk/auctions.php

Robert Bell & Co.
Old Bank Chambers
HORNCASTLE
01507 522222
www.robert-bell.org/auctions

Thomas Mawer & Son
Dunston House, Portland St
LINCOLN
01522 524984
www.thos-mawer.co.uk

Naylors Auctions
16, Meadow Lane
LINCOLN
01522 696496

John Taylors Auction Rooms
14-18 Cornmarket Chambers
LOUTH
01507 603648
www.johntaylors.com

John Taylors Auction Rooms
The Wool Mart
KIDGATE, LOUTH
01507 611107
www.johntaylors.com

Perkins, George Mawer & Co.
Corn Exchange Chambers, Queen St
MARKET RASEN
01673 843011
www.perkinsgeorgemawer.co.uk/general/information/

John Taylors Auction Rooms
13, Queen St
MARKET RASEN
01673 844249
www.johntaylors.com

Willsons Auctions
41, High St
BURGH-LE-MARSH, SKEGNESS
01754 810477
www.willsons-property.co.uk/auctions.asp

Hix & Son
28, Church St
HOLBEACH, SPALDING
01406 422777
www.hixandson.co.uk/html/auctioneering.html

Longstaff
Auction Rooms, Enterprise Way
SPALDING
Office address: 5, New Rd, Spalding
01775 765534
www.longstaff.com/auctions/

M. W. B. Auctions
Unit 8-9, Cradge Bank
SPALDING
01775 724337

Munton & Russell

16, Sheep Market
SPALDING
01775 722475
www.muntonandrussell.co.uk/auction.html

Batemans Auctioneers & Valuers
The Saleroom, Ryhall Rd
STAMFORD
01780 766466
www.batemans-auctions.co.uk

Naylors Auctions
20, St John's St
WAINFLEET
01754 881210

LONDON

Baldwin's
The Holiday Inn, Bloomsbury
LONDON, WC1
Office address: 11, Adelphi Terrace, London WC2N
Specialists in coins
020 7930 9808
www.baldwin.co.uk/auctions.html

Barnes Auctions
Old Sorting Office, Station Rd
BARNES, LONDON, SW13
020 8878 9223
www.andsotobid.com

Biblion Auctions
Grays Antiques Market, 1-7 Davies Mews
Nr Oxford St
LONDON, W1
Specialist book auctions within book centre
020 7629 1374
www.biblionauctions.co.uk

Bloomsbury Auctions
24, Maddox St
LONDON W1
020 7495 9494
Specialist book, ephemera and pens departments
www.bloomsburyauctions.com

Bonhams
101, New Bond St
LONDON, W1
020 7447 7447
www.bonhams.com

Bonhams
Montpelier Galleries, Montpelier St
KNIGHTSBRIDGE, LONDON, SW7
020 7393 3900
www.bonhams.com

Chiswick Auctions
1, Colville Rd, Off Bollo Lane
CHISWICK, LONDON, W3
020 8992 4442
www.chiswickauctions.co.uk

Christie's
8, King St, St James'
LONDON, SW1Y
020 7839 9060
www.christies.com

Christie's
85, Old Brompton Rd
SOUTH KENSINGTON, LONDON, SW7
020 7930 6074
www.christies.com

Comic Book Auctions Ltd
40-42, Osnaburgh St
LONDON, NW1
020 7424 0007
www.compalcomics.com

Criterion Auctioneers
53-57, Essex Rd
ISLINGTON, LONDON, N1
020 7359 5707
www.criterionauctions.co.uk

Criterion Riverside Auctions
41-47 Chatfield Rd
WANDSWORTH, LONDON, SW11
020 7228 5563
www.criterionauctions.co.uk

Dix, Noonan, Webb
16, Bolton St
LONDON, W1
Specialists in coins and medals. Sales held at top

London venues
020 7016 1700
www.dnw.co.uk

Stanley Gibbons
339, The Strand
LONDON, WC2
Specialists in stamps
020 7836 8444
www.auctions.stanleygibbons.com

Greenwich Auction Partnership
47, Old Woolwich Rd
GREENWICH, LONDON, SE10
020 8853 2121
www.greenwichauctions.co.uk

Harmers
Unit 11, 111, Power Rd
CHISWICK, LONDON, W4
Specialists in stamps
020 8747 6100
www.harmers.com

Holt's Auctioneers
Princess Louise House, Hammersmith Rd
LONDON, W6
Office address: Church Farm Barns, Wolferton Norfolk
Specialists in guns and related items. Sales are held in London
01485 542822
www.holtandcompany.co.uk

Hornsey Auctions
54-56 High St
HORNSEY, LONDON, N8
020 8340 5334

Kerry Taylor Auctions LLP (in Association with Sotheby's)
Unit C25, Parkhall Trading Estate Unit F26, 40, Martell Rd
DULWICH, LONDON, SE21
Specialists in costume and textiles
020 8676 4600
www.kerrytaylorauctions.com

Lloyds International Auction Galleries
Lloyds House, 9, Lydden Rd
EARLSFIELD, LONDON, SW18
020 8788 7777

Lots Road Auctions
71-73, Lots Rd
CHELSEA, LONDON, SW10
020 7376 6800
www.lotsroad.com

Luckner's
128, Druid St
LONDON, SE21
020 7252 3507
www.luckners.com

MacDougall's Arts Ltd
30a, Charles II St
LONDON, SW1
Specialists in Russian art
020 7389 8160
www.macdougallauction.com

Morton & Eden Ltd
45, Maddox St
LONDON, W1
Specialists in medals, coins and banknotes
020 7493 5344
www.mortonandeden.com

North London Auctions
Lodge House, 9-17 Lodge Lane
FINCHLEY, LONDON, N12
Be warned, the website makes strange sounds. Turn on the mute button if browsing at work
020 8445 9000
www.northlondonauctions.com

Phillips de Pury & Co.
Howick Place
LONDON, SW1
020 7318 4010
www.phillipsdepury.com

Rosebery's Fine Art Auctioneers
74-76, Knights Hill
WEST NORWOOD, LONDON, SE27
020 8761 2522
www.roseberys.co.uk

Francis Smith Ltd

107, Lots Rd
CHELSEA, LONDON, SW10
0800 195 7800
www.francis-smith.com

Sotheby's
34-35, New Bond St
LONDON, W1
020 7293 5000
www.sothebys.com

Sotheby's Olympia
Olympia, Hammersmith Rd
LONDON, W14
020 7293 5555
www.sothebys.com

Southgate Auction Rooms
55, High St
SOUTHGATE, LONDON, N14
020 8886 7888
www.southgateauctionrooms.com

Spink & Son Ltd
69, Southampton Row
BLOOMSBURY, LONDON, WC1B
020 7563 4000
Specialists in coins and banknotes, stamps and medals
www.spink.com

Woodford Auctions
209, High St
SOUTH WOODFORD, LONDON, E18
020 8553 1242

MERSEYSIDE

Anyone selling at auction or other antiques venues or car boot sales in Merseyside on a regular basis needs to register with Trading Standards to comply with the Registration Act

Cato Crane & Co.
6, Stanhope St
LIVERPOOL
0151 709 5559
www.cato-crane.co.uk

Bonhams

33, Botanic Rd
CHURCHDOWN, SOUTHPORT
Regional office
01704 507877
www.bonhams.com

Cromwells Auctioneers
The Grosvenor Salerooms
Rear of 91-97 Eastbank St
SOUTHPORT
01704 514505
General auctions, plus specialises in motorbikes
www.cromwellsauctioneer.co.uk

Outhwaite & Litherland
43, Hoghton St
SOUTHPORT
01704 538489
www.lots.uk.com

Nationwide Auctioneers
Unit 4, Millfield Business Park, Millfield Lane
HAYDOCK, ST HELENS
01942 713005

Kingsley Auctions Ltd
3-4, The Quadrant
HOYLAKE, WIRRAL
0151 632 5821
www.kingsleyauctions.blogspot.com

MIDDLESEX

Harrow Auctions
Victoria Hall, Sheepcote Rd
HARROW
0800 1444 226
www.harrowauctions.com

Northwood Missionary Auctions
Fairfield, Windsor Close
NORTHWOOD HILLS
All proceeds from the auctions go to charity so goods sold are being donated, not sold for your own benefit
01923 836634
www.nmauctions.org.uk

Bainbridge's
The Auction Room, Ickenham Rd

WEST RUISLIP
01895 621991
www.thecollectorscompanion.co.uk/bainbridges_homepage.html

Ruislip Manor Auctions
Ruislip Manor Football Club
RUISLIP
079 0563 2976

Richard J. Steel
The Cattle Market, High St
SOUTHALL
020 8574 1611

Staines & Stanwell Moor
Stanwell Moor Village Hall
Horton Rd
STANWELL MOOR
078 5051 3311

Hillingdon Auctions
51, Frays Ave
WEST DRAYTON
01895 447932

NORFOLK

Horners Auctioneers
Acle Gallery, Old Norwich Rd
ACLE
0800 975 4416 / 01493 750225
www.horners.co.uk

Keys Fine Art Auctioneers
Aylsham Salerooms, Palmers Lane
AYLSHAM
01263 733195
www.keys24.com

Case & Dewing
Memorial Hall, Norwich St
DEREHAM
Office address: Church St, Dereham
01362 692004
www.case-dewing.co.uk

Thomas William Gaze & Son
Diss Auction Rooms, Roydon Rd
DISS

01379 650306
www.twgaze.com

Barry L. Hawkins
Downham Market Auction Rooms
15 Lynn Rd
DOWNHAM MARKET
01366 387180
www.barryhawkins.co.uk

James Beck Auctions
Cornhall, Cattle Market St
FAKENHAM
Auction and Fleamarket
01328 851557
www.jamesbeckauctions.co.uk

Hunters Auctions (in Association with Patrick Plumpton)
30, Upper Market
FAKENHAM
01328 863091
www.huntersofnorfolk.com/auctions.html

Garry M. Emms & Co. Ltd
Great Yarmouth Salerooms, Beevor Rd
Off South Beach Parade
GREAT YARMOUTH
01493 332668
www.greatyarmouthauctions.com

Cruso & Wilkin
Snettisham Auction Centre, Common Rd
SNETTISHAM, KING'S LYNN
Office address: Waterloo St, King's Lynn
01485 542656
www.crusowilkin.co.uk

Tawn Landles
Blackfriars Chambers, Blackfriars St
KING'S LYNN
01553 772816
www.tawnlandles.co.uk/auctionsandchattels.html

Blyth & Co.
Norwich Auction Rooms, 40-42, Lothian St
NORWICH
01603 667984
www.blyths.com

Clowes & Nash Auctions
Norwich Livestock & Commercial Centre
Hall Rd
NORWICH
01603 504488

Knights Sporting Auctions
Cuckoo Cottage, Town Green
ALBY, NORWICH
Specialists in sporting goods & memorabilia and Wisden Cricketers' Almanacks
01263 768488
www.knights.co.uk

Bonhams
The Market Place
REEPHAM
Regional office
01603 871443
www.bonhams.com

Stephen Roberts (Auctioneers) Ltd
Watton Salerooms, Unit 10, Breckland Business Park, Norwich Rd
WATTON
01953 885676
http://homepages.tesco.net/stephen.roberts67/

Holt's Auctioneers
Church Farm Barns (Sandringham Estate)
WOLFERTON
Specialists in guns and related items. Sales are held in London
01485 542822
www.holtandcompany.co.uk

NORTHAMPTONSHIRE

J. P. Humbert Auctioneers Ltd
The Northampton Salerooms, The Nene Enterprise Centre, Freehold St
NORTHAMPTON
01604 712945
www.jphumbertauctioneers.com

J. P. Humbert Auctioneers Ltd
The Towcester Salerooms, Wood Burcote Rd
TOWCESTER
01327 359595
www.jphumbertauctioneers.com

Wilfords
The Saleroom, 74/76, Midland Rd
WELLINGBOROUGH
01933 222760
www.wilfords.org/index.html

NORTHUMBERLAND

Jim Railton
Nursery House
CHATTON, ALNWICK
01668 215323
www.jimrailton.com

Jack Dudgeon Auctioneer & Valuer
76, Ravensdowne
BERWICK-UPON-TWEED
01289 332700
www.jackdudgeon.co.uk

Hexham & Northern Marts
Tyne Green
HEXHAM
Antiques sales are held at their Rothbury Auction Centre
01434 605444
www.hexhammart.co.uk

Louis Johnson
Oswald House, 63, Bridge St
MORPETH
01670 513025
www.louis-johnson.co.uk

NOTTINGHAMSHIRE

Peter Young Auctioneers
Hillside, Beacon Hill
GRINGLEY-ON-THE-HILL
01777 816609

D. J. Auctions (Linked to Vectis)
Newark & Notts Showground
NEWARK
Office address: 26, Bracknell Rd, Thornaby Stockton-on-Tees, County Durham Specialist in toys
01642 649331
www.dj-auctions.co.uk

Northgate Auction Rooms Ltd
17, Northgate
NEWARK
01636 605905
www.northgateauctionroomsnewark.co.uk

Dreweatts
192-194, Mansfield Rd
NOTTINGHAM
Formerly Neale Fine Art Auctioneers
0115 962 4141
www.dnfa.co.uk

Arthur Johnson & Sons
The Nottingham Auction Centre
Meadow Lane
NOTTINGHAM
0115 986 9128
www.arthurjohnson.co.uk

Mellors & Kirk
The Auction House, Gregory St
NOTTINGHAM
0115 979 0000
www.mellorsandkirk.com

T. Vennett-Smith
Nottingham Racecourse, Colwick Park
COLWICK, NOTTINGHAM
Office address: 11, Nottingham Rd, Gotham Nottingham
0115 983 0541
www.vennett-smith.com

Bonhams
Chancery Court, 34, West St
RETFORD
Regional office
01777 708633
www.bonhams.com

C. B. Sheppard & Son
The Auction Gallery, 87, Chatsworth St
SUTTON-IN-ASHFIELD
01623 556310
www.sheppard-auctions.co.uk

OXFORDSHIRE

Mallams
Dunmore Court, Wootton Road
ABINGDON
01235 462840
www.mallams.co.uk

Bonhams
Globe House, Calthorpe St
BANBURY
Regional office
01295 272723
www.bonhams.com

Holloway's Auctioneers
49, Parsons St
BANBURY
01295 817777
www.hollowaysauctioneers.co.uk

J. S. Auctions
Cotefield Farm, Oxford Rd
BODICOTE, Nr BANBURY
01295 272488
At the time of writing, their temporary salerooms in Bicester could be about to move. See website or phone for updated details
www.jsauctions.co.uk

Mallams
Pevensey House, 27, Sheep St
BICESTER
At the time of writing, the auction is closed due to redevelopment of the site
01869 252901
www.mallams.co.uk

Hugo's Auction Ltd
Unit 114, Station Rd
CULHAM
01865 407787
www.hugos.biz

Bonhams
The Coach House, 66, Northfield End
HENLEY-ON-THAMES
Regional office
01491 413636
www.bonhams.com

Bonhams
39, Park End St

OXFORD
01865 723524
www.bonhams.com

Mallams
Bocardo House, 24a St Michael's St
OXFORD
01865 241358
www.mallams.co.uk

Jones & Jacob
Watcombe Manor Saleroom, Ingham Lane
WATLINGTON
01491 612810
www.jonesandjacob.com

PERTHSHIRE

Anyone selling at auction or other antiques venues or car boot sales in Scotland on a regular basis needs to register with Trading Standards to comply with the Registration Act

Lindsay Burns & Co.
6, King St
PERTH
01738 633888
www.lindsayburns.co.uk/home.asp

Iain M. Smith Auctioneers & Valuers
Unit 18, Perth Airport Business Park
SCONE, PERTH
01738 551110

ROXBURGHSHIRE

Anyone selling at auction or other antiques venues or car boot sales in Scotland on a regular basis needs to register with Trading Standards to comply with the Registration Act

Mainstreet Trading
Main St
ST BOSWELLS, MELROSE
01835 823978

RUTLAND

Jeff Dale
Oakham Auction Centre, 16b Pillings Rd

OAKHAM
01572 723569

Tennants Auctioneers
Mill House, South Street
OAKHAM
01572 724666
www.tennants.co.uk

SCOTTISH BORDERS

Anyone selling at auction or other antiques venues or car boot sales in Scotland on a regular basis needs to register with Trading Standards to comply with the Registration Act

Hall's Auctioneers
Ladhope Vale House, Ladhope Vale
GALASHIELS
01896 754477

Border Auctions Ltd
The Mill, Garfield St
HAWICK
01450 376170
www.borderauctions.co.uk

SHROPSHIRE

Bridgnorth Auction House
Unit 3, Salop St
BRIDGNORTH
01746 762226

Nock Deighton
Bridgnorth Livestock & Auction Centre
TASLEY, BRIDGNORTH
01746 762666 / 079 6751 4211
www.nockdeighton.co.uk/antiqueFurniture.php

Perry & Phillips
Old Mill Auction Rooms, Mill St
BRIDGNORTH
01746 762248

Mullock's Specialist Auctioneers & Valuers
The Old Shippon, Wall Under Haywood
CHURCH STRETTON
01694 771571

Specialists in sporting goods and ephemera. Sales
held at Ludlow Racecourse
www.mullocksauctions.co.uk

Walker Barnett & Hill
Cosford Auction Rooms, Long Lane
COSFORD
01902 375555
www.walker-barnett-hill.co.uk

Bowen Son & Watson
The Wharf Saleroom, Wharf Rd
ELLESMERE
01691 622534
www.bowensonandwatson.co.uk/Auctions.htm

McCartneys Portcullis Saleroom
The Livestock Market, The Ox Pasture
Overton Rd
LUDLOW
01584 878822
www.mccartneysauctioneers.co.uk

Barber & Son
Tower House Saleroom, Maer Lane
MARKET DRAYTON
01630 653641
Livestock and property auctions
www.barbers-online.co.uk

Hendersons Auctions
Minsterley Parish Hall
MINSTERLEY
Registered address: Myrtle Cottage, Pontesbury Hill, Pontesbury, Shrewbury.
Valuations available at the hall or home visits can be arranged
01743 792727
www.hendersonsauctions.co.uk

Brettells Auctioneers & Valuers
Newport Auction Rooms, Rear of 58, High St
NEWPORT
01952 815925
www.brettells.com

House 2 Auction
The Assembly Rooms
KNOCKIN, Nr OSWESTRY

Postal address: Pool Cottage, Stanwardine Baschurch
01939 260319 / 079 5096 0668
www.house2auction.co.uk

Halls Fine Art (Part of Humberts)
Welsh Bridge Salerooms
WELSH BRIDGE, SHREWSBURY
08451 309610
www.hallsestateagents.co.uk

Oaklands Auctions
Oaklands Farm, A49 Nr Hawkstone Park
WESTON-UNDER-REDCASTLE
SHREWSBURY
01948 841192
www.oaklandsauctions.co.uk

SOMERSET

See also Bristol (p193)

Aldridges of Bath
Newark House, 26-45 Cheltenham St
BATH
01225 462830
www.aldridgesofbath.co.uk

Bonhams
Queen Square House, Charlotte St
BATH
01225 788988
www.bonhams.com

Transport Collector Auctions
Budds Farm, High St
BARRINGTON
Specialists in transport-related goods, including models, car mascots, bicycles and ephemera
01460 55955
www.tc-auctions.com

Tamlyn & Son
Market St, Behind 56, High St
BRIDGWATER
01278 445251
www.tamlyn-son.co.uk

Adam Auctions
28, Adam St

BURNHAM-ON-SEA
01278 793709

Greenslade Taylor Hunt
75-77 High Street
BURNHAM-ON-SEA
01278 782326
www.gth.net/auctions

J. H. Palmer & Sons
Bank Chambers, 75-77, High St
BURNHAM-ON-SEA
01278 782326

Greenslade Taylor Hunt
1 High Street
CHARD
01460 283383
www.gth.net/auctions

Lawrences Auctioneers of Crewkerne
The Linen Yard, South St
CREWKERNE
01460 73041
www.lawrences.co.uk

Cooper & Tanner (Dennis Barnard)
Agricultural Centre, Standerwick
FROME
01373 831010
www.coooperandtanner.co.uk

Dore & Rees
The Auction Rooms, Vicarage St
FROME
01373 462257
www.doreandrees.co.uk

Ilminster Auctions
Rear of 21, West St, By Public Car Park
ILMINSTER
01460 54151

Greenslade Taylor Hunt
Cheapside
LANGPORT
01458 250000
www.gth.net/auctions

Vickery's Auctions

Highway Farm, Highway, Ash
MARTOCK
01935 823261

Chanin & Thomas
8, The Parade
MINEHEAD
01643 706666
www.chaninandthomas.co.uk/auctions.html

The London Cigarette Auction Co.
Sutton Rd
SOMERTON
Postal auction
01458 273452
www.londoncigcard.co.uk/auctions.html

Greenslade Taylor Hunt
The Priory Saleroom, Winchester St
TAUNTON
01823 332525
www.gth.net/auctions

McCubbing & Redfern
66/68 Southover
WELLS
01749 678099
ww.mccubbingandredfern.co.uk

Wellington Salerooms
Clifton House, Mantle St
WELLINGTON
01823 664815

Hosegood Ford
3, Fore St
WILLITON
01984 632040
www.hosegoodford.co.uk

Greenslade Taylor Hunt
22 Princes Street
YEOVIL
01935 423474
www.gth.net/auctions

McCubbing & Redfern
3, Court Ash
YEOVIL
01935 428101

www.mccubbingandredfern.co.uk

STAFFORDSHIRE

Richard Winterton Fine Art Auctioneers
Main Midland Saleroom, Hawkins Lane
BURTON-ON-TRENT
01283 511224
www.richardwinterton.co.uk

Bury & Hilton
Britannia St
LEEK
078 1125 8153 / 079 7643 0638
www.buryandhilton.co.uk/auctions.php

Hansons Auctioneers & Valuers Ltd
Lichfield Rugby Football Club, Cookfields
Tamworth Rd
LICHFIELD
Regular sales held at this venue. Contact the Derbyshire office at the number below for more details
01283 733988
www.hansonsauctioneers.co.uk

Richard Winterton Fine Art Auctioneers
Lichfield Auction Centre, Brookhay Lane
Hilliards Cross
FRADLEY PARK, Nr LICHFIELD
01543 251081
www.richardwinterton.co.uk

Cuttlestones
Penkridge Auction Rooms, Pinfold Lane
PENKRIDGE
01785 714905
Previously Richard Winterton Auctioneers
www.cuttlestones.co.uk

A.S.H. Auctions (Lee Sherratt)
St Peter's Church Hall, Grange St
Off Waterloo Rd
COBRIDGE, STOKE-ON-TRENT
Office address: 226, Cobridge Rd, Hanley, Stoke-on-Trent
01782 868061
www.ashauctions.com

Louis Taylor Fine Art Auctioneers
Lower Ground Floor, Britannia House
10, Town Rd
HANLEY, STOKE-ON-TRENT
01782 214111
www.louistaylorfineart.co.uk

Potteries Specialist Auctions
271, Waterloo Rd
COBRIDGE, STOKE-ON-TRENT
01782 286622
www.potteriesauctions.com

Wintertons Fine Arts
Uttoxeter Auction Centre, Short St
UTTOXETER
Partnered with Bagshaws
01889 564385
www.wintertons.co.uk

STIRLINGSHIRE

Anyone selling at auction or other antiques venues or car boot sales in Scotland on a regular basis needs to register with Trading Standards to comply with the Registration Act

Robertsons of Kinbuck
Main St
KINBUCK, DUNBLANE
01786 822603
www.robauctions-dunblane.co.uk

Auction Rooms Falkirk
Castle Laurie, Bankside
FALKIRK
01324 623000
www.auctionroomsfalkirk.co.uk

Kildean Auctions
Stirling Auction Mart
KILDEAN
01786 849988

SUFFOLK

Durrants
The Old School House, Peddlars Lane
BECCLES
01502 713490
www.durrants.com

Bonhams
21, Churchgate St
BURY ST EDMUNDS
Regional office with sales held at the nearby Athenaeum in the town
01284 716190
www.bonhams.com

Peter Crichton Auctioneers
6, Northgate Ave
BURY ST EDMUNDS
01284 701304
Specialists in vintage tractors and cars
www.petercrichton.co.uk

Lacy Scott and Knight
The Auction Centre, 10, Risbygate St
BURY ST EDMUNDS
01284 748624
http://data.bidmaster.co.uk/lsk/

Marshall Buck & Casson
The Auction Rooms, Unit E, Autopark
Eastgate St
BURY ST EDMUNDS
01284 756081

Mander Auctioneers
The Auction Room, Church St
CLARE
Formerly known as Dyson & Son
01787 277993
www.manderauctions.co.uk

Bannister & Co.
173, Hamilton Rd
FELIXSTOWE
01394 282828
www.bannisterco.com

Diamond Mills & Co.
Orwell Hall Saleroom, Orwell Rd
FELIXSTOWE
01473 218600
www.diamondmills.com

Boardman Fine Art Auctioneers
Station Rd Corner
HAVERHILL
01440 730414

Goldings
9, St Helens St
IPSWICH
01473 210200
www.goldingsauctions.co.uk

Lowestoft Auction Rooms (John M. Peyto & Co. Ltd)
36, Pinbush Rd
South Lowestoft Industrial Estate
LOWESTOFT
01502 531532
www.lowestoftauctionrooms.com

Russell Sprake, Lowestoft Porcelain Auctions
103, High St
LOWESTOFT
Specialists in Lowestoft Porcelain
01986 892736
www.lowestoftchina.co.uk

Toolshop
78, High St
NEEDHAM MARKET
Specialists in antique and useable tools
01449 722992
www.antiquetools.co.uk

Stowmarket Auctions
14, Old St
HAUGHLEY, STOWMARKET
01449 677166

Sworders (Incorporating Olivers)
The Saleroom, Burkitts Lane
SUDBURY
01787 880305
www.sworder.co.uk/olivers

Abbotts Auction Rooms
Campsea Ashe
WOODBRIDGE
01728 746323
www.abbottsauctionrooms.co.uk

Neal Sons & Fletcher
26, Church St
WOODBRIDGE
01394 382263
www.nsf.co.uk/auctions.htm

SURREY

Lawrences of Bletchingley
Norfolk House, 80, High St
BLETCHINGLEY
01883 743323
www.lawrencesbletchingley.co.uk

BCA (British Car Auctions)
Auction Centre, Blackbushe Airport
BLACKWATER, Nr. CAMBERLEY
Specialist car auctions, including classic cars
01252 877317
www.british-car-auctions.co.uk

Parkins Auction Rooms
18, Malden Rd
CHEAM
020 8644 6633

Wellers Auctioneers
70, Guildford St
CHERTSEY
01932 568678
www.wellers-auctions.co.uk

Rosan Reeves / Croydon Auction Rooms
145-151, London Rd
CROYDON
020 8688 1123

Cartel Auctioneers & Valuers
2, Tanners Court, Middle St
BROCKHAM, Nr DORKING
01737 844646

Crow's Auction Gallery
The Car Park, Rear of The Dorking Halls
Reigate Rd
DORKING
01306 740382
www.crowsauctions.co.uk

P. F. Windibank Auctions
The Dorking Halls, Reigate Rd
DORKING
01306 884556
www.windibank.co.uk

Cooper Owen

74, Station Rd
EGHAM
01753 855858
Specialists in entertainment-related goods
www.cooperowen.com

Alexander Auctions Ltd
Langley Bottom Farm, Langley Vale Rd
EPSOM
01372 270770

Dreweatts
Baverstock House, 93, High St
GODALMING
*Regional office, formerly known as Hamptons
Fine Art Auctioneers*
01483 423567
www.dnfa.com

Bonhams
Milmead
GUILDFORD
Regional office
01483 504030
www.bonhams.com

Clarke Gammon Wellers
The Sussex Barn, Loseley Park
GUILDFORD
01483 207570
www.clarkegammon.co.uk/fineartaandantiques

John Nicholson Auctions
The Auction Rooms, Longfield, Midhurst Rd
FERNHURST, HASLEMERE
01428 653727
www.johnnicholsons.com

Coys of Kensington
Manor Court, Lower Mortlake Rd
RICHMOND
*Auctions are held at various venues, including
Central London and Brands Hatch*
020 8614 7888
www.coys.co.uk/auctions/index.php

Kew Auctions
Richmond Station, Kew Rd
RICHMOND

Entrance within Richmond Station
020 8948 6677

Parkins Auction Rooms
18, Malden Rd
SUTTON
020 8644 6633

Wallington Missionary Auctions
Crusader Hall, Corner of Boundary Rd and Stanley Park Rd
WALLINGTON
Office address for donations: The mart at the rear of 105, Stafford Rd
All proceeds from the auctions go to charity so goods sold are being donated, not sold for your own benefit
020 8647 8437
www.wallingtonmissionary.org.uk

Ewbank Fine Art Auctioneers & Valuers
Burnt Common Auction Rooms, London Rd
SEND, WOKING
01483 223101
www.ewbankauctions.co.uk

SUSSEX

Mid Sussex Auctions Ltd
Glebe Farm Estates, Haywards Heath Rd
BALCOMBE
01444 819100
www.midsussexauctions.fsnet.co.uk

Burstow & Hewett
Abbey Auction Galleries, Lower Lake
BATTLE
01424 772374
www.burstowandhewett.co.uk

Salehurst Auctioneers
Bexhill Rd
NINFIELD, BATTLE
01424 893293

Gorringes
Terminus Rd
BEXHILL
01424 212994
www.gorringes.co.uk

Bellmans Auctioneers & Valuers
New Pound, Wisborough Green
BILLINGSHURST
01403 700858
www.bellmans.co.uk

Bonhams
19, Palmeira Square
BRIGHTON
Regional office
01273 220000
www.bonhams.com

Raymond P. Inman
98a Coleridge St, Adjacent to 43, Rutland Rd
HOVE, BRIGHTON
01273 774777
www.invaluable.com/raymondinman

Southern Independent Auctions Ltd (NAVA)
Regent House, The Hyde Business Park
LOWER BEVENDEAN, BRIGHTON
01273 696545
www.sia-group.co.uk

Henry Adams Fine Art Auctioneers
Baffins Hall, Baffins Lane
CHICHESTER
01243 532223
www.henryadamsfineart.co.uk

Stride & Sons
Southdown House, St John's St
CHICHESTER
01243 780207
www.stridesauctions.co.uk

Dreweatts Eastbourne Salerooms
46-50, South St
EASTBOURNE
Formerly known as Edgar Horns
01323 410419
www.dnfa.com

Eastbourne Auction Rooms
Auction House, Finmere Rd
EASTBOURNE
01323 431444
www.eastbourneauction.com

Watsons Auctioneers
Heathfield Auction Salerooms, Burwash Rd
HEATHFIELD
01435 862132
www.watsonsauctioneers.co.uk

Rosan & Co.
Springham Farm, Grove Hill
HELLINGLY
01435 810410

Denham's
The Auction Galleries, Dorking Rd, A24
WARNHAM, Nr HORSHAM
01403 255699
www.denhams.com

Gorringes (Incorporating Julian Dawson)
Lewes Auction Rooms, Garden St
LEWES
01273 478221
www.gorringes.co.uk

Gorringes
15, North St
LEWES
01273 472503

Wallis & Wallis
West St Auction Galleries, West St
LEWES
01273 480208
Specialists in tinplate and die-cast toys and militaria, arms & armour
www.wallisandwallis.co.uk

Peter Cheney
Western Rd Auction Rooms, Western Rd
LITTLEHAMPTON
01903 722264

South Downs Auctioneers
Gosdens Heath Barn
LODSWORTH, PETWORTH
01798 860960
www.southdownsauctioneers.co.uk

Rye Auction Galleries
Rock Channel
RYE
01797 222124
www.ryeauctiongalleries.co.uk

Ascent Auction Galleries
1, The Mews, East Ascent
ST LEONARDS-ON-SEA
01424 420275

Scarborough Fine Arts and Worthing Auction Galleries
Unit 2, Grange Industrial Estate, Albion St
SOUTHWICK
01273 870371
www.scarboroughfinearts.co.uk
www.worthing-auctions.co.uk

Gorringes
15, The Pantiles
TUNBRIDGE WELLS
Office and bookshop
01892 619670

Toovey's
Spring Gardens
WASHINGTON
01903 891955
www.tooveys.com

Campbells Auctions
44-46, High St
WORTHING
01903 238989
www.campbellsauctions.co.uk

Worthing Auction Galleries
See Scarborough Fine Arts, Southwick

TYNE AND WEAR

Anyone selling at auction or other antiques venues or car boot sales in Newcastle on a regular basis needs to register with Trading Standards to comply with the Registration Act

Boldon Auction Galleries
24a, Front St
EAST BOLDON
0191 537 2630
www.boldonauctions.co.uk

Anderson & Garland Newcastle
Anderson House, Crispin Court
Newbiggin Lane
WESTERHOPE, NEWCASTLE
0191 430 3000
www.andersonandgarland.com

Bonhams
30-32, Grey St
NEWCASTLE-UPON-TYNE
Regional office
0191 233 9930
www.bonhams.com

Thomas N. Miller Auctioneers
The Algernon Rd Auction Rooms
Algernon Rd
BYKER, NEWCASTLE-UPON-TYNE
0191 265 8080
www.millersauctioneers.co.uk

J. C. Featonby Auctioneers & Valuers
234-236, Park View
WHITLEY BAY
0191 252 2601

WARWICKSHIRE

Steven B. Bruce
Unit 5, Clayhall Farm, Honeybourne Rd
BIDFORD-UPON-AVON
01789 490450

Auction-Plus
Over Whitacre Village Hall
OVER WHITACRE, Nr COLESHILL
Office address: 40, Berrington Rd, Nuneaton
02476 394099
www.auction-plus.com

Warwick Auctions
The Coventry Auction Centre
3, Queen Victoria Rd
COVENTRY
02476 223377 / 223378
www.warwick-auctions.co.uk

Locke & England
18, Guy St
LEAMINGTON SPA

01926 889100
www.leauction.co.uk

Rugby Salerooms
6, Paynes Lane
RUGBY
01788 543445

Vectis Train Auctions
The Benn Hall, Newbold Rd
RUGBY
See also Vectis, County Durham
01642 767116
www.vectis.co.uk

Stoneleigh Auctions
Village Hall, Birmingham Rd
STONELEIGH
01788 536379

Bigwood Auctioneers Ltd
The Old School
TIDDINGTON, STRATFORD-UPON-AVON
01789 269415
www.bigwood.uk.com

Philip Bros.
The Saleroom, Bearley Rd
SNITTERFIELD, STRATFORD-UPON-AVON
01789 731114

Warwick and Warwick
Chalon House, Scar Bank, Millers Rd
WARWICK
Specialists in toys, medals, postcards, cigarette cards & tradecards, coins & banknotes and stamps
01926 499031
www.warwickandwarwick.com

WEST LOTHIAN

Anyone selling at auction or other antiques venues or car boot sales in Scotland on a regular basis needs to register with Trading Standards to comply with the Registration Act

D. J. Manning
Bridgeness Rd
BO'NESS

01506 827693
www.djmanning.co.uk

WEST MIDLANDS

See also Staffordshire and Warwickshire

Biddle & Webb Ltd
Ladywood, Middleway
BIRMINGHAM
0121 455 8042
www.biddleandwebb.co.uk

Fellows & Sons
Augusta House, 19, Augusta St
HOCKLEY, BIRMINGHAM
0121 212 2131
www.fellows.co.uk

Walton & Hipkiss
Parish Rooms, Belbroughton Rd
BLAKEDOWN
01562 886688
http://waltonandhipkiss.co.uk/auction

Carters Auctioneers
Dodford Village Hall, Priory Rd
DODFORD, Nr BROMSGROVE
01299 271130
Office address: 11, Church St, Cleobury Mortimer, Kidderminster
www.cartersauction.co.uk

Black Country Auctions
Baylies' Hall, Tower St
DUDLEY
01384 250220
www.blackcountryauctions.co.uk

Bonhams
The Old House, Station Rd
KNOWLE
01564 776151
www.bonhams.com

Old Hill Auctions
220, Halesowen Rd
OLD HILL
01384 411121

Fieldings Auctioneers Ltd
Mill Race Lane
STOURBRIDGE
01384 444140
www.fieldingsauctioneers.co.uk

Acres Fine Arts
28, Beeches Walk
SUTTON COLDFIELD
0121 355 1133

WILTSHIRE

Chippenham Auction Rooms
Unit H, Ivy Lane Industrial Estate, Ivy Rd
CHIPPENHAM
General auctioneers and specialists in vintage cars, motorbikes and automobilia
01249 444544
www.chippenhamauctionrooms.co.uk

Wessex Auction Rooms (Davis Meade & Partners)
Westbrook Farm, Draycot Cerne
CHIPPENHAM
01249 720888
www.wessexauctionrooms.co.uk

Gardiner Houlgate
The Bath Auction Rooms, 9, Leafield Way
CORSHAM
01225 812912
www.gardinerhoulgate.co.uk

Henry Aldridge & Son
Unit 1, Bath Rd Business Centre, Bath Rd
DEVIZES
General auctioneers and specialists in ocean liner memorabilia
01380 729199
www.henry-aldridge.co.uk

Hilditch & Co.
The Auction Rooms
Gloucester Rd Trading Estate
MALMESBURY
01666 822577
www.hilditchauctions.co.uk

Dreweatts

Hilliers Yard, High St
MARLBOROUGH
Regional office, formerly Hamptons Fine Art
01672 516161
www.dnfa.com

Finan & Co.
The Square
MERE
01747 861411
www.finanandco.co.uk

Harrison Auctions Ltd (Jubilee Auction Rooms)
Jubilee Auction Rooms
Fordbrook Business Centre
PEWSEY
01672 562012
www.jubileeauctions.com

Netherhampton Salerooms / Southern Counties Auctioneers
Salisbury Auction Centre, Salisbury Rd
NETHERHAMPTON, SALISBURY
01722 321215
www.salisburyauctioncentre.co.uk

Woolley & Wallis
51-61, Castle St
SALISBURY
01722 424500
www.woolleyandwallis.co.uk

May Auctioneers
Units 1, 3 & 4, The Delta Works, Salisbury Rd
SHIPTON BELLINGER
01980 846000
www.mayauctioneers.co.uk

Kidson Trigg Fine Art Auctioneers
Friars Estate Office and Auction Rooms
Friars Farm
Nr HIGHWORTH, SWINDON
01793 861000
www.kidsontrigg.co.uk

WORCESTERSHIRE

Anyone selling at auction or other antiques venues or car boot sales in Worcester City on a regular basis needs to register with Trading Standards to comply with the Registration Act

Clive Carter Auctions
Wribbenall Parish Rooms
BEWDLEY
01299 403999 / 079 7172 3617
www.clivecarterauctions.com

Clive Carter Auctions
Blakedown Parish Rooms
BLAKEDOWN, Nr KIDDERMINSTER
01299 403999 / 079 7172 3617
www.clivecarterauctions.com

Kidderminster Market Auctions Ltd
The Wholesale Market, Comberton Hill
KIDDERMINSTER
01562 741303
www.kidderminstermarketauctions.co.uk

The Classic Auction Co.
Severn Hall, Three Counties Showground
MALVERN
Office address: Highcroft, 101, Graham Rd, Malvern
Specialists in classic cars and automobilia but they also sell fine art and antiques
01684 562213 / 584922 (sale day)
www.theclassicauctioncompany.com

Doorbars (Philip Laney)
The Malvern Auction Centre, Portland Rd
Off Victoria Rd
MALVERN
01684 893933
www.invaluable.com/philiplaney

Philip Serrell Auctioneers
The Malvern Saleroom, Barnards Green Rd
MALVERN
01684 892314
www.serrell.com

Arrow Auctions
Bartleet Rd
WASHFORD, REDDITCH
01527 517707
www.arrowauctions.co.uk

Andrew Grant Fine Art Auctioneers
c/o 59-60 Foregate St
WORCESTER
Goods consigned to auction are sold through Drewatts. Valuation days are conducted at The Crown and Sandy Arms Hotel in Droitwich
01905 357547
www.dnfa.com/andrewgrant/

Griffiths & Charles
57, Foregate St
WORCESTER
01905 726464
Auctions held at venues including Severn Stoke Village Hall
www.griffiths-harles.co.uk/gc_auctions.html

YORKSHIRE

Anyone selling at auction or other antiques venues or car boot sales in North and/or South Yorkshire or Humberside on a regular basis needs to register with Trading Standards in each county to comply with the Registration Act

BBR Auctions
Elsecar Heritage Centre
ELSECAR, Nr BARNSLEY
Specialists in bottles, pot lids, breweriana, kitchenalia, pharmacy and also sells Twentieth Century china
01226 745156
www.onlinebbr.com/auctions

Wilbys Fine Art and Auctions
6a, Eastgate
BARNSLEY
01226 299211
www.wilbys.net/fineart.htm

Dale Wood & Co. Auctioneers & Valuers
20, Station Rd
BATLEY
01924 479439
www.dalewoodauctions.co.uk

Bonhams
Market Chambers, 14, Market Place
BEDALE
Regional office

01677 424114
www.bonhams.com

M. W. Darwin & Sons
The Dales Furniture Hall, Bridge St
BEDALE
01677 422846
www.darwin-homes.co.uk/html/auctions.html

De Rome's
12, New John St, Westgate
BRADFORD
01274 734116

John Raby & Son
21, St Mary's Rd
MANNINGHAM, BRADFORD
01274 491121

J. Harrison Auctions
14, Churchill Building
Churchill Rd
DONCASTER
01302 341774

Tudor Auction Rooms
Tudor House, 28, High St
CARCROFT, DONCASTER
01302 725029
www.tudorauctionrooms.co.uk

Wilkinson's Auctioneers Ltd
The Old Salerooms, 28, Netherhall Rd
DONCASTER
01302 814884
www.wilkinsons-auctioneers.co.uk

Dee Atkinson & Harrison
The Exchange Saleroom, Exchange St
DRIFFIELD
01377 253151
www.dahauctions.com

Calder Valley Auctioneers
Fairlea Mill, Ellenholme Rd
LUDDENDEN FOOT, HALIFAX
01422 886648
www.caldervalleyauctioneers.co.uk

Christopher Matthews

Information and Auction Directory

23, Mount St
HARROGATE
01423 871756

Morphets
6, Albert St
HARROGATE
01423 530030
www.morphets.co.uk

Tennants Auctioneers
34, Montpelier Parade
HARROGATE
01423 531661
www.tennants.co.uk

Thompson Auctioneers (Harrogate Ltd)
The Dales Saleroom, Levens Hall Park
Lund Lane
KILLINGHALL, HARROGATE
01423 709086
www.thompsonauctioneers.com

Gilbert & Baitson
389-395, Anlaby Rd
HULL
01482 500500
www.gilbert-baitson.co.uk

Hartleys Auctioneers & Valuers
Victoria Hall, Little Lane
ILKLEY
Formerly known as Andrew Hartley Fine Arts
01943 816363
www.hartleysauctions.co.uk

Bonhams
Hepper House, 30, Park Square West
LEEDS
Regional office. Sales are held at the Great Yorkshire Showground, Harrogate or goods can be sent to other Bonhams salerooms
0113 204 5755
www.bonhams.com

Gary Don
Curtis Buildings, Berning Ave
LEEDS
0113 248 3333
www.garydon.co.uk

Tennants Auctioneers
The Auction Centre
LEYBURN
01969 623780
www.tennants.co.uk

Boulton & Cooper
St Michael's House, Market Place
MALTON
01653 696151
www.boultoncooper.co.uk/index.php?core=fine_arts

Cundalls
Milton Rooms, Market Place
MALTON
Office address: 15, Market Place, Malton
General auctioneers and specialists in railwayana
01653 697820
www.cundalls.co.uk/auctions.shtml

Hawleys Auctioneers
Albion House, Westgate
NORTH CAVE
01430 470654
www.hawley.karoo.net

Hutchinson Scott
The Grange
MARTON-LE-MOOR, RIPON
01423 326236
www.hutchinson-scott.co.uk

Paul Beighton Auctioneers
16-18 Woodhouse Green
THURCROFT, Nr ROTHERHAM
01709 700005
www.pbauctioneers.co.uk

David Duggleby Scarborough
The Vine St Salerooms
SCARBOROUGH
01723 507111
www.davidduggleby.com

Ward Price Ltd
The Royal Auction Rooms, 14-15, Queen St
SCARBOROUGH
01723 353581

A. E. Dowse & Son
Cornwall Galleries, Scotland St
SHEFFIELD
0114 272 5858
www.aedowseandson.com

Shalesmoor ELR Auctions
The Nichols Building
SHALESMOOR, SHEFFIELD
0114 281 6161
www.elrauctions.com

Sheffield Railwayana Auctions
Now located in Bedford with some auctions in Derby
01234 325341
www.sheffieldrailwayana.co.uk

D. Wombell & Son
The Auction Gallery, Northminster Business Park, Northfield Lane
UPPER POPPLETON
01904 790777
www.invaluable.com/Wombells

John Walsh & Co.
55, Jenkin Rd
HORBURY, WAKEFIELD
01924 271710
www.john-walsh.co.uk

Malcolm's No. 1 Auctioneers

The Trustee's Hall, High St
BOSTON SPA, Nr WETHERBY
No longer holding regular auctions but still doing valuations for probate and insurance, buying antiques and working as a freelance auctioneer
01977 684971 / 077 7413 0784
www.malcolmsno1auctions.co.uk

David Duggleby Whitby
See their Scarborough auction house where all sales are now being held
WHITBY
01723 507111
www.davidduggleby.com

Richardson & Smith
West Cliff Salerooms, 19, Silver St
WHITBY
01947 602298
www.richardsonandsmith.co.uk

John Simpson
4, Forest Grove, Stockton Lane
YORK
01904 424797

Summersgill Auctioneers
8, Front St
ACOMB, YORK
01904 791131
www.summersgill.com*

* No auction house has been charged for entry in these free listings. If salerooms would like their details included or updated in future editions, please contact Fiona Shoop, Auction Book, Pen & Sword Books Ltd, 47, Church St, Barnsley, South Yorkshire, S70 2AS.

Permissions

I would like to thank the following for their kindness and generosity in allowing me to use their images:

BCA – BCA (British Car Auctions)
Auction Centre, Blackbushe Airport
BLACKWATER, Nr. CAMBERLEY
01252 877317
www.british-car-auctions.co.uk

BN – Bonhams
101, New Bond St
LONDON, W1S
020 7447 7447
www.bonhams.com

CH – Cheffins
Clifton House, 1-2, Clifton Rd
CAMBRIDGE
01223 213343
www.cheffins.co.uk

DN – Dreweatts
Donnington Priory Salerooms
DONNINGTON, NEWBURY
Formerly known as Dreweatt Neate
01635 553553
www.dnfa.co.uk

ESS – Estate of Stanley Shoop

LW – Lawrences Auctioneers of Crewkerne
The Linen Yard, South St
CREWKERNE
01460 73041
www.lawrences.co.uk

SW – Sworders
14, Cambridge Rd
STANSTED MOUNTFITCHET
01279 817778
www.sworder.co.uk
TH – Thomaston Auction Place Auction Galleries
Route 1, Thomaston,

MAINE 04861
USA
www.thomastonauction.com

WW – Woolley & Wallis
51-61, Castle St
SALISBURY
01722 424500
www.woolleyandwallis.co.uk

INDEX

Auction houses and places listed in the directory are not mentioned here unless they are also part of the main text.

Accessories 15, 62
Accountant 180
Account/s 132, 139, 169, 170, 172, 179
A.D. 120, 183
Ancient 113, 163
Antiques 8, 11, 24, 25, 29, 40, 41, 42, 62, 68, 98, 101, 140, 146, 172, 185
Centre/s 16, 40, 70, 100, 185, 186, 191
Dealer/s 15, 16, 19, 25, 93, 139, 149, 152, 155-156, 172, 174
Fairs 16, 18, 21, 23, 62, 63, 64, 65, 66, 69, 70, 100, 104, 106, 108, 139, 185, 186, 191
Markets 100
Press / Publications 21, 93, 136, 164, 187-188
Trade 8, 20
World 18, 81, 84, 117, 139, 155, 187
Antiques & Collectables 35, 136
Antiques Roadshow, The 105
Antiques Trade Gazette 32, 43, 85, 93, 136, 162, 187, 188
Apostle spoons 183
Appliances 62, 68
Appraisal 110, 183
Arcade game 45
Art 19, 40, 44, 64, 184, 213
Russian 214
Art Deco, *see also* Deco 16, 41, 44, 63, 72, 125, 127
Artfact 23, 85, 95, 188
Article/s 8, 11, 18, 20, 47, 108, 183
Artist/s 20, 33, 64, 119, 135, 176
Arts and Crafts 105, 107
Assay 184

Atari 150
Attwell, Mabel Lucie 126
Auction/s [most pages]
Car 68, 69, 223, 224, 228
Classic car 68, 195, 204, 224, 228, 229, 233
Commercial 68
Estate 8, 10, 114, 143-181, 184
General 19, 25, 41, 42, 43, 44, 45, 46, 64, 65, 68, 111-112, 113, 162, 163, 164, 175
House/s [most pages]
Internet 18, 69, 71, 78, 80, 81-85, 93, 101, 116, 119
Specialist 18-19, 20, 21, 25, 36, 42, 43, 44, 45, 64, 66, 101, 105, 109, 111, 113, 161-162, 163, 164, 175, 176
Trickery 30, 60
Auctioneer [most pages]
Auctioneer's discretion 120, 121, 183
Austin Morris 69
Autograph/s 21, 36, 66, 175, 183
Albums / Books 36, 125, 183

Backstamp/ed 51, 59, 65, 67, 72, 110, 183, 188
Bank account 169, 179
Banker's draft 48
Banknotes 214, 215, 227
BCA 69, 224, 233
Beatles, The 112, 117, 190
Bed and breakfast 15
Beds 15, 46
Benefactors 104, 148, 151
Bequeathed 145
Bequest 145
Bereaved 8
Beswick 65, 66, 105

Bid 11, 22, 30, 31, 32, 33, 41, 47, 51, 53, 54, 56, 58, 60, 61, 68, 74, 75, 76, 78, 79, 80, 81, 82, 83, 84, 86, 87, 88, 89, 93, 98, 100, 121, 129, 184, 186
Bidding 26, 31, 32, 33, 37, 47, 50, 51, 56, 58, 60, 61, 63, 64, 66, 74, 75, 76, 77, 82, 84, 86, 87, 88, 89, 90, 91, 121, 122, 186
Absentee 54, 183
Commission 44, 53, 54, 61, 74, 78-79, 80, 82, 84, 89, 183, 186
Phone 78, 79, 80, 82, 83
Bird/s 107
Bath 19, 63, 64
Endangered 108
Stuffed 107, 108
Birmingham Guild of Handicraft 107
Bisque 183
Bloomsbury Auctions 20, 161
Blue and white 44, 62, 66, 161
Bonhams 11, 24, 25, 26, 102, 110, 176, 190
Books 8, 11, 18, 20, 27, 41, 43, 64, 98, 100, 113, 149, 153, 154, 160, 161, 164, 172, 183, 213
Auctions 20, 161, 203, 206, 213
Children's 62
Dealers 153
First Editions 21
Hardback 153, 156
Paperback 153
Sales 161
Bottles 163, 230
Bouncing bids 33, 34, 74, 82, 88, 98
Box/es 21, 33, 34, 35, 36, 45,

49, 50, 64, 66, 68, 70, 90, 125, 127, 135, 150, 158, 171, 172, 183, 185
Knife 182
Breakfast at Tiffany's 43
Breweriana 230
Bronze 186
Bubble wrap 49, 50, 90
Burleigh 71
Business 8, 20, 23, 24, 28, 33, 34, 35, 36, 41, 44, 45, 51, 52, 56, 59, 68, 111, 124, 137, 138, 139, 140, 147, 155, 171, 178, 185
Buyer/s 8, 15, 17, 22, 23, 24, 25, 26, 27, 28, 30, 31, 32, 33, 35, 41, 43, 44, 45, 46, 47, 51, 52, 54, 55, 56, 60, 61, 73, 74, 76, 79, 81, 83, 84, 86, 87, 88, 92, 97, 98, 99, 104, 105, 106, 107, 111, 113, 116, 117, 119, 120, 124, 125, 129, 130, 133, 134, 136, 137, 138, 161, 162, 163, 165, 166, 175, 178, 183, 189
Buyer's premium 25, 26, 40, 45, 62, 66, 76-77, 78, 89, 128, 141, 183, 184
Buying at auction 16, 24, 39-101, 139, 140

Cab 24, 25
Cabinet/s 52, 53, 56
  Display 66
Cambridge 164, 189
Camera 31, 45, 60
Car/s 23, 49, 53, 68, 69, 71, 92, 166, 172, 175, 220, 223
  Boot sales 18, 101, 115, 139, 149, 151, 153-154, 155, 156, 157, 191
  Classic 68, 195, 204, 224, 229
  Park 23, 24, 30, 32, 33, 52, 139
  Toy 65
Cards 68, 93, 183, 185
Career 8
Carlton Ware 59, 99
Carpets 19, 40, 64, 84, 166
Cash 18, 38, 47, 48, 68, 75, 76, 105, 131, 132, 157, 172, 189

Cash in the Attic 86
Catalogue/s 11, 18, 21, 26, 27, 28, 29, 33, 34, 35, 40, 44, 49, 52, 54, 55, 57-59, 60, 61, 73, 74, 76, 77, 81, 84, 85, 86, 92, 95, 109, 113, 114, 116, 117, 118, 119, 121, 125, 126, 127, 132, 134, 137, 138, 141, 158, 160, 162, 169-170, 173-176, 183, 184
Cataloguer 26
Cataloguing 8, 44, 104, 109, 110, 112, 113, 118, 119, 121, 126, 127, 134, 156, 170, 173, 175, 176
Caveat Emptor 61, 185
Centrepiece 41, 183, 185
Chairs 19, 38, 45, 49, 72, 107, 122, 177, 190
  Rocking 177, 178
Charity shop/s 149, 151, 152, 153, 154, 156, 157, 168
Charlotte Rhead 33, 41
Cheffins 11, 20, 46, 161, 162, 164, 166, 189, 193
Cheque/s 18, 47, 48, 90, 132, 169, 170, 179
Chess 63
Chests of drawers 55
China 11, 27, 36, 43, 44, 50, 51, 56, 61, 62, 65, 67, 70, 71, 72, 95, 113, 117, 161, 183, 188, 230
Chinese porcelain 66
Chintz 183
Chip and Pin 48
Christmas 117
  Decoration 67
Clarice Cliff 63
Clothes 149, 153, 155, 156, 171
  Vintage 15, 93, 149, 154
Coins 44, 213, 214, 215, 227
Collecting goods 47, 49, 50, 61, 90, 91, 130, 153, 156
Collection/s 11, 26, 36, 63, 65, 102, 114, 115, 144, 145, 147, 150, 157, 158, 159, 160, 161, 164, 165, 167, 168, 169, 172, 176, 184
Commission 18, 25, 26, 44, 76, 109, 114-116, 124, 125, 128, 132, 133, 134, 141, 144, 150,

161, 170, 173, 179, 183
Bid 44, 53, 54, 61, 74, 78-79, 80, 82, 83, 84, 89, 183, 186
Rate 109, 112, 114-116, 132, 156, 160, 161, 173, 179
Complain/t 31, 61, 97, 125, 134, 159
Computer/s 47, 75, 82, 150, 169
Consultant 26, 29, 110, 176
Conventions 100
Cookers 19
Copper 105, 187
Corgi cars 183
Cover 76, 125, 183
Crazing 183
Credit card/s 47, 48, 75, 76, 90, 98
Crockery 15, 19, 40, 62, 64, 67, 68, 70, 149
Crystal 135, 149
Cupboards 55, 137
Curtains 19, 40, 42, 64, 65
Cutlery 19, 68, 149, 185
Cuttings 183
Czech Republic 71

Damage/d 22, 30, 34, 49, 52, 54, 55, 56, 58, 59, 61, 72, 73, 83, 90, 93, 97, 134, 135
Dealers 15, 17, 18, 20, 22, 23, 25, 30, 31, 32, 34, 35, 40, 41, 42, 44, 46, 52, 55, 56, 60, 62, 66, 73, 74, 79, 82, 87, 91, 92, 93, 95, 99, 108, 111, 117, 123, 138, 139, 144, 145, 150, 152, 153, 156, 157, 158, 160, 161, 163, 164, 165, 185, 190
Records 153
Specialist 42, 63, 149, 153, 156
Death 145, 146, 164
Certificate of 169
Debit cards 48, 79
Deco, see also Art Deco 63, 70, 71, 124
Decorating 68
Decoration 67, 68, 113, 183, 185
DEFRA 108
Defraud 139, 168

Information and Auction Directory

Denby 66
Descriptions 57, 74, 83, 87, 98, 99, 109, 114, 118, 119, 125, 126, 127, 128, 134, 162, 172, 173-174, 175, 176
Designer/s 63, 107, 135, 149, 154, 156
Desks 55, 75, 77, 90
Details 47, 59, 60, 75, 76, 110, 121, 128, 136, 137, 161, 164, 169, 170, 171, 185
Diamond 18, 25, 65, 81, 106, 204
Diaries 21, 66
Die/d/s 8, 119, 142, 144, 145, 155, 158, 159, 164, 167
Die-cast 183, 226
Dinner
  Plate 66
  Services 18, 62, 66, 67, 70, 71, 72, 105
Dolls 65, 98
Dominic Winters 20, 161
Dorothy 43
Double-glazing 19, 40, 64
Dress 43, 112
Driving licence 47, 75
Dyson (vacuum) 19, 64

E-mails 22, 36, 75, 85, 95, 96, 119, 125, 132, 169, 170
EBay 22, 36, 69, 78, 81-85, 101, 104, 116, 119, 149, 150, 152
  Live 22, 54, 78, 79, 81-85, 93
Edwardian 57, 77, 106
Edwards, Charles 106
Egyptian 135
Electrical goods 40, 45, 64
Ellis, Aline 67, 165
Embossed 71, 183
Entertainment 40, 43, 112, 117, 224
Epergne/s 62, 183
Ephemera 20, 21, 36, 66, 113, 164, 176, 183, 213, 220
Eras 15, 98, 127
Estate 8, 11, 16, 17, 144, 145, 147, 148, 149, 151, 156, 157, 158, 159, 160, 161, 164, 166, 167, 168, 169, 170, 171, 172, 173-178, 179, 181, 189

Auction/s 8, 10, 114, 143-181, 184
  Protect the 16, 123, 144, 145, 146, 147, 161, 167, 173-178, 181
Estate agent 112, 114, 168
Estimate/d 21, 25, 26-27, 29, 32, 34, 36, 43, 59, 66, 84, 89, 94, 104, 109, 112, 114, 115, 116, 120, 121, 122, 126, 127, 128, 130, 133, 134, 135, 136, 145, 175, 177, 178
Etching/s 184
Evershed, Kitty 58, 63
Executor/s 148, 151, 167, 168, 169, 172, 175, 179
Expert 8, 21, 40, 62, 64, 82, 84, 104, 110, 114, 135, 161
Expertise 44, 52, 56, 57, 59, 63, 66, 75, 110, 111, 113, 119, 174, 175, 189

F&G 40, 59, 184
Fabric 15, 56, 93
Fake/s 33, 59, 88, 98, 99, 183, 185
Family/ies 8, 15, 29, 144, 145, 146, 147, 148, 150, 155, 157, 159, 160, 166, 167, 168, 170
Fashion buyers/designers 15
Fee/s 21, 69, 76, 78, 115, 125, 128, 130, 132, 133, 152, 167, 179, 180, 183, 185
Figural/es 22, 63, 65, 95, 105, 112, 125, 126, 183, 184 186
Film 15, 43
Filming 11, 45
Fine Art 25, 40, 44
Folio/s 19, 55, 56, 64-73, 91, 92, 125, 127
Form 47, 48, 78, 132, 137, 140, 180, 183, 184
Fowlmere 189
Framed and glazed 40, 59, 184
French polishing 61
Fridges 40
Funeral 152, 156
Furniture 15, 16, 17, 19, 40, 42, 46, 49, 55, 61, 62, 63, 64, 68, 71, 81, 84, 90, 93, 107, 153, 156, 172, 178

Games 33, 68, 69
  Board 68
  Children's 68
  Garden 64
  Centre 19, 63, 64
  Ornaments 19, 40, 62, 64
  Statuary/es 19
Garibaldi 20, 175
Garland, Judy 43
Gavel 184
George II 98
George III 27
George IV 36, 175
Glass 43, 61, 67, 106, 135, 149, 163, 183, 184, 185, 186
Gold 184, 185
Gorringes 11, 25, 27, 81, 111, 163, 186, 225, 226
Graduating levels 114
Guns 180, 214, 217

Hallmark 184, 185
Halls 33, 49
  Village 49, 54, 109, 130, 131
Hammer 68, 76, 184
Hammer price 26, 76, 160, 165, 183, 184
Health and safety 49, 107
Heir/s 8, 144-148, 152, 156, 159, 167-170, 173-177, 179-180
Hepburn, Audrey 43
History 16, 63, 110
Hobby 8
Home 8, 15, 16, 18, 24, 40, 41, 47, 64, 71, 75, 90, 139, 144, 145, 151, 155, 158, 166, 168, 171, 189
  Move/ing 8, 15, 16, 48, 93, 123, 139
Hotels 71, 189, 190
House 19, 45, 68, 69, 70, 71, 93, 98, 148, 150, 151, 152, 153, 156, 159, 164, 165, 166, 167, 168, 169, 171, 177, 189
  Clearance 139, 149, 153
  Sales 46, 166, 189
Household goods 40, 153, 155
Humpen 96
Hunt/ing 83, 133, 180

ID 47, 48, 75, 80
Ikea 15
Inherit/ed 138, 167, 169, 180
Inheritance 16, 104, 154, 159, 164, 165, 169
Inlaid/y 182, 184, 185
Insurance 36, 50, 65, 76, 93, 98, 115, 116, 128, 132, 134, 135, 136, 176
Interior designer/s 15, 42, 44, 62, 63
Internet 21-22, 50, 72, 79, 81-85, 93, 95, 104, 116, 127, 150
  Auctions 18, 36, 69, 71, 78, 81-85, 101
Investment 57, 64, 72, 92
Islamic 135
  Art 135
  Glass 163
Ivory 107, 108, 185

Jewellery 16, 23, 24, 25, 27, 40, 43, 44, 63, 81, 84, 106, 148, 149, 156, 162, 163, 185
  Costume 63
Jigsaws 68, 69
Job lots 17, 18, 19, 34, 55, 56, 60, 61-62, 63, 64, 65, 66, 67, 68, 84, 91, 92, 97, 98, 106, 123, 124-125, 127, 144, 145, 149, 150, 165, 173, 185
Journalist 11, 31, 60
Jug 33, 71, 106, 135

Keys 63
Kidner, George 11, 110
Kitchenalia 149, 230
Knocker 155-156

Labels 22, 29, 55, 56, 60, 61, 91, 107, 153, 167, 183
  Swapping 55, 60
Lang, Faust 127
Late entries 162
Lawnmowers 19, 64
Lawyer/s 17, 138, 144, 145, 146, 148, 150, 167, 168, 180, 181
Lennon, John 112
Letters 21, 35, 36, 66, 120, 136, 137, 183
Lewes 11, 25, 81, 111, 163, 186
Lieberich, Nikolai Ivanovich 186
Lighting 42, 61, 63
Linen 40, 42, 68
Lion passant 185
Lion rampant 185
Lithograph 185
Live eBay 22, 54, 78, 79, 81-85, 93
Llandudno 68
Local interest 67
Location 8, 20, 112, 135
London 16, 24, 63, 191
Lot/s [most pages inc 185]
  Job, see job lots
  Numbers 27, 28, 60, 61, 91
  Pulling 82, 125, 126-128, 150, 174-175
  Unsold 33, 129-130, 132, 134, 153, 173, 177
  Withdrawing 34, 121, 126, 128, 134, 137, 170, 174-175, 181
Lottage 18, 76, 115, 116, 124, 125, 132, 150, 179, 185
Loungers 64
Loupe 185
Lowestoft Porcelain 223

Magazine/s 15, 43, 101, 183, 187
  Fan 101
  Magic Roundabout, The 69
Mailing lists 43, 95
Majolica 29, 113, 121, 132, 138
Market 15, 21, 22, 25, 26, 27, 42, 44, 46, 65, 67, 69, 70, 71, 73, 80, 81, 83, 84, 85, 95, 96, 98, 99, 104, 113, 116, 120, 121, 122, 126, 140, 150, 152, 153, 157, 161, 164, 165, 176, 185, 186
  Antiques 100
  Housing 16
Marquetry 94, 185
Mattresses 46, 93
Medals 44, 62, 213, 214, 215, 227
Memories/y 10, 16, 146, 147, 158, 159, 169, 171, 175, 177, 181
MIB 127, 185
Military goods 164, 207
Mint 185
Mint in box 127, 185
Minton 50
Misdescription/s 47, 51, 57, 128, 138, 173
Money laundering 48
Moorcroft 63
Moss, Kate 15
Motorbikes 215, 228
Movie posters 100
Music shops 63
Musical instruments 18, 63, 106

Nef 185
Negotiate/ing better rates 114-116, 160, 179
Network 40, 44
New (goods) 45, 70
Newlyn 105, 187
Newsletter/s 22, 85, 95, 96
Newspaper/s 21, 50, 90, 101, 116, 134, 171, 183, 187
Nicked 185

Obituary 156, 164
Ocean liner 228
Offer 33, 129, 130, 156, 189
Office 131, 184, 190, 191
Olivier, Laurence 175
Onassis, Jacqueline 16
Opium pipes 67
Oriental 66, 113, 161
  Porcelain 66
Ornament/s 66, 127, 156
Ovens 68

Packaging 21, 47, 49-50, 90, 97, 98, 179, 183
Paddle 75, 89, 185
Paintings 20, 27, 33, 45, 48, 49, 51, 62, 64, 84, 90, 93, 119, 135, 147, 148, 159, 163, 176, 177, 184, 186
  Animals 64
  Landscapes 64
  Portraits 64

Information and Auction Directory 239

Palmerston 175
Paper trail 17, 36, 98, 141, 145, 157, 170, 172
Paperwork 17, 28, 29, 36, 77, 104, 107, 119, 132, 137, 139, 141, 144, 145, 149, 156, 161, 169, 170, 172, 181, 183
Papier maché 83
Paragon 71
Parking 22, 24, 55, 73, 84, 93, 154
Parquetry 118, 185
Pay/ing 8, 24, 26, 30, 32, 33, 40, 41, 45, 46, 47, 48, 52, 53, 57, 60, 61, 63, 64, 65, 66, 68, 74, 75, 76, 78, 80, 84, 88, 89, 90, 91, 94, 95, 98, 109, 114, 116, 131, 132, 134, 136, 138, 139, 140, 141, 150, 152, 153, 156, 169, 172, 173, 177, 179, 180, 183
PAYE 139
Payment 47, 55, 56, 75, 76, 90, 97, 104, 116, 131, 132, 133, 172
  Slip 48
Pearls 40
Peel (Robert) 175
Pens 41, 186
Pepper caster 185
Pepper pot 185
Period drama 15
Phillips 26, 102, 110, 176
Phone/s 36, 47, 75, 78, 79, 80, 93
  Mobile 150
Photos/Photographs 11, 29, 60, 97, 111, 116, 117, 118, 127, 128, 132, 134, 147, 158, 164, 167, 172, 179
Piano/s 63, 192
Pictures 20, 23, 40, 41, 43, 50, 55, 59, 64, 65, 73, 92, 97, 116, 117, 137, 184
Pin number 48
Pitch rent 153
Pocket/s 149, 169
Police 51, 98, 99
Poole 66
Porcelain 66, 183, 223
Porter/s 19, 22, 23, 24, 33, 36, 49, 51-53, 55, 56, 59, 60, 73, 74, 90, 91, 92, 93, 135, 137
Post/ed 18, 47, 50, 83, 95, 97, 125, 130, 132, 136, 140, 152, 169, 170, 172, 179
Postage 18, 71, 85
Postcards 21, 68, 166, 176, 183, 203, 227
Pot lids 230
Potter, Beatrix 65, 66, 105
Potter, Harry 21
Pottery 21, 51, 99
  Studio 22, 34, 63, 67, 83, 112, 120
Price guide 95, 153
Primary market 15, 62, 185
Print/s 27, 184, 185
Probate 145-146, 167-168, 181
Prop buyers 15

Racecourse 189, 190
Radio 8, 170
Railwayana 192, 204, 231, 232
Rain 23, 93
Receipt/s 36, 47, 90, 137
Record/s (paper) 28, 29, 36, 57, 60, 75, 78, 91, 104, 113, 119, 136, 139, 140, 145, 148, 156, 157, 158, 169, 170, 172, 179
Records (music) 153, 156
Recycling 149, 154, 172
Refund 92, 97, 98
Regency 182
Register, to 24, 47, 48, 55, 56, 73, 74, 75, 83, 80, 89, 138, 139, 140, 141, 180, 185
Registration Act 185, 191
Relief work 183
Rembrandt 135
Removal firm/s 92-94, 158, 169, 171, 172, 179
Reserve/s 27, 29, 33, 51, 55, 69, 74, 89, 116, 120-123, 129, 130, 132, 134, 136, 144, 145, 166, 173, 176-177, 178, 183, 184, 185
Restaurants 61, 68
Restaurateur/s 19, 68
Restoration 61
Restored 72
Restorer 72
Reticello 185
Reynolds, Debbie 43
Ring/s (illegal) 30-33, 34, 74
Ring/s (jewellery) 18, 40, 65, 106, 148
Ringer/s 37, 185
Rocking horse 46
Royal Albert 105
Royal Doulton 66, 70, 99, 112
  Lambeth Ware 111
Royal Dux 71
Royal Winton 55
Rubbish 62, 146, 149, 154
Rugs 19, 40, 64, 82, 84

Sale agreement 114, 179
Sale of Goods Act 98
Saleroom 11, 24, 30, 41, 48, 49, 50, 51, 52, 54, 57, 60, 61, 64, 74, 75, 83, 85, 89, 90, 91, 92, 95, 105, 107, 109, 111, 114, 115, 116, 123, 127, 129, 130, 132, 133, 134, 136, 161, 163, 165, 166, 169, 178
Sales 21, 22, 24, 32, 33, 41, 43, 49, 59, 63, 64, 70, 76, 82, 83, 84, 93, 95, 104, 106, 111, 113, 114, 116, 117, 118, 121, 122, 125, 127, 129, 131, 132, 134, 156, 162, 163, 164, 165, 166, 168, 178, 179, 185
  General 21, 24, 41, 43, 45, 162
  Particulars 121, 134, 169, 179
  Specialist 21, 42, 44, 45, 64, 104, 106, 109, 111, 113, 117, 150, 161, 162
Salt cellar 186
San Demos 190
Savoy Hotel 16, 63
School 15, 86
Scrapbooks 183
Scratch/es 51, 55, 61, 86, 88
Seasonal goods 67
Second/s 51, 186
Secondary market 185
Security 91, 92, 97, 109, 136, 150, 151, 156, 164
Self-assessment 140
  Forms 139, 180

Self-employed 139-141
Selling at auction 8, 16-19, 20-21, 24-29, 30-36, 57, 95, 100, 103-141, 143-181, 185, 189, 191
Shelley 71
Shippers 92-94, 96, 116
Shipping 95
Shop display 68
Shops 15, 16, 24, 40, 45, 60, 62, 64, 185, 186
Showground 189, 190
Silver 27, 30, 37, 87, 106, 112, 141, 184, 185
Sketch/es 112, 125, 184, 186
Smoking-related 67
Society of Fine Art Auctioneers 97
SOFAA 97
Solicitor 167, 168
Sotheby's 191
Specialist 20-21, 22, 36, 41, 42, 45, 46, 63, 66, 69, 73, 89, 100, 101, 106, 107, 109, 110, 114, 123, 160, 161, 162, 163, 163, 164, 165, 175
Auctioneers 43, 44, 66, 161, 164
Auctions 18-19, 20, 25, 41, 42, 43, 44, 45, 66, 68, 101, 105, 109, 111, 113, 161, 162-163, 176
Buyers 44
Dealers 42, 63, 149, 153, 156
Sales 21, 24, 42, 43, 45, 46, 104, 106, 111, 112, 113, 117, 150, 174
Sport 87, 117, 194, 217, 220
Staff 11, 19, 23, 24, 34-35, 36, 52, 91, 189
Stall rent 104
Stamps 43, 214, 215, 227
Stately homes 16
Stealing 35, 91, 152, 153, 156
Stereoscopic viewer 166
Stevens and Williams 106
Stickers 51, 55, 60
Storage 49, 64, 67, 116, 128, 130, 150-151, 165, 169, 170,

172, 179
Stourbridge 106
Students 15, 40
Stuffed 107
Animals 107
Birds 107, 108
Summer 117
Susie Cooper 72
Sylvac 164

Table/s 19, 45, 49, 60, 62, 70, 118
Settings 62
Tax 104, 132, 138, 139-141, 144, 145, 168, 179-180, 181
Capital Gains 139, 140, 180
Man 36, 140, 141, 169
Office 17, 138, 139, 140, 180
Tea 51, 172
Caddy 178
Services 18, 70, 71, 105
Set/s 70, 187
Teapot 29, 125
Teddy bears 65
Televisions (TVs) 40
Terms and conditions 47, 57, 76, 78
Ts&Cs 47, 49, 57, 59, 64, 76, 77, 128, 129, 130, 131, 132, 134
Textiles 214
Thatch/ed cottage 11, 69
Theft 49, 92, 136, 137, 168, 170
Tools 211, 223
Tortoiseshell 108, 178
Toys 65, 117, 162, 164, 183, 196, 217, 226, 227
Trade 8, 34, 41, 42, 43, 60, 109, 136, 162, 174
Trading Standards 98, 99, 191
Trains 127, 227
Model 65
Transport/ed 70, 104, 107, 164, 190, 220
Trick/s 8, 33, 34, 41, 60, 61, 91-92, 122, 156
Tuscan Ware 70

Ugly mugs 68

Unsigned 66, 67, 184
UPVC doors 19, 64
Utility bill 47, 75
Vacuum cleaners 19, 40, 64
Valuer 110, 124, 128, 137, 157, 158, 161, 163, 168
VAT 26, 40, 62, 76, 77, 78, 89, 115, 122, 128, 132, 141, 179, 183, 184
Vehicle/s 23, 68, 92
Vendor 129, 132, 135, 186
Vestas 186
Victoria 135, 175
Victorian 16, 36, 57, 63, 64, 71, 106, 117, 172, 177
Viewing/s 24, 54-60, 68, 73, 74, 83, 91, 92, 93, 97, 109, 127, 134, 137, 138, 166, 175, 189
Vintage 19, 65, 69, 204, 223, 228
Clothes 15, 93, 149, 154, 156
Wine 117, 204
Violin/s 63, 106

Wade 63, 99, 102, 126, 127, 128
Whimsies 105, 127, 128
Wardrobes 71
Washing machines 64, 153
Watercolours 184, 186
Websites 21, 22, 25, 43, 81, 82, 84, 85, 101, 116, 117, 119, 140, 187, 188
Wedgwood Fairyland 61
White elephant 70
Wilberforce 175
Will/s 145, 146, 147, 167-169, 177
Windows 19, 64
Wine 117
Labels 183
Vintage 117, 204
Winnie the Pooh 65, 161
Wisden Cricketers' Almanacks 217
Wizard of Oz, The 43
Wrong leg, the 79, 186

Yogurt 19, 64